Praise for *Sun Tzu Said...*

Dialogue requires honesty. Prior to reading *Sun Tzu Said: Classic Warfare for the Modern Mind* I was very skeptical of the book's content as I had read no less than four translations and interpretations of Sun Tzu's *Art of War* targeting both military and business interest groups. However, I am offering this testimonial as I was delighted with the contemporary interpretation of Sun Tzu's treatise. Authors Kane and Wilder offer an extremely fresh translation culminating with modern usable commentary of pros and cons of how this timeless wisdom can and most certainly will impact your life in near and long-term situations. This book is not only applicable to those interested in history, military personnel, law enforcement officers, and martial arts practitioners but for the individual of any age who wants to gain an edge in self-protection and situational awareness and most important, strategic life planning. It might be a stretch to say this book will save your life, but I am convinced it can preserve and prolong it when the lessons the authors present are acted upon. I am planning on purchasing this book for each of my children to facilitate their own education and training. In short, if you had to choose one variant of Sun Tzu's collected work, this one should be at the top of the pile for consideration. I loved it. — **Jeffrey-Peter Hauck**, MSc, JD, Police SGT (Ret.), LPI, CPT USA, Professor of Criminal Justice

---

"The timeless wisdom of Sun Tzu is revisited through 21st century lenses—geopolitical, corporate, social, and personal—and is distilled into crisp and tangible takeaways that are meaningful in today's complex world. Great lessons that apply in business, and negotiations! For the win—Put this book on your Must-Read list! You lose—If you don't!" — **Canda S. Rozier**, SVP Global Procurement & Real Estate

---

"Kane and Wilder dive deep into the works of Sun Tzu offering interpretations for today's modern world. The authors skillfully approach this task by delivering thought-provoking historical, political, sporting, and business-related vignettes, capped by simple do's and don'ts, mirroring Tzu's principles. A great desktop companion for the strategist in an ever-challenging and turbulent environment." — **David A. Davies**, Security Consultant and Author

---

"I went to the bookshelves and counted; and I have 36 different versions of The Art of War. Why in the world would I have that many? And more so, why in the world would I ever want to read another version? The answer is simple: I like the different translations, annotations, and interpretations different authors and versions bring to the ancient text by Sun Tzu. Probably the most famous work of strategy ever written, Sun Tzu's Art of War has influenced military and business leaders alike. And now, in Sun Tzu Said, Kane and Wilder share commentary that will help readers appreciate how these timeless principles transcend warfare and apply to competitive situations of all kinds. The authors' modern insights into the text provide practical and pragmatic guidance for military leaders, martial artists, law enforcement officers, lawmakers, leaders, educators, and businesspeople. You don't need over thirty editions of The Art of War like I have, but you need this one!" — **Alain Burrese**, J.D., Director of Active Defense Training for Reflex Protect, Author of Survive A Shooting and other titles

---

"This book addresses a major gap in current business literature by combining business theories such as Porter's Five Forces with historical military strategies. It helps show how complex theories can actually apply to daily business activities. By presenting how each point can lead to success ("For the Win") or failure ("You lose"), the authors show how each point can be put into practice and create the link between theory and actual performance." — **R. Reis Sherin**, Doctorate of Management

---

"Sun Tzu Said brings a fresh perspective to the ageless wisdom of Sun Tzu by adding a touch of modern in easy to digest short narratives. A must read for the modern warrior and anyone looking to enhance insight in the modern world by connecting with ancient wisdom."
— **Andrew Lange**, US Army Combat Veteran, Operation Iraqi Freedom; VP Business Development, Sitel Group

---

"A fresh and modern take on the ancient wisdom of master Sun Tzu, this edgy book is packed with useful examples of feasible strategy and tactics that anyone can apply to accomplish their objectives." — **Nir "300" B.,** Israeli counterterror operative and owner of LOTAR Combat®

"This is an excellent read for the busy professional. Lawrence and Kris have written practical and relatable advice. Their humor makes the read easy and fun. Last week I was assigned a high-profile project for something I have never done before. After feeling sorry for myself and anxious about the daunting tasks ahead, I looked around and spotted Sun Tzu Said. Quickly I began devouring the pages, copying down 'For the Win' statements and pasting them across my office. In a matter of hours, my attitude transformed and I felt armed, prepared, and excited." — **Mary Zampino**, VP, Content, Research, and Analytics, Sourcing Industry Group

SUN TZU SAID

Classic warfare
for the
modern mind

Copyright © 2020 by Lawrence A. Kane and Kris Wilder.

Cover design and interior layout by Kami Miller.

Illustrations by Kris Wilder.

All rights reserved. No part of this publication may be reproduced, distributed or transmitted in any form or by any means, including photocopying, recording, or other electronic or mechanical methods, without the prior written permission of the publisher, except in the case of brief quotations embodied in critical reviews and certain other noncommercial uses permitted by copyright law. For permission requests, write to the publisher, addressed "Attention: Permissions Coordinator," at the address below:

Stickman Publications, Inc.
Burien, WA 98146
www.stickmanpublications.com

ISBN-13: 978-0-578-75158-0

First Print Edition March 2020

Disclaimer:

Information in this book is distributed "As Is," without warranty. Nothing in this document constitutes a legal opinion nor should any of its contents be treated as such. Neither the authors nor the publisher shall have any liability with respect to the information contained herein. Further, neither the authors nor the publisher has any control over or assume any responsibility for websites or external resources referenced in this book. When it comes to martial arts, self-defense, violence, and related topics, no text, no matter how well written, can substitute for professional, hands-on instruction. These materials should be used for *academic study only*.

SUN TZU SAID

Classic warfare
for the
modern mind

**Sun Tzu
Lawrence A. Kane
& Kris Wilder**

Table of Contents

Introduction	ix
Chapter 1: Laying Plans	1
Chapter 2: Waging War	27
Chapter 3: Attack by Stratagem	49
Chapter 4: Tactical Dispositions	71
Chapter 5: Energy	93
Chapter 6: Weak Points and Strong	117
Chapter 7: Maneuvering	157
Chapter 8: Variation in Tactics	197
Chapter 9: The Army on the March	213
Chapter 10: Terrain	263
Chapter 11: The Nine Situations	297
Chapter 12: The Attack by Fire	371
Chapter 13: The Use of Spies	397
Thank you!	440
Bibliography	441
About the Authors	447
Lawrence A. Kane, ECOP, CSP, CIAP	447
Kris Wilder, BCC	448
Authors' Note	449
Other Works by the Authors	451
Non-Fiction Books:	451
Fiction Books:	458
DVDs:	459

Introduction

Two of the most celebrated military strategists in history are Sun Tzu (544 – 496 BC) a Chinese general and Miyamoto Musashi (1584 – 1645) a Japanese samurai warrior.

Sun Tzu is an honorific that means "Master Sun." According to historians, his given name was Wu. His mastery of military strategy was so exceptional that he reportedly transformed 180 courtesans into skilled soldiers in a single training session in order to secure a generalship with King Ho-Lu. While that particular episode was likely exaggerated, historians agree that King Ho-Lu, with Sun Tzu at his side, defeated the powerful Ch'u state in 506 BC, capturing their capital city of Ying. He then headed north and subdued the states of Qi and Chin to forge his empire. Sun Tzu recorded his winning strategies in a book titled *Art of War* sometime around 510 BC. It is the earliest surviving and most revered tome of its kind, one that is still referenced throughout the world today, and forms the basis for this book.

Miyamoto Musashi was born Shinmen Takezō. He grew up in the Harima Province of Japan. Arguably, the greatest swordsman who ever lived, Musashi slew his first opponent, Arima Kihei, at the age of 13. Considered Kensei, the sword saint of Japan, Musashi killed more than sixty trained samurai warriors in fights or duals during the feudal period where even a minor battle injury could lead to infection and death. He was the founder of the *Hyōhō Niten Ichi-Ryu* style of swordsmanship, which translates as "two heavens as one" or "two-sword style." Like most samurai, he was skilled in the peaceful arts as well, an exceptional poet, calligrapher, and artist. Two years before he died, Musashi retired to a life of seclusion in a cave where he codified his winning strategy in the famous *Go Rin No Sho* which, in English, means *The Book of Five Rings*.

These two masters' timeless wisdom has been studied throughout the ages by prominent historians, warriors, and businesspeople alike, yet they took two very different directions with their works. You see, Sun Tzu wrote top-down, speaking primarily to military leaders, heads of state, and (to some degree) captains of industry, whereas Miyamoto Musashi wrote bottom-up, speaking more to individual warriors and entrepreneurs. For that reason, many readers tend to gravitate toward Musashi's work, yet there is as much if not more to be learned from Tzu's writings. This is why we deeply explore Sun Tzu's *Art of War* here, making his strategy relevant to, and accessible for, everyone.

Sun Tzu's methods are so powerful that proficiency in them can turn an adversary's aims into one's own, coopting their strategy, which when executed masterfully yields victory without the need for fighting. For instance, Master Tzu thought of successful campaigns largely in terms of conquering an enemy's spirit rather than through more mundane means of taking their turf, slaughtering their soldiers, and destroying their possessions. Indeed, history shows that triumphant generals virtually never prevail by annihilating opposing forces, but rather by subduing their adversary's will to fight and accepting his (or rarely her) surrender.

Psychological dominance and manipulation, implemented through such tactics as splitting alliances, evading battle, and attacking by surprise, are strategies commonly employed by the military yet they effortlessly translate into individual actions for those who study martial arts or self-defense as well. Clearly, these very same precepts function flawlessly in many aspects of business such as contract negotiations, acquisition strategies, and marketing campaigns too. Whether we are elite warriors or simply ordinary citizens, Sun Tzu's wisdom is valuable for us all. He speaks to everyone.

This book is designed to create not only thought but action. It's not something to display on one's bookshelf, but rather to internalize and use. We started with the classic 1910 translation of *Art of War* written by Dr. Lionel Giles of the British Museum in London and add both modern and historical insight and examples of how the master's wisdom can be put into use in our everyday lives. In this fashion, the *Art of War* is made accessible for the modern mind, simultaneously entertaining, enlightening, and practicable.

Sun Tzu's passages often play off of and reinforce each other, even going so far as to be repetitious at times, so some sections had to be combined or altered slightly in order to make the most sense for readers. We cite his original passage number before each quote, so wherever you see two or more numbers before "Sun Tzu wrote:" you will know that we have combined quotations to make the concept easier to read and internalize. Additionally, references to certain anachronistic practices had to be adapted a bit to assure that they remain relevant. Nevertheless, while we have taken a touch of literary license, we remained true to the intent of the original work, demonstrating applications for military leaders, martial artists, law enforcement officers, lawmakers, leaders, educators, and businesspeople.

In this way, ancient Chinese wisdom becomes accessible for influential individuals in today's modern world.

Enjoy!

Chapter 1: Laying Plans

In this chapter, we discover the value of preparation to assure success in most any endeavor be it in the boardroom or on the battlefield. We cannot afford to learn through trial-and-error under pressure, but rather must know what we're facing and how best to approach it before we do battle. Five constant factors, the moral law, heaven, earth, the commander, and method & discipline are instrumental in determining the outcome of any confrontation. We must deeply consider these elements and plan accordingly.

1. Sun Tzu wrote:

"The art of war is of vital importance to the state."

The ability to fight a successful war and threaten to wage a successful war is instrumental for any successful government. Like a child on the playground, without this ability, a country becomes subject to the whim and will of its more powerful neighbors. While mastery of the art of war is vital, waging war is costly. Once unleashed, bloodshed cannot end until one side is destroyed or their will to fight is extinguished. This is why fighting is the final projection of the state… or the individual.

Both inter-state and interpersonal conflicts tend to ebb and flow in intensity. As long as there is still room to escalate so too is there an ability to deescalate. The possibility of a peaceful solution remains viable. The Defense Readiness Condition (DEFCON) scale, for instance, has five levels. These status alerts indicate the readiness of the United States military and are adjusted up or down based on world conditions, rarely approaching critical levels save for incidents such as the Cuban Missile Crisis in 1962 which nearly led to nuclear war between the US and USSR, or Iraq's invasion of Kuwait in 1991 which sparked the first Gulf War.

For the Win: Gauge wisely. Not every offense is a trumpet calling for war.

You Lose: Rush through the doorway of battle needlessly and your demise will be swift.

2. Sun Tzu wrote:

"It is a matter of life and death, a road either to safety or to ruin. Hence it is a subject of inquiry which can on no account be neglected."

Violence amongst nations or individuals is a serious endeavor, yet like any other subject, it can be studied, evaluated, and mastered. We cannot afford to learn through trial-and-error, but rather must know with certainty what we're facing and how to best approach it before we fight. After all, all participants in a fight go in thinking they can win, yet the aftermath invariably proves that only one of them was correct.

Fighting carries serious risks, even for professionals such as soldiers, bouncers, or bodyguards, let alone for civilians. Win or lose there will be consequences. For instance, we might beat down the other guy only to land in jail and find ourselves spending our life's savings trying to stay out of prison. Our health, wealth, and reputation are threatened every time we choose to use something other than words to resolve a dispute. Therefore, we must not only know how to fight but also understand what's worth fighting for as well.

For the Win: The proposed value of fighting must outweigh the guaranteed losses you will have from engaging in battle.

You Lose: Ignoring the adage, "He won the battle, but lost the war." Shortsighted actions fail when they do not advance your long-term goal.

3. Sun Tzu wrote:

> *"The art of war, then, is governed by five constant factors, to be taken into account in one's deliberations, when seeking to determine the conditions obtaining in the field."*

There are too many "what ifs" to account for in the heat of battle. We must work big to small, starting with strategic principles that are mastered before we need to concern ourselves with individual tactics. Knowing the five constant factors that govern warfare allows us to pursue our endeavor in the optimal fashion.

Mastering the art of war is a challenge, but even commonplace things like learning to read can be difficult. As children, we discover how to identify the alphabet, associate sounds with the letters, build words, discover word families, decode grammar rules, and decipher spelling patterns before ultimately being able to make any sense of the gobbledygook written on a page or displayed on a screen. Like mastering the mechanics of reading, once the strategy is internalized, tactics can be employed without much conscious thought. This is a giant leap toward mastery.

For the Win: Take a true measurement of your situation, understand what it means, and act accordingly.

You Lose: Failing to understand your measuring tool and its structure when appraising your situation creates errors that quickly build toward disaster.

4. Sun Tzu wrote:

"These five constant factors are: (1) the moral law, (2) heaven, (3) earth, (4) the commander, and (5) method & discipline."

These five factors are: (1) Alignment with cultural norms and values, (2) blessings of Divine Providence (or luck), (3) the field we find ourselves fighting on, (4) the make-up and fortitude of our leader, and (5) how we have trained and prepared ourselves for success or failure. Whenever we plan to fight it is vital to know not only the battlefield but also the rules of combat as well.

While it may not seem like it to the casual observer, war has rules. For inter-state conflicts, the Geneva Conventions, which are enforced via the International Criminal Court, are a good example of strictures that proscribe certain behaviors in battle and its aftermath. A series of treaties negotiated between 1864 and 1949 that were concluded in Geneva Switzerland, these protocols outline international protections for civilians in warfare, proper treatment of wounded combatants, recognition of the International Red Cross, and appropriate handling of prisoners of war, among other important issues. Similarly, our conduct in interpersonal conflicts and business ventures is also regulated. Breaches of the protocol are adjudicated via criminal and civil laws which may vary from jurisdiction to jurisdiction.

For the Win: The five constant factors are like stars in the night sky by which you can navigate. These five constants are gifts, use them.

You Lose: Like a ship sailing off the medieval navigational map never to be seen again, ignoring these five constants, through ignorance or negligence, will lead you astray.

5,6. Sun Tzu wrote:

"The moral law causes the people to be in complete accord with their ruler, so that they will follow him regardless of their lives, undismayed by any danger."

Any successful leader must be in alignment with their people, and the people must be in alignment with their leader. All must adhere to norms of the greater culture in order to succeed. Break the norms of our culture and we risk everything. In many places, if we do something rude or inconsiderate, we could be fired from our job or ostracized from our community. This can impact our ability to earn a living, maintain relationships, or even stay in our home.

Within certain elements of society, however, the impact of straying beyond the norm is more immediate and severe. The term that violence professionals, such as law enforcement officers, security personnel, bouncers, and bodyguards use for this is "educational beat-down." If we learn the intended lesson it may only hurt for a while, yet repeated inappropriate behavior could lead to serious injury or death. Understanding societal norms are necessary for our success. This applies to every individual in every element of society.

For the Win: The greatest commanders treat high and low in accordance with social norms. Shared values and goals assure unity.

You Lose: Believe that, "All animals are equal, but some animals are more equal than others." As George Orwell demonstrated in *Animal Farm*, actions that countervail the moral law court disaster.

7. Sun Tzu wrote:

> *"Heaven signifies night and day, cold and heat, times and seasons."*

No matter how much we plan and prepare, some elements of a fight are not within our control. Accepting what we can control and what we cannot control not only allows for better planning but also helps lower the stress level in our lives.

There is no point in worrying about things that we cannot control nor is there any value in praying that Divine Providence will resolve all our problems. Instead, we need to recognize risks and opportunities and be flexible within our strategy to latch onto those that prove beneficial. A nimble mind remains open to possibilities, even in the heat of battle, be it physical or metaphorical. We must identify openings where we might land a blow or find an opportunity to escape as well as recognize any changes in dynamics such as the deployment of a weapon, intervention by third parties, or hazardous obstacles that might constrain our movements.

For the Win: See and know the variable(s) over which you have no control. Act with attention, and observation, leaving anxiety and worry behind.

You Lose: A blackout drunk is as beneficial as worrying about what cannot be controlled; both are useless and dysfunctional.

8. Sun Tzu wrote:

"Earth comprises distances, great and small, danger and security, open ground and narrow passes, and the chances of life and death."

Terrain plays a significant role in the battle. The field of combat contains many parts; how we choose to see and use them can determine a win or a loss. Unlike competing in a pristine boxing ring or sparring in an orderly *dojo,* real-life battlefields are fraught with risks and opportunities that stem from the terrain.

Consider the famous battle of Thermopylae where King Leonidas and a small force of Spartans (and other Greek hoplites) used a narrow mountain pass to hold off the entire might of the Persian army for three days in 480 BC before eventually being slaughtered to the last man. Their heroic last stand was memorialized in the film 300, yet few remember that that same location played an instrumental role in the Greek invasion of Gaul in 279 BC, the Roman defeat of Antiochus III in 191 BC, and the Allied New Zealand assault on German forces in 1941 during the Second World War. We must know our territory, choose our ground, and whenever possible leverage this understanding for our benefit. This goes as much for creating and implementing playbooks in corporate negotiations as it does for fisticuffs in the alley behind our favorite drinking establishment.

For the Win: Knowing the terrain allows you to use territory to your benefit. In sports this is the "home field advantage."

You Lose: Being ignorant of your surroundings creates a staple of comedy. The idiot only prevails in the make-believe demesne of the movies. You cannot afford to be unenlightened.

9. Sun Tzu wrote:

> *"The commander stands for the virtues of wisdom, sincerity, benevolence, courage, and strictness."*

Stupidity, deception, nastiness, timidity, and sloppiness are poor traits in a leader or any person regardless of his or her role. We can fake it for a while perhaps, but feckless or deceitful individuals who cannot be trusted will ultimately be discovered and brought down. Leadership is not about ourselves, but rather about what we can accomplish for our team.

Leadership is all about setting an example that others wish to follow, so regardless of title, rank, or position everyone is a leader in many aspects of their lives. Furthermore, many endeavors cannot be performed by one person alone. As humans we are social animals who need community and collaboration to become our best selves. And, under duress, we have a tendency to band together for strength and protection. Consequently, these five virtues should be sought, trained, and tended, even strictness which can be considered discipline. We are far better for embracing them.

For the Win: All organizations reflect their leadership. Model what you wish others to follow. Exercising wisdom, sincerity, benevolence, courage, and strictness charts the path from mediocrity to greatness.

You Lose: Poor leaders pitch and yaw with the gusts in the storm. Ignoring the five virtues of leadership creates a rudderless organization that goes nowhere fast.

10. Sun Tzu wrote:

"By method and discipline are to be understood the marshaling of the army in its proper subdivisions, the graduations of rank among the officers, the maintenance of roads by which supplies may reach the army, and the control of military expenditure."

Any significant endeavor requires planning and organization; we simply cannot count on getting from here to there on luck alone. Keep order of ourselves and our team, making sure that we are not derailed from logistical oversights or lack of resources. Supply lines must remain open.

If we do not take proper care of ourselves, we eventually become useless. We must be ready and able to perform when needed, applying the right tools and resources to achieve our goals whatever they may be. For instance, without proper conditioning, we cannot expect to prevail in a fight or escape to safety, so staying in good physical shape not only safeguards our health but also our wellbeing. Staving off physical threats, building a business, or completing our education, these endeavors all require preparation and forethought. We must both know what must be done and be regimented in our approach to completing it.

For the Win: Supply lines must remain healthy. The Roman roads provisioned the empire, even as the unpaved Ho Chi Minh Trail (an elaborate system of mountain and jungle paths used by North Vietnam to infiltrate insurgents and supplies into South Vietnam, Cambodia, and Laos) supplied the Communist rebellion.

You Lose: Cities in decay have crumbling infrastructure, hampering the means of effective distribution. This weakness undermines every aspect of society.

11. Sun Tzu wrote:

"These five heads should be familiar to every general. He who knows them will be victorious; he who knows them not will fail."

This section refers once again to the constant factors of moral law, heaven, earth, the commander, and method & discipline. The reason they are called "heads" in this instance is that each element is equally important as the other four, directing our actions as if it were a head sitting atop our body. Just as a body cannot survive without its head, a person cannot hope to succeed in battle without this vital understanding.

These five factors are constant, consistent, and interrelated. In peacetime, they bring order to our lives, whereas in a war they guide our plans for battle. Nevertheless, our best-laid plans can and often will be confounded by our adversaries so adopting a plan-do-check-act approach keeps us from being overly locked into our preparations while simultaneously facilitating continuous course-correction based on the conditions we face at any given time. Plan and implement our strategy, monitor its effectiveness, and make any adjustments necessary to remain on track as things progress. Flexibility wins battles.

For the Win: Communication creates strength. In the best organizations, relationships are fortified with clear exchanges of ideas and information.

You Lose: Hide, withhold vital information, and you sow the seeds of deception and mistrust.

12, 13. Sun Tzu wrote:

"Therefore, in your deliberations, when seeking to determine the military conditions, let them be made the basis of a comparison, in this wise: (1) Which of the two sovereigns is imbued with the moral law? (2) Which of the two generals has most ability? (3) With whom lies advantages derived from heaven and earth? (4) On which side is discipline most rigorously enforced? (5) Which army is stronger? (6) On which side are officers and men more highly trained? (7) In which army is there the greater constancy both in reward and punishment?"

All adversaries are not created equal. Use these seven considerations to measure opposing sides, gauge their strengths and weaknesses, and plan accordingly. Fights rarely happen in a vacuum; conflicts escalate toward violence. This affords us an opportunity to prepare.

Focusing on these seven questions helps us assure readiness, guiding our options based on an analysis of the adversaries we may face. This concept is not just useful in a fight. In business, for instance, we might develop a playbook that identifies the unmet need, value proposition, account team, compensation structure, and negotiating strategy of ourselves and other bidders to help assure success in a sales campaign. In this fashion, we hope to discover and take advantage of strengths, weaknesses, opportunities, and threats—our adversary's and our own.

For the Win: When taking the measure of an adversary scrutinize the five virtues. This template reveals both strength and weakness.

You Lose: Without these five virtues as a guide you will focus like a child on the jingling car-keys held within your view, missing the profound for the superficial.

14. Sun Tzu wrote:

"By means of these seven considerations I can forecast victory or defeat."

Entering into conflict or competition we can use these seven considerations to reliably measure ourselves and others, knowing in advance more often than not what the outcome will be. Use these factors to understand the other party, asking ourselves, "Do either of us have the ability to take what we want?" This can inform a strategy to capitulate, compete, or cooperate.

For instance, applying Porter's Five Forces, a business model created by Harvard Business School professor Michael Porter (1947 –) commonly used to evaluate competition intensity, attractiveness, and profitability of an industry or market, we can help position our organization for success. This involves measuring levels of competition, the likelihood of new entrants into our desired market space, the power of suppliers, the power of customers, and the threat of substitute products to architect our winning business model.

For the Win: We call it painting a room, but anybody who has actually painted a room will tell you that it should be called, "Prepping a room for painting." Far more time goes into the preparation than the painting. Like painting, we must prepare ahead of time to be successful in any endeavor.

You Lose: Seeking battle without proper preparation is tantamount to walking through the chute at a slaughterhouse. The only consolation is that your death will be swift.

15. Sun Tzu wrote:

"The general that hearkens to my counsel and acts upon it will conquer, let such a one be retained in command! The general that hearkens not to my counsel nor acts upon it, will suffer defeat, let such a one be dismissed!"

A wise leader knows that he or she can chart the course toward victory, but others must embrace the plan and carry it out. It is imperative to have the right people with the right knowledge, skills, and experience in power positions to successfully execute their leader's vision. Those who best fit the needs of the role must be maintained; those who cannot live up to our expectations must be let go.

A collection of individuals who operate as one team can be far more powerful and productive than some group of talented individuals acting alone. This is as true in business and on a sports team as much as it is with elite military operators and violence professionals. But, in order to be successful, all team members must hold tightly to a common goal, believing in a shared vision so strongly that they are willing to sacrifice, subordinating their individual desires for the greater good of the team. Those who cannot, or will not, will contaminate the group, pulling others down with them if they are not dismissed.

For the Win: To win you must have buy-in. This cannot be formed from words alone. Don't just say it, do it… only then can you inspire others to follow.

You Lose: Let others come to say that you, "Talked the talk, but didn't walk the walk." Phonies never prevail over the long run.

16. Sun Tzu wrote:

"While heading the profit of my counsel, avail yourself also of any helpful circumstances over and beyond the ordinary rules."

There is no single font of all wisdom. The best ideas cannot be implemented everywhere or cover every conceivable possibility. Consequently, whenever we encounter wisdom, we owe it to ourselves to pick it up and consider it thoughtfully before adopting or setting it aside.

We can discover great ideas in virtually all aspects of our lives. Blindly following the advice of a single individual, no matter how learned, risks missing out on other important thoughts, ideas, and perspectives disseminated by others. The philosophies of Sun Tzu, Machiavelli, Clausewitz, Socrates, Aristotle, or any other luminary thinker are impressive in and of themselves, but far more powerful when considered more holistically by comparing and contrasting one with the others. Those who embrace continuous learning, formally and informally, are on average more successful than those who do not.

For the Win: You must be both well-read and broadly experienced. These allows for adroitness in battle. Leverage multiple resources to make good decisions.

You Lose: Be a scientist rather than an artist. Narrow focus is useful in hard science where expertise in the immutable laws of nature is essential. Art, however, is the ability to draw from diverse realms to create something fresh and fascinating.

17. Sun Tzu wrote:

"According as circumstances are favorable, one should modify one's plans."

Rigidly following one's preconceived plans courts disaster as risks go unmitigated, issues go unaddressed, and opportunities go unfulfilled. As circumstances change, we must be willing to modify our plans accordingly.

A flexible mind is a Zen concept of remaining open to new concepts and ideas. It is neither indecisive nor unsure, merely open. And, it is a powerful tool in conflict. In war, our success or failure often hinges on our ability to identify and exploit opportunities in a timely manner, just as it does in business, sports, or martial arts. If a situation changes for the better, we must be ready to alter our plans and promptly take advantage. Meditation and mindfulness can help us move past habituation and become more open to these possibilities as they arise.

For the Win: Different levels of experience require different skills. A supple mind can adapt as needed.

You Lose: Rigidity and inflexibility are raw acts of ego. Conceit clouds decision-making, ultimately leading to your destruction. Ask Captain Ahab (the protagonist in Herman Melville's 1851 novel *Moby Dick*).

18. Sun Tzu wrote:

"All warfare is based on deception."

The stronger force does not always prevail, nor the strongest combatant. If we can convince an adversary to believe and take action on something untrue, we create an advantage where otherwise we may have had none. Deception and deceit are integral to successful warfare.

When fighting for our lives we may not always win, but we cannot afford to lose. Lying, cheating, and deception, any tactic may be employed in order to prevail. Consider the American Revolutionary War (1775 – 1783) in which British forces held every advantage in training, equipment, and numbers, yet they marched over open ground in straight volley-lines while the American insurgents sniped at them from the tree lines. Their hit-and-run guerrilla tactics confounded and ultimately vanquished a vastly superior force. Doing the unexpected gives us a leg up in any venture.

For the Win: Misdirection, obfuscation, lies, and deception, these are fundamental to the art of war. Win fast, with minimum exposure, these are the tools to meet your goal.

You Lose: Not engaging in deception during times of war is an act of betrayal to yourself and your people.

19. Sun Tzu wrote:

"Hence, when able to attack we must seem unable, when using our forces we must seem inactive, when we are near we must make the enemy believe we are far away, and when far away we must make him believe we are near."

Confounding the enemy in war is paramount. We become a ghost, appearing unexpectedly, attacking, and vanishing again to haunt our adversaries. We lie, we cheat, using dirty tricks to win. But that's on the battlefield. Self-defense in the civilian world is a different beast.

Self-defense is an "affirmative defense" in the United States, meaning that if we choose that route we admit to an underlying crime in court and argue that we should not be punished because it (the assault, homicide, or whatever) was justifiable under the circumstances. Not only does this strategy shift the burden of proof from the prosecution to the defense, but it also means that we had to act appropriately during the encounter or we will lose in court. This means that while deception in self-defense may include feints, misdirection, or obfuscation, surprise attacks make us the bad guy ethically as well as in the eyes of the law. Assassins cannot legitimately claim self-defense.

For the Win: Make physical fighting your last resort. It is expensive and messy, even when necessary.

You Lose: If you fight and are swept up by the law, you will find yourself in a bad situation. No matter your perspective on the event, the courts may have a different view. A 30-second fight could easily mean 30 months of legal fees.

20. Sun Tzu wrote:

*"Hold out baits to entice the enemy.
Feign disorder and crush him."*

Give the enemy the illusion of an opportunity that is too good to pass up and he or she will fall into our trap. To make deception appear real, it is best to dust it with a grain of truth. For instance, those who practice classical martial arts will notice that the opening move of their forms often involves a defensive-looking posture used to feigned weaknesses and invite an attack where and when the practitioner is best prepared to defend against it.

Human psychology hasn't changed much between when these ancient arts were codified and what we encounter on the streets today. In fact, analysis of police reports indicates that enraged individuals tend to lead with a right-hand punch to the head, even when they're left-handed. This starts fights far more than any other technique since the adversary's face best represents what a person is angry at and wishes to destroy. We can take advantage of tendencies like this to feign disorder and disrupt a threat's designs.

For the Win: When the strong look weak, treat this pretense as a lie.

You Lose: Taking the bait is like a river trout hitting a shiny lure. The trout can't help itself, and certainly does not understand what happened, yet it becomes your dinner nonetheless.

21. Sun Tzu wrote:

"If he is secure at all points, be prepared for him. If he is in superior strength evade him."

Meticulous research uncovers an adversary's strengths, numbers, and formations. Knowing with certainty at what points he is best prepared to thwart or launch an attack simultaneously identifies the cleverest to counter to his intents. Like a good boxer, we can slip an adversary's punch, but we must know from where it will originate before making the attempt. Even as professional tournament fighters review each opponent's history and tendencies in order to formulate their strategy, so too must we understand how bad guys think and act to remain safe on the street.

Consider, for instance, that fringe areas near heavily traveled public places are where the majority of crimes take place. This includes parking lots, bathrooms, stairwells, ATM kiosks, and the like, especially at night. In order to attack us, however, the threat (or threats) must close distance or control our movement so that they can get into range to strike. Being aware of potential ambush sites and pre-attack indicators such as closing, cornering, herding, or surrounding give us time and options to formulate a viable response.

For the Win: There's nothing cowardly about avoiding a fight. It is good to run away, evading a superior opponent.

You Lose: Let your ego spur you to fight not because it is necessary or unavoidable, but simply because you want to fight and even if you prevail you will ultimately lose.

22. Sun Tzu wrote:

"If your opponent is of choleric temper, seek to irritate him. Pretend to be weak that he may grow arrogant."

Whatever the adversary's natural mental state, we must use it to trick him or her into an action that works best for us. If an adversary is a slave to his emotions, for instance, he may as easily be manipulated to serve our needs. We've all heard of "good cop/bad cop" which takes advantage of this strategy as law enforcement professionals investigate crimes, but manipulating the other guy's emotions is useful in much of our everyday lives as well.

Consider negotiations. Everything from navigating violence to asking for a raise to buying a car or home involves some sort of negotiation. We can deescalate a social violence threat by offering a face-saving way out, manipulate a business deal by appealing to another's greed, or demand concessions after provoking an inappropriate outburst that puts a rival's job in peril. This strategy is a powerful tool and we should use it wisely.

For the Win: Listen to the other person's emotions, acknowledge their words, and confirm you have heard what they said. In this you will perceive the path to victory.

You Lose: Let your emotions dictate and you will quickly discover that you are no longer leading the dance.

23. Sun Tzu wrote:

"If he is taking his ease give him no rest. If his forces are united separate them."

A weary adversary will want to rest. A scattered opponent gains strength by bringing his resources together. Harry him mercilessly, disrupting these designs. Sleep deprivation impairs memory, retards cognition, decreases effectiveness, and leads to careless errors.

Research indicates that sleepiness doubles the risk of sustaining an occupational injury and directly leads to more than 100,000 automobile accidents in the United States every year. If an adversary is tired, we can use this to our advantage. Conversely, we must exercise caution to assure that we get sufficient rest to operate at peak performance ourselves. People who are sleep-deprived lose aerobic endurance and may experience higher cortisol (a stress hormone) levels as well as decreased human growth hormone production. In addition to lowered mental acuity, this diminishes our body's ability to repair damaged tissues and recover from injuries.

For the Win: Get there the faster and with more, not everything, just more than your opponent.

You Lose: Let your opponent establish the pace and you become a stick swept away in the current. You've lost control of your destiny.

24. Sun Tzu wrote:

"Attack him where he is unprepared, appear where you are not expected."

If an adversary can brace for our strike, we will face a hard-fought battle. Clearly, it is best to use the element of surprise in our attack. This principle works both ways; criminals do not want to fight; they want to win. Consequently, they use the element of surprise to set victims up for attack

If we are singled out, the bad guy(s) will typically use dialogue, deception, distraction, and destruction to take us down. Dialogue allows an adversary to control distance, deception disguises his predatory intent, distraction sets up the attack, and destruction is the physical assault, rape, robbery, or murder that he commits. Nevertheless, it is rare for victims to be caught totally unaware. Even when sucker-punched, most assault victims report that they saw the blow coming yet did not have time to react. Consequently, our level of awareness and preparedness should ratchet up whenever a stranger is close enough to strike, at least until we give him a thorough once-over and dismiss any threat.

For the Win: Strike the weakest with your strongest. This is not about perceptions of fair play; it is about winning.

You Lose: Even coyotes know to circle around a bear, evade its mighty claws, and strike from the rear. Demonstrate that you're dumber than a coyote and you deserve to reap what you sow.

25. Sun Tzu wrote:

"These military devices leading to victory must not be divulged beforehand."

It's good to be underestimated. We cannot show everything we have before a battle. If we do, our adversary will take our measure and go into the fight fully prepared. That is by no means a winning recipe.

Presence, the use of body language that warns potential adversaries of our readiness and ability to act yet poses no threat to another's ego can stave off a criminal assault. We appear too costly to make a good victim, yet there's no sense in laying all of our proverbial cards on the table. This is why most civilians who own firearms prefer concealed over open carry. If bad guys know we have a gun they may ambush with overwhelming force to counter the threat that our weapon represents. Sure, the presence of a gun may stave off violence, but it's better to have it and not need it than to advertise and invite trouble.

For the Win: Understand that predators who display are not hunting, they're mating. It's the hunter who's trying to blend in we must watch for.

You Lose: Predators that surprise their prey, eat. Those who do not go hungry. Exercise poor situational awareness and become a victim.

26. Sun Tzu wrote:

"Now the general who wins a battle makes many calculations in his temple ere the battle is fought. The general who loses a battle makes but few calculations beforehand. Thus, do many calculations lead to victory and few calculations to defeat. How much more no calculation at all! It is by attention to this point that I can foresee who is likely to win or lose."

When the stakes are high, the wise never improvise. Calculation is the highest form of preparation before a battle. We all know that no plan survives contact with the enemy, so our strategy must be holistic, sensible, and well thought out. When others are involved, the strategy must be clearly communicated too. Rarely would we share our plan in its entirety, but we must assure that each member of our team knows his or her role and does exactly what we expect them to do at the moment when we need them to act.

In this fashion, our intent is realized no matter how much extemporization becomes necessary in the heat of the moment. Doing this effectively calls for thorough planning. Whenever we have the luxury of time to prepare, we must make the most of it. Calculate, analyze, and be ready for every contingency. Clarity of vision, mission, and strategy sets us up for success in nearly any endeavor as our whole team may act in concert to carry out our plan.

For the Win: Know the goal and suit the proper tactics to meet it; all else is meaningless.

You Lose: "We'll just make it up as we go along," said the surgeon to the soon to be dead patient. Only fools improvise when everything is on the line.

Chapter 2: Waging War

In this chapter, we discover the value of experience and proficiency in knowing our objective, intuiting what resources we will need, and setting our plans right the first time. Any significant undertaking requires investments in capital, equipment, and personnel. We must acquire what's needed for the job, but when we can simultaneously appropriate an adversary's resources to serve our needs, we place ourselves in a superior position. Nevertheless, if we fall short, we raise doubts about ourselves, our endeavor, and the likelihood of achieving results. The quality of the leader is the point around which the destiny of the enterprise or nation and its people circle.

1. Sun Tzu wrote:

"In the operations of war where there are in the field a thousand swift chariots, as many heavy chariots, and a hundred thousand mail-clad soldiers with provisions enough to carry them a thousand li *(~ 500 kilometers), the expenditure at home and at the front, including entertainment of guests, small items such as glue and paint, and sums spent on chariots and armor, will reach the total of a thousand ounces of silver per day. Such is the cost of raising an army of 100,000 men."*

War is expensive. We cannot afford to be miserly and expect to win. Most any worthwhile venture, be it in business, war, or our personal life, is expensive. We can look at the necessary layout of funds as a cost that we must pay or as an investment. Investment is the path to success, yet we must be prudent in reaching for too much at once lest we bite off more than we can chew and choke on our gluttony.

Consider debt-to-income ratio. It is often used by lenders to measure our ability to manage the monthly expenditures we must make to repay whatever we have borrowed. It is calculated as the sum of our monthly debt payments divided by our gross monthly income. Any debt-to-income ratio below 43% represents a lower risk of default, hence tends to be rewarded with favorable interest rates and loan conditions. Borrowing too much, which drives that ratio up, makes us a credit risk. Just as countries can be bankrupted by overextending military operations so too can individuals by taking on too much debt, even in pursuit of a worthy cause.

For the Win: War is expensive and nobody can escape its costs. Make the adversary lose more than you, and do so as quickly as possible.

You Lose: If you cannot recognize this formula for the win, making the opponent quickly lose more than you, you are the one who is losing.

2, 3. Sun Tzu wrote:

"When you engage in actual fighting if victory is long in coming then men's weapons will grow dull and their ardor will be damped. If you lay siege to a town you will exhaust your strength. Again, if the campaign is protracted the resources of the State will not be equal to the strain."

Long battles are bad; long wars are worse. Winning quickly is best for both the soldiers and the state. Prolonged battles sap our spirit, strength, and support. Sadly, at times they are necessary. Whenever possible it's best to chunk major endeavors into small components where we can celebrate periodic victories or correct our course along the way toward our final goal. This keeps our momentum rolling.

For lofty personal projects such as earning a black belt, completing a degree, or starting a successful business it is best to do this via SMART goals. This acronym stands for (1) specific, (2) measurable, (3) achievable, (4) relevant, and (5) time-bound, and helps assure that we are able to see progress, stay on track, and ultimately finish as strong as we started. Without this methodical approach it's easy to lose momentum, hit a plateau, or give up before achieving our goal.

For the Win: The spirits of your warriors must be held high. The longer the war, the farther the warrior's energy will fade. You must reinforce it.

You Lose: If you lose emotional momentum, you are losing. It may not show instantly, but it will become clear soon enough.

4. Sun Tzu wrote:

"Now, when your weapons are dulled, your ardor damped, your strength exhausted, and your treasure spent other chieftains will spring up to take advantage of your extremity. Then no man, however wise, will be able to avert the consequences that must ensue."

People willingly follow the example of strong leaders, yet whenever we are perceived as tired or weak, others may be tempted to take advantage of this infirmity and usurp our position. If it gets to this point, we will have failed. History rarely favors the weak. Consider Louis XVI (1754 – 1793), the king of France whose monarchy was overthrown during the French Revolution.

Louis' reign was weakened by a series of missteps including the acquisition of heavy debt from supporting the colonists during the American Revolutionary War, organized political unrest, burdensome taxes, and accusations of scandalous behaviors against his queen-consort Marie-Antoinette (1755 – 1793). Together these events brought France to the verge of bankruptcy and discredited the monarchy. In September of 1792, a National Convention declared the country a republic, throwing Louis XVI out of office. He was found guilty of treason and executed at the guillotine in January of 1793. His consort Marie Antoinette was executed nine months later.

For the Win: Never confuse weakness with compassion. Great leaders show no weakness, yet all great leaders are compassionate.

You Lose: Fail the inevitable test of strength and you have jeopardized not just yourself but also everyone who has supported and allied with you.

5. Sun Tzu wrote:

"Thus, though we have heard of stupid haste in war, cleverness has never been seen associated with long delays."

Preparation and delay are two separate things, yet they can easily be confused one for the other. We must act decisively, taking advantage of opportunities as they arise. The proverb of "striking while the iron is hot" hearkens back to a blacksmith at his forge. If he delays in shaping the metal while it is in a pliable state the iron soon cools and hardens to the point where his opportunity is lost. A late strike and it cracks or shatters, so he must lose productivity by re-heating the metal once again.

Smart people prepare, dullards repeatedly delay. It is silly to make important determinations without first understanding pertinent facts and data, but this does not mean waiting until we know everything. For example, due to the speed of modern business most decisions need to be made with at best 80% of the relevant information. Analysis paralysis is unacceptable. There is almost never a perfect answer, so we await one at our peril. Gather enough information to make an informed choice and move forward.

For the Win: Know when the time is right by astute measure of yourself and your enemy.

You Lose: Delay is often the avoidance of the inevitable. When the inevitable appears, it does so on its terms, not yours.

6. Sun Tzu wrote:

"There is no instance of a country having benefited from prolonged warfare."

A long fight, be it amongst individuals or states, will cost us on every level—health, wealth, and spirit. It is prudent to end the confrontation quickly. Unlike tournament competitions, real fights are brutal and short. Consider fighter pilots by way of example.

During World War II, Korea, and Vietnam aerial dogfighting was vital to the war effort. Enemy fighters closed on each other with missiles and guns blazing where those pilots with exceptional skill (and a little luck) won out. With the evolution of technology dogfighting has become exceedingly rare. Nowadays it's all about spotting and destroying the enemy before he or she even knows that we're a threat. Acquire the enemy first, strike first, and he'll never know what killed him. A popular advanced medium-range air-to-air missile built by Raytheon is the AIM-120D which was first deployed in 2008. It is a fire-and-forget weapon that travels at supersonic speeds with a lethal range of over 97 nautical miles. When you fly a plane armed with these missiles it's more of an assassination than a fight.

For the Win: Avoid protracted engagements. Prolonged battles make your forces weak.

You Lose: Enter a battle with no strategy or exit plan and you will fall into the trap of prolonged warfare. Disease, dysfunction, and defeat will soon follow.

7. Sun Tzu wrote:

"It is only one who is thoroughly acquainted with the evils of war that can thoroughly understand the profitable way of carrying it on."

Fighting is a specialized skill. While everybody makes judgments about violence, few have the experience and first-hand knowledge to produce an informed opinion. Those are the folks we should listen to. Creation of strategies for fighting and rules that govern one's behavior during a confrontation is best left to violence professionals, yet politicians, pundits, and keyboard warriors all feel inclined to pontificate about the subject. This can be explained by the Dunning-Kruger Effect.

Coined in 1999 by Cornell psychologists David Dunning (1961 –) and Justin Kruger (1972 –), the Dunning-Kruger Effect is a cognitive bias where people who are incompetent at something are unable to recognize their shortcomings. Ironically, not only do folks fail to recognize their own incompetence, but they're also likely to feel certain that they actually know what they're talking about. Consequently, we must be careful where we get advice from and how much credence we give it.

For the Win: You must spend extended time in an environment to truly understand that environment.

You Lose: Simply being smart is insufficient. Context is essential for understanding. Naively assuming that innate intelligence is transferable to any situation turns even the smartest person into a fool.

8. Sun Tzu wrote:

"The skillful soldier does not raise a second levy, neither are his supply-wagons loaded more than twice."

Skill and experience mean knowing our objective, intuiting what resources we need, and getting it right the first time. If we fall short, we raise doubts about ourselves, our endeavor, and the likelihood of achieving results. It takes skill and resources to win a fight, build a business, or do virtually anything worthwhile. Whatever our profession, successful individuals develop the expertise necessary to create and execute plans that achieve our goals.

The accountant has his spreadsheets, the mechanic his tools, so too must those concerned with their personal safety acquire the right knowledge, skills, and ability to prevail. Remaining safe on the street requires a holistic understanding of the nature of the threats we may face and the various resources necessary to thwart them. A black belt alone does not ward off danger. Neither does a knife, gun, or club. If we are truly concerned about self-defense, we must become experts at situational awareness, avoidance, de-escalation, fighting, and a host of other tools of the trade.

For the Win: Clarity and experience are the cornerstones of getting a task done right the first time.

You Lose: Lackadaisical arrangements and false confidence leave openings for the enemy to exploit.

9. Sun Tzu wrote:

"Bring war material with you from home, but forage on the enemy. Thus, the army will have food enough for its needs."

Any significant undertaking requires resources. We must acquire and bring what's needed for the job, but when we can also appropriate the other guy's supplies to serve our needs, we place ourselves in a superior position. Whenever we find ourselves in a fight, we not only bring the skills and equipment we have carried into the battle but also whatever we are able to appropriate from our adversaries.

We cannot afford to overlook what our adversary has brought to the game; it creates both risks and opportunities. For instance, if we were to find ourselves unarmed and facing a blade-wielding adversary, and we be able to disarm the threat we now have a weapon we could use against him. Or, we may be able to grab a hold of impromptu weapons that level the playing field, striking with found objects such as sticks, rocks, bricks, or bottles. We may also be able to use the terrain against our enemy by smashing him into a hard surface like a curb, parked vehicle, bolder, or tree. With a little creativity, we rarely run out of resources.

For the Win: Found resources are necessary. Alliances, groups, memberships and relationships are opportunities not burdens. Use them.

You Lose: When you see only one use for your environment you lose the ability to forage. You cannot exploit ripe opportunities that others have not yet perceived.

10. Sun Tzu wrote:

"Poverty of the State exchequer causes an army to be maintained by contributions from a distance. Contributing to maintain an army at a distance causes the people to be impoverished."

War is costly. In order to win we must first have our financial house in order or we will suffer and so too will those around us. According to the Small Business Administration, a third of all new business in the United States fail within the first two years and a little over half of them go out of business within their first five years. As economic cycles ebb and flow these failure rates can reach as high as 80%.

A significant contributor to these sad statistics is the fact that many entrepreneurs are unable to acquire sufficient initial capital to keep their enterprise afloat until they have developed a profitable model with repeat customers and sustained revenue streams. Further, new business owners often underestimate how much money they will truly need, or materially misunderstand their expected cash flow. Before starting a new venture, it is imperative to ascertain the full resources our business will require, both startup costs as well as ongoing business needs. Most enterprises take a year or two to get going, so we'll need enough funds to cover everything we need to spend until profits from sales can recoup our initial investment and cover all of our recurring costs.

For the Win: Know people will only contribute for a limited amount of time, even in a winning effort. Act swiftly and in total.

You Lose: Acting like a drug-addict, continuously begging others for help, is a strategy doomed to failure. Support will quickly dry up as your unreliable nature is revealed.

11. Sun Tzu wrote:

"On the other hand, the proximity of an army causes prices to go up and high prices cause the people's substance to be drained away."

It is expensive to prepare for battle, yet the price of open conflict can quickly become exorbitant. As resources are rapidly consumed to provision the troops, they become scarcer, which in turn causes prices to inflate. The longer the battle, the faster this cycle escalates, impacting military and civilian populations alike.

War has a profound impact on the economy, tax structure, and monetary policy of both affected and unaffected governments as well as civilian populations worldwide. Throughout history, economic, political, and cultural disruption has a tendency to create rising levels of inflation due to increases in demand for, as well as shortages of, critical products and services. While government spending stimulates demand, it simultaneously shifts civilian work to war production which causes a decline in the aggregate supply of many commodities which in turn drives up the cost we must pay for them. Unless revenue increases through mechanisms like taxes or asset seizures, financing a war adds significant inflationary pressures to the economy. This may be tolerated in the short term but it often ends badly over the long run.

For the Win: An army in warfare becomes a ravenous beast. It can purchase what it needs and take what it wants. Know this and prepare accordingly.

You Lose: If an army is deployed nearby, sooner or later it will be eating at your table.

12. Sun Tzu wrote:

"When their substance is drained away, the peasantry will be afflicted by heavy exactions."

The people, property, and purse we are fighting for will be exhausted with time. An ever-increasing burden on the populace sparks unrest, opening up the war to a second front at home. Knowledge, skill, and ability tend to follow a bell-curve, with a small number of outstanding individuals at one end, a few ne'er-do-wells at the other, and most everyone else in-between.

This means that when it comes to the most important assignments we look toward our A-Team to do the heavy lifting. It's good to reward the best employees with the most meaningful assignments, but we must take caution not to overload them with work. As the old adage says, "Never push a loyal employee to the point where he no longer cares." In the heat of the moment, it's natural to expect more, to push for long hours and extra effort to meet important goals and deadlines. Just like medieval peasants supporting their liege lord's war effort, in the short-term people can and will step up, but overburdening them overlong will eventually backfire.

For the Win: The exhaustion that comes with spikes in your workload should be noted and marked on your calendar, assuring that your team will not become overburdened.

You Lose: If the team's exhaustion is a surprise to leadership, you are following a poor leader.

13, 14. Sun Tzu wrote:

"With this loss of substance and exhaustion of strength, the homes of the people will be stripped bare and three-tenths of their income will be dissipated. While government expenses for broken chariots, worn-out horses, breast-plates and helmets, bows and arrows, spears and shields, protective mantles, draught-oxen and heavy wagons, will amount to four-tenths of its total revenue."

The waste of war affects both the citizens and the military. The longer the campaign, the more wealth that must be poured into repairing and replacing supplies expended in battle. This creates a hardship for combatants and non-combatants alike.

A superordinate goal such as conquering a hated adversary, winning a league championship, or earning a transformational business deal can inspire a collection of ordinary individuals to put forth extraordinary efforts. Arduous work, grueling hours, low pay, deferred benefits or compensation, it can all be tolerated in pursuit of a shared vision so long the endgame remains in sight and measurable progress is being made. We must, therefore, assure that every expenditure furthers our long-term goal so that we will not inadvertently undermine our endeavor.

For the Win: The cost of war is high. Act fast; the people will not tolerate a protracted financial burden.

You Lose: Dragging out military action, tapping the people's purse for extended periods of time, is the height of folly. This ends with your head on a pike.

15. Sun Tzu wrote:

"Hence a wise general makes a point of foraging on the enemy. One cartload of the enemy's provisions is equivalent to twenty of one's own and likewise a single picul (a "shoulder-load" weighing approximately 133 pounds) of his provender is equivalent to twenty from one's own store."

Foraging from an enemy's provisions creates a twofold victory, simultaneously lightening the burden on one's own populace while depleting the adversary's ability to support their war effort. Not every struggle has to become a zero-some game with a winner and a loser, sometimes we can grow the proverbial pie rather than compete for the largest slice, but we must know what scenario we face going in.

Members of a strategic alliance may steal from the enemy yet they will not cannibalize each other's resources because they must work together to win the war. Nevertheless, there's a chain of command that establishes who leads and supports the effort, and to what degree. Sometimes it's a power dynamic where the strongest player wins, whereas other times it is more of a joint partnership. For instance, if we're representing an enterprise with significant buying power and negotiating for commodity products or services it's easy to compete suppliers against each other to obtain the best price. A common tactic for this is the use of a reverse auction where the lowest bidder earns the contract. Coercive tactics like these are valuable, yet used in the wrong circumstances, such as where we need collaborative innovation from our suppliers, they will spectacularly fail.

For the Win: Create and maintain healthy relationships with suppliers and customers alike. Fair trade is good trade.

You Lose: Deceive a companion or colleague in trade and you not only ruin that relationship but also your reputation. No one wants to do business with a swindler.

16. Sun Tzu wrote:

> *"Now in order to kill the enemy our men must be roused to anger, that there may be advantage from defeating the enemy they must have their rewards."*

It's not easy to kill. Emotions are necessary to take the battle to the enemy, and clear rewards must await heroes after the battle. Scientists who study primitive, midbrain processing have long known that well-balanced individuals have a powerful resistance against killing other people. This dynamic is an evolutionary survival mechanism that prevents our species from destroying itself during territorial and mating rituals.

According to historians, when US soldiers had a clear shot at their enemy only 20% of them actually fired during World War II (WWII). Due to changes in training procedures such as the use of psychological conditioning and practicing against human-shaped targets rather than circular bull's-eyes this rate increased to about 55% during the Korean War and then climbed up to more than 90% by the end of the Vietnam War. In order to take a life, we must be able to overcome our natural resistance to killing, be it through rage, fear, or survival instincts during sudden violence, or through specialized training that helps desensitize professional warriors and prepares us for enduring conflict.

For the Win: As ugly as it is, the enemy must be seen as different. We can only destroy that which we disdain.

You Lose: This inability to kill, even when necessary, reduces you to a beggar.

17. Sun Tzu wrote:

"Therefore in chariot fighting when ten or more chariots have been taken, those should be rewarded to who took the first. Our own flags should be substituted for those of the enemy and the chariots mingled and used in conjunction with ours. The captured soldiers should be kindly treated and kept."

Some will strike more boldly than their peers on the battlefield; reward them first so that others may see their example and follow. Appropriate captured resources and use them against our foe, but treat prisoners well. An enterprise is only as good as its people, so attracting the best talent is imperative. The military uses medals, service ribbons, and badges to distinguish significant accomplishments by service members. Likewise, civilian enterprises look for ways to acknowledge outstanding personnel, but many are not particularly proficient at it.

According to exit interviews, a prime reason that people leave their organization is a lack of recognition for their contributions. Ineffectual management plays an important as well, of course; these two factors play hand-in-glove. Some folks are inspired by challenging assignments whereas others are motivated by monetary reward, so it's not the form of recognition so much as how and when we give it that matters most. Sincere, meaningful, relevant, and timely recognition that is adaptable to individual needs and desires is best.

For the Win: Capture and repurpose. Treat prisoners well; they no longer threaten your plans and may even be persuaded to your cause.

You Lose: Total destruction is the realm of chaotic barbarians. Take that route at your peril.

18. Sun Tzu wrote:

"This is called using the conquered foe to augment one's own strength."

Conscripting captured personnel increases one's own resources while depleting the enemy's strength. Throughout recorded history wars have traditionally been fought by a core force of seasoned professionals supported by levies of conscripts or draftees. Impressment, instituted via "press gangs" was the tradition of enlisting men into a military against their will, a practice which peaked in the early 1800s but lasted well into the 19th century.

Certain criminal gangs use similarly heavy-handed tactics to recruit new members even today. In a much less repressive manner, business and academic enterprises often attempt to poach talented employees away from their rivals. Whenever we are able to convert, coerce, or co-opt people to our cause it creates a twofold win. We gain a valuable resource while our adversaries lose access to their most talented personnel.

For the Win: Absorb every resource appropriately.

You Lose: When you aim to "burn it all to the ground" without considering its use to your cause, you sacrifice valuable opportunities.

19. Sun Tzu wrote:

"In war, then, let your great object be victory, not lengthy campaigns."

Our goal must be to win and to do so quickly. While a prolonged encounter is no good in war, this principle holds true in a street fight as well. The adversary will be doing everything he or she can to win in a fight. We cannot afford to make that threat's job any easier. Unlike sparring in the safety of a training hall, street fights often end with life-altering consequences.

We cannot get too smart for our own good, trying fancy or flashy techniques or tournament applications that fail to end the fight swiftly. We must think, "Him down now!" This is our mindset. We must keep things simple and direct, putting the adversary down as quickly and ruthlessly as possible so that we may escape to safety.

For the Win: When your plan is ready, execute it swiftly.

You Lose: Your hesitation demonstrates a lack of confidence.

20. Sun Tzu wrote:

"Thus it may be known that the leader of armies is the arbiter of the people's fate, the man on whom it depends whether the nation shall be in peace or in peril."

The quality of the military leader is the point around which the destiny of the nation and its people circle. A title like CEO, President, Director, or the like is respected but carries tremendous responsibility. The person in charge holds a higher purpose than those in their care since their actions impact not only themselves but also everyone around them.

In the fifth century BC, Lao-Tzu (601 – 514 BC) wrote, "The highest type of ruler is one of whose existence the people are barely aware… The sage is self-effacing and scanty of words. When his task is accomplished and things have been completed, all the people say, 'we ourselves have achieved it!'" This is the difference between a leader and a manager. We do not have to be in charge to lead, but we do need to set a good example. If we are always looking out for the welfare of those in our sphere of responsibility while keeping the endgame in mind it's hard to go wrong.

For the Win: You must be confident in your position and plan. All must see this conviction demonstrated through action.

You Lose: By failing to recognize that you set the tone through every action you take; you lose the ability to influence your men and women. This may be challenging, but it is the armor of leadership that you must boldly wear.

Chapter 3: Attack by Stratagem

In this chapter, we discover the significance of strategy, the way in which we prepare ourselves to deal with our adversaries. If our strategic foundation is strong, appropriate tactics can be employed over the course of any battle. We spontaneously react to each circumstance and prevail because we know when to fight and when not to fight, how to handle both superior and inferior forces, how to assure that our side is animated by the same spirit throughout all ranks, how to prepare and take the enemy unprepared, and how to assure that our capacity is not interfered with by our leaders or malefactors who would intervene. This is why attacking with stratagem is not only imperative, it is the only course for victory.

1. Sun Tzu wrote:

"In the practical art of war the best thing of all is to take the enemy's country whole and intact, to shatter and destroy it is not so good. So, too, it is better to recapture an army entire than to destroy it, to capture a regiment, a detachment or a company entire than to destroy them."

Wars are often fought over resources, so everything destroyed in battle can be considered a loss to both sides. Burning and destroying is the lowest form of warfare. Every captured piece of land has resources that the victor can use. Consequently, a wise general destroys as little as possible while breaking his or her enemy's will to fight.

Conversely in a self-defense situation, our aim must not be to kill or cripple the adversary but rather to remain safe or to thwart the threat and escape to safety. In this fashion, we are not forced to consume our own resources attempting to win a legal battle after the physical fight. Perhaps we can avoid conflict altogether, but if not, we may be able to eliminate the threat in a way that does not create adverse consequences. In other words, we must choose to escape rather than fight, fight rather than kill, and only destroy the adversary as a last resort.

For the Win: Understanding the hierarchy of fighting, killing, and destruction is necessary for adroit warfare at every level.

You Lose: Acts of vengeance destroy vital resources. This is the small-minded undertaking of an immature leader.

2. Sun Tzu wrote:

"Hence to fight and conquer in all your battles is not supreme excellence. Supreme excellence consists in breaking the enemy's resistance without fighting."

Fighting is expensive. Far better to conquer an enemy's will than to kill their soldiers and destroy their resources. Mastery of the art of fighting without fighting is the highest skill in warfare. This concept works in everyday life as well. For instance, "presence," colloquially body language, is the art of doing nothing skillfully. When social violence threatens, our body language (and verbal skills when necessary) prevents or diverts the attention of threats who want to monkey dance. In asocial violence, particularly in predatory ambushes, these same skills keep us off the victim list.

Whenever we are perceived as a hard target, threats consider us too dangerous to warrant the risk of attack. As such certain skills must be habituated, correct posture, how we move, how we scan, and what we naturally do with body positioning. Done right, we may never even realize how well our presence works; bad guys recognize our capability and quietly move on.

For the Win: Defeat the enemy's will and they cannot fight.

You Lose: Leave an ember of hope in your opponent's heart that they may prevail and it can become a flame that ignites their triumphant resurgence.

3. Sun Tzu wrote:

"Thus the highest form of generalship is to balk the enemy's plans, the next best is to prevent the junction of the enemy's forces, the next in order is to attack the enemy's army in the field, and the worst policy of all is to besiege walled cities."

The way to win the mind of the enemy is to have them question their ability, their plan, thus diminishing their will. When this cannot be done it is preferable to engage in a way that can drive a swift victory rather than a sustained and costly struggle. This process can be described mathematically. Response time in a fight is a summation of how long it takes us to perceive a threat, choose a response, set that response into motion, and then strike the adversary. This concept, known as Boyd's law, after US Air Force Colonel John Richard Boyd (1927 – 1997), illustrates the Observation, Orientation, Decision, and Action (OODA) loop and applies to everything from dogfights amongst fighter jets to fistfights amongst individuals.

As a confrontation begins, we observe ourselves, our surroundings, and the threat(s). This takes time, which delays immediate action, even if only by milliseconds. Next, we must orient ourselves with a mental image of the situation, building on past experiences and training to interpolate our environment before deciding how best to respond. Because it is impossible to process information as quickly as we perceive it, there is also an orientation delay that precedes action. Once we select an appropriate response, there is another delay between thought and action. A person who can consistently go through this cycle faster than his adversary gains the advantage. This is the value of training.

For the Win: Make the enemy flinch. Countervail their plans; do not let them muster their full forces before you meet in battle.

You Lose: Charging headlong into battle flips the order of action. Even if you prevail it will be the costliest victory possible.

4. Sun Tzu wrote:

"The rule is not to besiege walled cities if it can possibly be avoided. The preparation of mantlets, movable shelters, and various implements of war will take up three whole months and the piling up of mounds over against the walls will take three months more."

Any siege is tedious and expensive. Fighting a fortified opponent violates the principle of winning swiftly. Even in modern warfare, urban house-to-house engagements are arduous and fraught with peril. It takes a highly-trained, well-coordinated team to clear each building.

Flipping the equation, this means that in a self-defense situation we're most secure in our own homes. Intimately knowing the neighborhoods where we live, work or attend school, and frequent creates an advantage if we're ever attacked. On our home turf, we can build relationships with others who may help ward off threats and will know ambush locations, escape routes, and other environmental factors that can be turned to our advantage.

For the Win: It is expensive and dangerous to engage an entrenched enemy. Find another path to victory.

You Lose: Heavily fortified enemies are immobile by choice. In surrounding them you play into their game not your own. This is a recipe for disaster.

5. Sun Tzu wrote:

"The general, unable to control his irritation, will launch his men to the assault like swarming ants with the result that one-third of his men are slain while the town still remains untaken. Such are the disastrous effects of a siege."

Emotions are expensive for commanders and deadly to our troops. Life-and-death matters must be handled with reason and perspicacity. Be it in business or in personal protection, the better we prepare, the keener our strategy, the less we have to rely on suboptimal, hasty, or impassioned decisions. We must plot, plan, and execute.

Consider mergers and acquisitions, hostile takeovers, and shareholder revolts. Like siege warfare of old, these business battles must be perfectly executed or they become long, drawn-out affairs that exhaust resources on all sides. Thoroughly examine the target company's strategic alignment, cultural fit, performance, and market position, identify industry trends and opportunities, understand workforce impacts, and evaluate likely customer reactions before taking any action. With diligence and swift action, we create value.

For the Win: Knowing both how and when to strike are key components of a complete leader.

You Lose: Heavy losses are the reward for petulant leaders who take imprudent or inopportune action.

6. Sun Tzu wrote:

"Therefore the skillful leader subdues the enemy's troops without any fighting, he captures their cities without laying siege to them, and he overthrows their kingdom without lengthy operations in the field."

The best battle is no battle. The best siege or protracted campaign is, of course, none. Find victory by seeking the swiftest end to any conflict. Just as bad guys use dialogue, deception, distraction, and destruction to take us down, so too can we adopt these tactics to turn the tables on our enemies. If we must fight, we must fight dirty.

Misdirection, obfuscation, and trickery can be tools of war, business, and self-defense. This means, for example, that we must fight with our minds and mouths as much as with our fists and feet. Clever words can de-escalate a tense situation, create confusion or doubt, stave off bloodshed until help arrives, or momentarily distract an adversary to facilitate our counterattack and escape. Even a *kiai*, or "spirit shout" found in classical martial arts, can startle and disorient our foe making it easier to land a disabling strike.

For the Win: Take all necessary means to subdue the enemy without lifting your sword. This is the first act.

You Lose: Jumping ahead in the equation from the least-cost way out of your predicament to the most expensive solution does a disservice to all.

7. Sun Tzu wrote:

"With his forces intact he will dispute the mastery of the empire, and thus without losing a man his triumph will be complete. This is the method of attacking by stratagem."

Planning well, understanding the moment, this is the highest form of battle. Mastery of strategy brings total victory. Our strategy is a plan of action, a high-level, policy-based approach for obtaining our goals. Tactics, on the other hand, are expedient means of achieving our ends. In other words, strategy is what we do to prepare for contact with the adversary while tactics are actions that we carry out during the course of battle.

We cannot think of and plan for every eventuality ahead of time, so if all we have is tactics, we will have a tendency to freeze in that critical moment when things begin to go south or the adversary catches us by surprise. This rarely ends well. If our strategic foundation is strong, on the other hand, appropriate tactics can be employed without much conscious thought. We spontaneously react to most any situation and prevail. This is why attacking with stratagem is the only course for victory.

For the Win: Win swiftly using deception to leave the enemy's resources intact and you multiply your victory.

You Lose: Without using trickery, deception and lies, you are nothing more than an incompetent pugilist, and a bruised and bloodied one at that.

8. Sun Tzu wrote:

"It is the rule in war, if our forces are ten to the enemy's one to surround him, if five to one to attack him, if twice as numerous to divide our army into two."

Superior forces have more options. We may surround the adversary and force his surrender without a fight. Overwhelming resources can help us prevail in most any fight. Nevertheless, we must use them wisely. For example, one might think that modern technology, armor, and weapons guarantees victory over any tribal culture living in near stone-age conditions, but this is not always the case. There is a lot we can learn about this from the death of Portuguese explorer Ferdinand Magellan (1480 – 1521).

Despite having warships, cannons, swords, and armor at his disposal, Magellan was beaten to death by a group of nearly naked natives armed with bamboo spears and rattan sticks in the Philippine Islands on March 17, 1521. Lured onto a long, shallow beach, he was ambushed in the surf where his men were weighed down by their heavy armor and wet clothing. Worse, the fight took place beyond the range of his standoff naval weaponry. Since all his tactics and equipment were built around a strategy he could no longer employ, he lost before the fight even began.

For the Win: War is a game of numbers. Measuring your resources is important. Measuring the enemy's numbers is equally vital. Understanding changes in either and how they may impact your plans is imperative.

You Lose: Become blind to the dynamic flow of the battlefield and you will lose. Elements once counted upon can easily change or even disappear.

9. Sun Tzu wrote:

"If equally matched we can offer battle, if slightly inferior in numbers we can avoid the enemy, if quite unequal in every way we can flee from him."

We must know when it makes sense to fight and when it is more prudent not to fight. On equal terms, we can engage in battle, but when faced with superior forces it is better to escape to fight another day. David and Goliath notwithstanding, it is exceedingly rare for an inferior force or individual to prevail in a battle against a bigger, stronger, or more numerous adversary.

Sometimes we do have to fight, at least long enough to deal with the immediate threat, but running away as soon as practicable can be the best alternative in mismatched conflicts. Be aware and leave an area if trouble seems to be brewing. We can walk away normally if we only have a feeling that things are not right, evading potential or developing threats by crossing the street, turning and walking back the way we came from, turning down another street, or otherwise moving toward a safer location. If actual trouble becomes apparent, we should move away from it quickly but calmly. If the trouble starts after us, that's the time to run.

For the Win: To seal your victory, avoidance and flight are just as valid as combat. Seek the least cost avenue to success.

You Lose: Battle is but one path to victory. Failing to look for alternate means to prevail is negligent; failure to act in alternate ways once discovered is just plain stupidity.

10. Sun Tzu wrote:

"Hence, though an obstinate fight may be made by a small force in the end it must be captured by the larger force."

If we are small, we may hang on despite the odds, but not for long. Overwhelming force virtually always prevails. We cannot afford to let our desire to fight draw us into a battle that we cannot expect to win without luck. This holds true for war and self-defense just as much as it does in business, or pretty much any aspect of life.

Sometimes this means checking our ego and keeping firm control of our temper so that we do not engage in the "*escalato* follies." *Escalato* is the game of one-upmanship whereby events escalate into violence unless one player or the other accepts a face-saving way out. This is easier said than done at times, but that's only one side of the equation. The other guy(s) plays a vital role too, and that can lead to the need to physically remove ourselves from danger. There are two components to this sort of tactical withdrawal, evasion, and escape. Evasion allows us to avoid or deal with an immediate threat, while escape gets us away to safety.

For the Win: Mass is often the determining factor in warfare. When all other elements are equal, history favors the larger force.

You Lose: If you point to the biblical story of David and Goliath as an example of small overcoming large, know that narrative represents an anomaly. Depending on this incredibly rare outcome to apply in your situation is ridiculous.

11. Sun Tzu wrote:

"Now the general is the bulwark of the State. If the bulwark is complete at all points the State will be strong, if the bulwark is defective the State will be weak."

A country only remains viable to the extent that it can secure and defend its borders. The general and his armies are the cornerstones of any nation's defense, yet it takes leadership and alignment across the entire government to assure success. Like any successful individual, a leader must be balanced.

An unbalanced general can lead his troops, his government, and his fellow citizens to ruin. Conversely, an unstable structure or entrenched bureaucracy operating at odds to the greater good can undermine even the most capable leader. We must be able to share our vision and mission, build alliances, and work in concert in order to achieve our goals. And, we must guard against those treacherous "allies" who would work at cross-purposes to our designs.

For the Win: Only the best leaders are fit to lead through crisis; all others must be discarded regardless of alliance or relationships.

You Lose: When loyalty to unworthy individuals puts your goals in jeopardy, the battle is already lost.

12, 13. Sun Tzu wrote:

"There are three ways in which a ruler can bring misfortune upon his army: (1) by commanding the army to advance or to retreat being ignorant of the fact that it cannot obey. This is called hobbling the army."

An inappropriate command can send an army into disarray. A general's commands must align with the capabilities of his army. We must set their hearts and intents toward our purpose in advance. This takes esprit de corps, a sense of unity, or common spirit existing in the members of a team which inspires enthusiasm, devotion, and strong regard for the honor of the group.

The term *"esprit de corps"* describes a collection of individuals who truly operate as one team. Together they hold tightly to the common goal that has been set before them such as securing a victory on the battlefield, rolling out a new product, building a program, or winning a sports championship. They believe in the collective vision so strongly that they are willing to sacrifice, subordinating their individual desires for the betterment of the team and the goal. This takes leadership from above, deference from below, and enough will and self-discipline from everyone to make it happen.

For the Win: Great leaders do not meddle in the day-to-day affairs of their team. They set a vision, empower underlings, and get out of the way.

You Lose: If you put good people and plans in place yet cannot leave well enough alone, you undermine trust. Constantly tinkering, meddling, and interfering sets your team up to lose.

14. Sun Tzu wrote:

"(2) by attempting to govern an army in the same way as he administers a kingdom being ignorant of the conditions which obtain in an army. This causes restlessness in the soldier's minds."

Commanding an army is not the same as running a government (or corporation for that matter). Generals must both deserve and earn the respect of their troops, yet the government has no such requirement. Leaders who rise through the ranks understand what motivates their underlings and can conduct themselves accordingly.

Most people cannot in good conscience follow a leader who in the heat of the moment proves him- or herself feckless, dishonest, or unethical. Thankfully most people have a pretty good moral compass, however, so once we understand a situation knowing the right thing is easy. While doing the right thing can be hard, it tends to get simpler when we consider how our actions might look from an outsider's perspective. If we wouldn't mind seeing our actions revealed on the front page of The Wall Street Journal or some other prestigious national periodical, we're probably on the right track.

For the Win: Commanders must demonstrate the tone needed for success. This is a vital part of leadership; if this role is left unfilled it will fill itself in unpredictable ways.

You Lose: When commanders fail to set the tone, administrators will fill the void with their self-serving agenda. Undirected bureaucracy rarely serves the greater good.

15. Sun Tzu wrote:

"(3) by employing the officers of his army without discrimination through ignorance of the military principle of adaptation to circumstances. This shakes the confidence of the soldiers."

Running an army by rote is a formula for failure. As the old adage goes, "No plan survives contact with the enemy." As leaders we must be flexible in how we execute our strategies, making adjustments based on the conditions we face along the way.

Successful leaders never assume that everything will go according to plan. That means that we must put good people in place and trust our team to make good choices. We are also savvy enough to know that people are, well, people, and things can go sideways if we are not paying attention. Monitoring is not micromanaging. We must be mindful not to meddle except where we are truly needed and there is no option but to course-correct. Problems are normal; so long as they are following our strategy, we can let our team deal with the details accordingly.

For the Win: Know that life is not a straight line going from A to B. To project this delusion of straight-line solutions onto a battlefield is senseless.

You Lose: When a commander confuses rigidity with discipline, adaptability is lost. In this fashion you cannot win.

16. Sun Tzu wrote:

"But when the army is restless and distrustful, trouble is sure to come from the other feudal princes. This is simply bringing anarchy into the army and flinging victory away."

If we begin to lose our grip, others will intervene and aid in our downfall. The German word *"schadenfreude"* means taking pleasure in another's failure. Sometimes we enjoy other people's shortcomings simply because it makes us feel better about our own imperfections, but occasionally it's more nefarious than that.

Certain individuals actively strive to actively take advantage of others when they are most vulnerable. This may be desirable in war, perhaps even in business on certain occasions, but we must guard against letting those with nefarious intent know when our lives or those of members of our teams are in disarray. In this fashion it's harder for an adversary to turn us into their victim.

For the Win: Keep order in all aspects of your life. As a leader it is part of your profession, unavoidable. Order keeps the vultures at bay.

You Lose: Show disorganization and you will draw the vultures of the world to your door. They will fly in from both outside and inside your organization to feed on the chaos.

17. Sun Tzu wrote:

"Thus we may know that there are five essentials for victory: (1) he will win who knows when to fight and when not to fight, (2) he will win who knows how to handle both superior and inferior forces, (3) he will win whose army is animated by the same spirit throughout all its ranks, (4) he will win who, prepared himself, waits to take the enemy unprepared, and (5) he will win who has military capacity and is not interfered with by the sovereign."

We must know when violence is the right answer. If we measure ourselves and our adversaries well, light a fire under our men, surprise the enemy, and keep outsiders from interfering with our plans we will ultimately prevail. The dynamics of interpersonal conflict and violence are complex, yet despite advances in technology, the nature of humans remains much the same today as it did in Sun Tzu's time.

Good situational awareness can usually keep us out of trouble, but when faced with an unavoidable threat we may still be able to stave off violence with presence alone. Bad guys rarely want to tangle with those who appear skillfully prepared to defend themselves. We can use words to defuse many situations or apply calming or directive touch to reach a resolution without injury. But not always. Empty-hand restraint may be required if we need to control a situation without seriously hurting anyone. Other times, less-lethal or even lethal force is necessary to save our lives or protect our loved ones. Holistic self-defense means developing a skill set that allows us to manage threats at all levels of force.

For the Win: Keen observation, strong spirit, swift action, and no interference from interlopers, these are key elements for the win.

You Lose: Poor information, inconsistent messaging, sporadic action, and overthinking… these are the elements of a certain loss. Admire the chaos rather than seeking solutions and you cannot prevail.

18. Sun Tzu wrote:

"Hence the saying: 'If you know the enemy and know yourself you need not fear the result of a hundred battles. If you know yourself but not the enemy for every victory gained you will also suffer a defeat. If you know neither the enemy nor yourself you will succumb in every battle.'"

Ignorance of our enemy's capabilities makes us irresponsible. Ignorance of our own skills makes us reckless. To a warrior, these are foolish shortcomings, and fools fall fast in fights, yet if we truly know both ourselves and our enemy, we need never fear the outcome of battle. This principle applies just as much to mental or spiritual battles as it does to physical fights.

As the old saying goes, "People seldom hit what they do not aim for." Given the right opportunity, most folks will step up or down to expectations. Setting lofty yet achievable goals for ourselves and those in our charge affords an opportunity to grow, to learn what we're truly made of. Done responsibly, it is far better to aim high and fail than it is to never aim at all and live with regret.

For the Win: The harsh light of examination is essential for victory. Honestly measure yourself and your opponent, acting with full knowledge and lucidity.

You Lose: Deceive yourself with respect to your strengths and weakness, or underestimate your enemy, and you will arrive at the battlefield with all the resilience of an afternoon shadow. You will fight with the strength and potential of a silhouette, which is to say practically none.

Chapter 4: Tactical Dispositions

In this chapter, we discover that he who is destined to defeat fights first and afterwards looks for victory. Of all the elements of conflict, tactics are the most easily understood, thus focused on the most, yet tactics without strategy are a hodgepodge with no clear application. The goal is understood, to defeat the adversary, but the cohesive plan that assures victory is lacking. All the rudiments of battle must be taken into account and then bound together by strategy to assure success upon the battlefield. Thus, to secure ourselves against defeat lies in our own hands, yet the opportunity of defeating the adversary is provided by our enemy himself. In war the victorious strategist only seeks battle after the victory has already been won.

1. Sun Tzu wrote:

> *"The good fighters of old first put themselves beyond the possibility of defeat and then waited for an opportunity of defeating the enemy."*

Our strategy is strong, our supplies abundant, now the only question becomes when to strike. With aptitude, diligence, and discipline we can place ourselves beyond the possibility of defeat in almost any endeavor. Consider Tom Dempsey (1941 –), who was born with no toes on his right foot and no fingers on his right hand, yet dreamed of playing American football. He dedicated himself to mastering the only position he could attain with limited mobility and ball-handling capability, a kicker.

An undrafted free-agent, Dempsey earned a spot on the New Orleans Saints NFL team where in 1970 he won a game with a 63-yard field goal, a record which stood for 43 years until it was eventually broken by Matt Prater in 2013. Dempsey identified what he could do in the context of the sport, had a modified shoe built that could accommodate his deformity, and then intelligently applied himself to becoming the best kicker in the game. In addition to his record-breaking field goal, he was selected to the Pro Bowl, tapped as a First-Team All-Pro, and inducted into the New Orleans Saints Hall of Fame.

For the Win: With focus and process, the map to victory can be revealed and the future reasonably assured.

You Lose: Having a dream is important. But, a dream without any process for achievement quickly becomes a nightmare of anxiety, fear, and failure.

2. Sun Tzu wrote:

> *"To secure ourselves against defeat lies in our own hands but the opportunity of defeating the enemy is provided by the enemy himself."*

Worrying about what we cannot control is worthless. We must secure what is ours and continuously prepare such that we may take advantage of openings offered by others as they arise. This idea of having no concern, other than observation, with things that are beyond our control runs deep within the Stoic Philosophy. A movement that grew out of the Hellenistic period designed to help practitioners overcome their destructive emotions, Stoics focused on actions over words.

We need not adhere to the Stoic way to adopt this pragmatic perspective, however. As Miyamoto Musashi (1584 – 1645) wrote, "Respect Buddha and the gods without counting on their help." The idea is not so much to discount what we cannot control, but rather to be aware of the moment we are in, shift our attention to the things that matter most, and constantly be prepared to take advantage of opportunities as they present themselves.

For the Win: When you release the things that are outside of your control you are able to bring more focus to the things you can affect.

You Lose: Simply because you cannot control an item today does not mean you should not keep an eye on it tomorrow; situations change and advantage may be seized with time.

3. Sun Tzu wrote:

"Thus the good fighter is able to secure himself against defeat but cannot make certain of defeating the enemy."

Even the best prepared individuals must face the realization that we cannot control every contingency. We may avoid defeating ourselves, but this does not always guarantee our victory. Although a winning track-record buoys confidence, it may not carry us through novel or unaccustomed challenges.

Consider that every advertisement for financial or investment services includes a disclaimer along the lines of, "Past performance does not guarantee future performance." This proviso is set in place to protect a company against legal action if their client makes a lower return or loses money on their investment. Risk exists in almost every endeavor. No matter how well we prepare, no matter what we are told or believe, we must take this fact into account.

For the Win: Ultimately your resources are your own and should be used to build your best self.

You Lose: By focusing on the enemy and failing to shape your own forces you flip the proper order of preparation upside down.

4. Sun Tzu wrote:

"Hence the saying, 'One may know how to conquer without being able to do it.'"

No matter how well we have prepared, the earth and the heavens choose… and the enemy gets a vote. We may know exactly how to succeed but never get the opportunity to put our plans into action. Before we engage, we must know how serious a loss in battle can be—to us, our men, and our country.

In an interview with former Central Intelligence Agency Director William Joseph Gates (1913 – 1987), he made a comment about surgical military strikes and swift war. The general thrust of his observations pointed out that war, in any capacity, is unlikely to go perfectly as planned. The conflict often takes more resources, more time, and more men than anticipated when it was charted out in the war room. Nevertheless, sometimes the opposite occurs and everything falls into place swiftly. Sometimes we just get lucky. For instance, the United States Navy had its aircraft carriers out on drills on December 7th, 1941 when the Japanese attacked and sank the moored ships at Pearl Harbor. Despite a heavy loss in men and equipment, this fortuitous timing left the American fleet with its most valuable ships and ability to project force over great distances largely intact.

For the Win: There is a difference between "book smart" and "street smart." This is the chasm between theory and practice. Victory in battle requires practical application of the art of war.

You Lose: Without the tempering of experience, your best plans will fail in application.

5. Sun Tzu wrote:

"Security against defeat implies defensive tactics, ability to defeat the enemy means taking the offensive."

Whenever we fight, we must push the enemy. As the adage states, the best defense is a good offense. Fighting defensively is a losing proposition. Siege warfare is the ultimate defensive action of a person, a city-state, or a business enterprise. Under siege we are left with little option but to attempt to repel assaults as they occur, expending vital resources to at best hold our own as initiative favors the adversary.

Unless we are able to start a successful counteroffensive all we can hope for is to delay the inevitable unless reinforcements arrive or some outside force bails us out of trouble. For instance, in 52 A.D. Vercingetorix (82 – 46 BC), a Gallic king found himself and 80,000 of his men under siege by a force of 60,000 Romans at the fortress of Alesia. The Romans, under the leadership of Julius Caesar, rebuffed a spirited counterattack by his forces, the siege continued, and Vercingetorix was ultimately defeated, brought to Rome in chains, and ultimately executed six years later. Likewise, in most any violent encounter, a skillful aggressor may overwhelm and defeat a defensive fighter.

For the Win: You must use aggressive defense. In any defensive position, maintain the ability to strike when the right opportunity presents itself.

You Lose: Playing not to lose, in practical reality, is playing to lose slowly. This is no path to victory.

6. Sun Tzu wrote:

"Standing on the defensive indicates insufficient strength; attacking, a superabundance of strength."

If we are forced into a defensive posture it means that our strength is inferior to that of our adversaries. Superior forces initiate attack. When someone attacks us, we can be sure that they have taken our measure, found us wanting, and believe that they can win.

Violence on the street is nothing like competition in the ring. Criminals never desire a fair fight; they want to secure our resources with minimal risk and effort. They want to win, and to do so convincingly. This means that they carefully select victims who appear to be easy targets, those who are small, weak, or inattentive. Consequently, defense does not deter a committed attacker nearly as much as the ability to fight back.

For the Win: Even in defense you must threaten, and that threat must be understood by the enemy.

You Lose: Adopting a fully defensive position, without the ability to strike, signals victimhood.

7. Sun Tzu wrote:

"The general who is skilled in defense hides in the most secret recesses of the earth, he who is skilled in attack flashes forth from the topmost heights of heaven. Thus, on the one hand we have ability to protect ourselves on the other a victory that is complete."

Offense produces victory, but if we must play defense it is prudent to hide our power until it is ready to be unleashed. We must follow these strategic principles even in defense, staving off damage while preparing for our counterstrike.

If we must fight defensively, it is best to adopt the attitude of the assassin, sniper, or a spy. We must be wily, not show our full strength until it is needed, and then strike swiftly and decisively in a flash to assure our victory. For instance, if we hold a weapon, we must keep it out of the adversary's sight until it is put to use. In this fashion, we turn the tables on our adversary through surprise, aggression, and skill.

For the Win: If the battle is imminent hide your weapons. The enemy should never see all that you can bring to battle, only feel it when caught by surprise.

You Lose: Letting your opponent acquire accurate information regarding your resources is a failure of duty.

8. Sun Tzu wrote:

"To see victory only when it is within the ken (comprehension) of the common herd is not the acme (pinnacle) of excellence."

Seeing the obvious is by no means the key to brilliance. Perceiving what everybody else sees is not only focusing on the obvious, it is also the act of a herd animal. And, sadly, a herd is only as intelligent at its dumbest creature. While the herd affords a certain degree of safety in numbers it also follows the comfortable path, the obvious route, making it easy for predators to plan where and how to cut from the herd and pick off members of the group.

Astute observation, the ability to grasp what others cannot, is key for self-preservation when we find ourselves part of a crowd. For instance, during an active shooter incident escape is paramount for those who are unarmed as the chances of successfully striking back are small. While the panicked throng attempts to fight their way through a door or window, an astute observer might create his own exit through a convenient wall by kicking his or her way through the sheetrock.

For the Win: Not everybody can see the forest for the trees, yet as a leader you must see all elements of the battle and discern their relationships to one another.

You Lose: When you fail to understand the elements of battle by your own accord, you cannot react with alacrity. You will become lost, unable to see what is shown, to appreciate the insight of others. In this fashion your plans become meaningless and un-implementable.

9. Sun Tzu wrote:

"Neither is it the acme of excellence if you fight and conquer and the whole empire says, 'Well done!'"

Praise is appealing, yet it often comes from those that have not done the hard work. The praise of others is fine but fleeting. Consider, who still remembers who was the Most Valuable Player in the 1988 World Series? The adulation of others should not be given much weight in our own self-appraisal. We already know what we do well.

Constructive criticism, on the other hand, can help expose weaknesses we may not be aware of, vulnerabilities that may be exploited by our adversaries. When we set our ego aside, listen to the criticism, and think well and hard upon its merits we become stronger. True leaders are intrinsically motivated, we do not need the accolades of others, yet we can continuously improve and evolve when we understand and work to overcome our flaws.

For the Win: Alignment with an ascendant goal is an underpinning of a leader's leader.

You Lose: Seek honors to gratify your ego and you become a politician, not a leader.

10. Sun Tzu wrote:

"To lift an autumn hair (the fur of a rabbit which is finest in the fall season) is no sign of great strength, to see the sun and moon is no sign of sharp sight, to hear the noise of thunder is no sign of a quick ear."

It is not through observation of everyday events that we attain great insight but rather through a deep study of the forces behind the scenes that make things happen. We must look behind the obvious to understand not only what we observe but also why. This illuminates deeper meaning.

For instance, a robber might steal our wallet at gunpoint, a burglar might break into our house and abscond with our jewelry while we're on vacation, or an embezzler might purloin our coffers at work. Clearly, what's happening is important at the moment, but isn't it better to understand why we were selected, to know the attributes, oversights, or inattentions that led to victimhood? Only in this fashion may we address our shortcomings and prevent a reoccurrence.

For the Win: Viewing the content and the context of a moment brings insight. The experienced leader uses all available resources to assist in decision-making.

You Lose: Focusing on the obvious brings little insight. You cannot lead if you do not understand.

11. Sun Tzu wrote:

"What the ancients called a clever fighter is one who not only wins but excels in winning with ease."

Mastery of strategy and tactics not only allows us to win but also to make our victories appear effortless. Winning is good but total victory, that effortless-appearing triumph that few can emulate, is far better. Oftentimes this "effortless" excellence brings unexpected opportunities.

For example, in 458 BC Lucius Quinctius Cincinnatus (519 – 430 BC) was appointed Dictator of Rome in order to rescue a consular army that was surrounded by the Aequi on Mount Algidus. At the time of his appointment, he was working a small farm. Cincinnatus assumed total power, put down the rebels, and then vacated his position and returned to farming after he finished less than a year later. The embodiment of the Roman virtues of manliness and devotion to the Republic, Cincinnatus was so well respected that the Roman people reportedly made him their dictator a second time 18 years later to check the tyrannical ambitions of Spurius Maelius (? – 439 BC).

For the Win: The clever fighter is prepared for any eventuality. With sound strategy you can respond to whatever you face with assuredness.

You Lose: A protracted battle indicates a lack of preparation. The tactical approach is useful in certain situations, but far from a panacea. Ultimately it leads to failure.

12. Sun Tzu wrote:

> *"Hence his victories bring him neither reputation for wisdom nor credit for courage."*

When victory appears too easy, we may not get the credit we deserve despite the fact that it was our mastery of the art of war that led to an easy triumph. Preparation, resilience, discipline, and grit are vital aspects of success, yet others around us perceive only the result, not the process of achieving it.

A challenge is that people often observe in others what they imagine about themselves. If it looks easy, surely anyone can accomplish the same thing with a little determination, luck, or perseverance. Consequently, if our victory appears effortless, many will believe that it stemmed from good fortune rather than through wisdom, courage, or skill. Little credit for our expertise will come our way.

For the Win: Swift victory is the goal, and this success alone is fulfilling regardless of any accolade earned from your endeavor.

You Lose: By confusing praise, admiration, or appreciation with victory, you vainly chase after things that do not matter.

13. Sun Tzu wrote:

"He wins his battles by making no mistakes. Making no mistakes is what establishes the certainty of victory for it means conquering an enemy who is already defeated."

If our preparation and execution are mistake-free, we are destined to prevail. In everyday life, we learn and grow from mistakes, yet in combat, any error may be our last as the adversary seeks to exploit our misstep. This is why training and preparation are so critical for survival. Without arduous, realistic practice our proficiency degrades unacceptably under adrenal stress during a life-or-death encounter.

Counter-ambush and other reality-based instruction using firearms loaded with Simmunition® non-lethal training ammo, ShocknifeTM training knives, pepper spray, and similar tools that can inflict pain without serious injury add a measured level of risk that conditions a better-trained response in participants than rubber guns, plastic knives, and other inert tools. This helps us learn to deal with both conflict and adrenaline, giving us a leg up during any violent confrontation.

For the Win: Mistakes will almost always be made, strive for the least impactful errors.

You Lose: Mistakes can be born of ignorance, inaction, or misplaced action. All of these can be within your control, unless you fail to adequately prepare ahead of battle, in which case you are responsible for your failure.

14. Sun Tzu wrote:

"Hence the skillful fighter puts himself into a position which makes defeat impossible and does not miss the moment for defeating the enemy."

We must place ourselves in a position where we cannot lose and then wait for the optimal moment to attack before we strike. Tournaments, duals, and other mutual forms of combat (typically social violence) afford ample warning of what is about to happen so we can usually prepare and respond judiciously. Ambush (typically predatory violence), on the other hand, changes everything.

Distance, timing, type, and direction of attack, these critical factors are all selected by the adversary when he strikes first. He or she will assault us without warning, attacking from a range and bearing where his weapon or empty-handed techniques will cause the most damage and disruption. This can be an insurmountable advantage if we are not highly-skilled, experienced, and at least a little bit lucky. It is also an approach we can emulate should the need arise.

For the Win: Great generals create the circumstances where their victory is preordained.

You Lose: There is no second place in a real fight. Failure to stack the deck in your favor means failure in everything that matters.

15. Sun Tzu wrote:

"Thus it is that in war the victorious strategist only seeks battle after the victory has been won, whereas he who is destined to defeat first fights and afterwards looks for victory."

Engaging in battle primed for victory assures that we will win whereas going into battle with the intent to fight means that we are set to lose. Violence professionals, such as soldiers, law enforcement officers, bouncers, and bodyguards move through the world differently than ordinary individuals. United States Marine General James "Mad Dog" Mattis (1950 –) summed it up nicely when he said, "Be polite, be professional, but have a plan to kill everybody you meet."

For example, career criminals have knowledge, skill, practice, and experience at putting victims into positions of extreme disadvantage so that they can have their way with them (e.g., assault, robbery, rape, or whatever). Unless we have equivalent experience and practice at recovering from positions of severe disadvantage, an ambush attacker has an almost insurmountable advantage. So, awareness, avoidance, de-escalation, and counter-ambush skills are vital for self-defense.

For the Win: Work the battle plan in reverse, moving from the ultimate goal backward through the various options for achieving victory and it will become obvious which choices are better than others.

You Lose: Thinking, "We will go to war and win," is folly. It is the incorrect order for planning, a fool's errand.

16. Sun Tzu wrote:

"The consummate leader cultivates the moral law and strictly adheres to method and discipline thus it is in his power to control success."

A military enterprise is only as strong as its weakest warrior. Tolerance is for peacetime. Lack of order and structure cannot be abided in war as those who embody this weakness will suck the discipline from any fighting force. The same principle holds true in all aspects of life. Discipline and direction are paramount.

People seldom hit what they do not aim at. Crafting a vision and mission for ourselves and our enterprise helps articulate our purpose, values, and actions necessary to stay on track and achieve our goals. Further, the shorter, more concise a plan is the more likely it is to be followed. Verbose statements are far easier to write than pithy ones, but simultaneously far less useful, so we must set aside however much time it takes to digest every word and get it exactly right. Thus, we inform our actions with a strategy in all aspects of our lives.

For the Win: Keep the discipline of the greats who have come before.

You Lose: Failure to recognize that you must lead in all aspects of behavior at all times leaves a weak link that will be exploited by your enemies.

17. Sun Tzu wrote:

"In respect of military method we have, firstly, measurement, secondly, estimation of quantity, thirdly, calculation, fourthly, balancing of chances, and fifthly victory."

We must measure, estimate, then weigh the two, figure our chances, and when we find all in our favor, strike. Our physicality, physique, posture, the way we stand and move, even the way we breathe gives clues to astute observers about who we are and how we might handle ourselves during a violent confrontation. What others can perceive of us, we can observe in those around us as well.

This principle is not solely about size or fitness level, however. A smaller person intimidates differently than a bigger one does, even if they are equally skilled, yet dangerous people give off a certain vibe, oftentimes even when they're "ghosting," trying to hide it, that others can pick up and act upon. Conversely, certain people have the kind of aura that makes others want to avoid disappointing them, so bad things rarely come their way. In this fashion, it is possible to take another's measure and decide the winner without actually having to fight. Measuring others, calculating shrewdly, and balancing our changes lets us know when it is or is not prudent to fight.

For the Win: With prudent measurement you will know when you may safely engage and when you must avoid battle to win.

You Lose: Small, barking dogs signal that they are eager for a fight, having no sense of the battle for which they are setting their course.

18. Sun Tzu wrote:

"Measurement owes its existence to earth, estimation of quantity to measurement, calculation to estimation of quantity, balancing of chances to calculation, and victory to balancing of chances."

Earth comprises distances, great and small, danger and security, open ground and narrow passes, and the chances of life and death. Through prudent observation and analysis of earth, we are able to ascertain the paths to victory, balance the odds in our favor, and prevail. The battlefield we choose should be one of our liking where the odds favor our endeavor, yet once selected it is unlikely to change much during the course of the battle. We are committed to seeing our plan through to victory, strategic withdrawal, or defeat.

This reinforces why strategy is supreme and tactics secondary. Sure, we must apply tactics effectively in order to implement our strategy, but if the strategy itself is flawed we extinguish our chances for victory. Consider, for instance, Eastman Kodak's failure to embrace digital photography. Despite inventing the world's first digital camera in 1975, Kodak focused on maintaining its profitable photographic film sales and at one time the company owned 80% of the US market and was a major player worldwide. As digital photography grew in popularity, however, film sales spiraled downward and were eventually suspended in 2006 after 74 years of production. Kodak declared Chapter 11 bankruptcy in 2012.

For the Win: The battlefield is the tool of measurement, with its own spans and units. Use it wisely.

You Lose: The battlefield was there before you arrived and will be there after you leave. When you fail to use it, it will use you. Or the enemy will. Either way you lose.

19. Sun Tzu wrote:

"A victorious army opposed to a routed one is as a pound's weight placed in the scale against a single grain."

Losing a significant battle not only destroys vital men and resources but also crushes the spirit of the losing side's remaining forces. Losing a fight can be scary. It can leave physical as well as emotional scars, even spark psychological disorders. Oftentimes victims are motivated to purchase a gun, carry a knife, or study martial arts to create to regain their lost sense of power and control. The fact of the matter is, however, that guns, knives, and martial arts skills do not ward off danger.

Weapons can help us deal with violence more effectively, but only in select circumstances. Self-defense is not about fighting. It is really about not being there when the other guy(s) wants to fight. It's only when we've screwed up our self-defense that fighting skills and tools come in handy. It's best to be safe, but if we cannot it's important to be dangerous enough to extricate ourselves from peril. As LOTAR Combat's motto states, "If you can't be safe, be deadly!" That is sound advice.

For the Win: Win the first contact.

You Lose: A loss at initial contact will crush morale of the unskilled, and challenge the will of the skilled. You cannot afford to fail at first contact with the enemy.

20. Sun Tzu wrote:

"The onrush of a conquering force is like the bursting of pent-up waters into a chasm a thousand fathoms deep."

If we have momentum, we may become impossible to stop. Momentum in battle is significant. Prussian general and military theorist Carl von Clausewitz (1780 – 1831) called it the "concentration principle," striking at a moment when the center of gravity is dense and resources can be focused for an effective, disabling assault.

Consider the blitzkrieg (lightning war) offensive carried out by the German military during WWII. This strategy was designed to leverage momentum by creating psychological shock through the employment of surprise, speed, and superiority in firepower and equipment. It proved effective at flustering and disorganizing the opposing side's forces. Though largely associated with the Nazis, this principle of victory through overwhelming swift action was not their invention. The same tactic was used by historical figures such as King Alexander the Great (356 – 323 BC), Holy Roman Emperor Frederick II (1194 – 1250), and Napoleon Bonaparte (1769 – 1821) too.

For the Win: "Get there the fastest with the most." This, or something very much like this has been said by every coach of every sport across the planet at one time or another, because it is true. This is how you win.

You Lose: Show up late for the battle. End of story… and of you as well.

Chapter 5: Energy

In this chapter, we discover that leading many men is much the same as leading a few. The secret is in how we organize and mobilize our forces. Using a deep understanding of the laws of nature determines our best course of action in any situation. This allows us to harness energy through momentum and timing, multiplying our resources and guaranteeing our results via a finite set of direct and indirect tactics that can be utilized in virtually limitless combinations. These ambush and counter-ambush tactics bait adversaries into thinking they have an advantage until we successfully spring our trap upon them.

1. Sun Tzu wrote:

"The control of a large force is the same principle as the control of a few men, it is merely a question of dividing up their numbers."

An army, no matter how large, is nothing more than a collection of smaller units. The same can be said of any enterprise—the whole is merely a sum of its parts. It is how we organize the team's structure that makes all the difference. Create a clear strategy while distributing authority to carry it out and even the most titanic organizational challenge becomes manageable.

Large is difficult to control, large goals, large groups, large undertakings. To meet this test, we must break our processes, our tasks, and our teams down into smaller elements that can be managed more easily. Clarity of vision and purpose allows us to simplify, distribute, and manage the complex. Dividing does not mean reducing; we must know this difference.

For the Win: Keep your sizes manageable. Forces must be able to move swiftly in order to win.

You Lose: Massive organizations are inefficient, slow, and bloated. Without agility you cannot prevail over the long run.

2. Sun Tzu wrote:

"Fighting with a large army under your command is nowise different from fighting with a small one, it is merely a question of instituting signs and signals."

Irrespective of troop size, the principles of command remain the same. Nevertheless, we must tailor our communication such that larges forces can coordinate as effectively as small squads. We all know that communication can be haphazard even in the best of times. What is said and heard may not be the same thing when individuals are not fully engaged dialogue, yet in times of stress, our ability to communicate effectively degrades even farther.

Critical incident stress can cause a loss of dexterity, complex motor skills, and depth perception, but under extreme conditions, people may experience hyper-vigilance, loss of rational thought, hearing loss, memory loss, or even the inability to consciously move or react. Multi-layered communication is needed to circumvent the adverse impacts of adrenaline. For example, when law enforcement officers or security personnel have to physically restrain an out-of-control individual they often use physical cues as well as words to communicate with each other.

For the Win: Keep communication clear, clean and simple. Ensure that there is no room for confusion or hesitation.

You Lose: Unclear communications require clarification, which slows you down. Even worse, confusion causes incorrect or inappropriate action. Both are a waste.

3. Sun Tzu wrote:

"To ensure that your whole host may withstand the brunt of the enemy's attack and remain unshaken— this is effected by maneuvers direct and indirect."

If our adversary strikes the initial blow, we must maneuver to thwart their advantage, keeping our forces intact for an overwhelming counterstrike. If we find ourselves under attack and overwhelmed, we need a way to speedily and decisively turn the tables on our adversary. This can be a challenge even for highly trained individuals, as an action is faster than reaction. Nevertheless, a method that works reliably, even for untrained individuals, is more of a mindset than a technique.

We must turn fear into anger, unexpectedly retaking the offense. Colloquially, this means going "ape-sh!t" on the adversary. A sudden, startling, and ferocious counterattack gives even an untrained individual a decent chance of regaining control of the situation. A significant challenge, however, is that this tactic only works once. We must make full advantage of it the first time we try as we will not get a second chance.

For the Win: When receiving a blow, hold order, keep ranks, and do your best to break the attacker's pattern. In this fashion countervailing force can flip the equation in your favor.

You Lose: Reeling from a blow is expected, yet collapsing from the initial blow makes for a rout. You cannot afford to buckle under the initial assault.

4. Sun Tzu wrote:

"That the impact of your army may be like a grindstone dashed against an egg—this is effected by the science of weak points and strong."

The science of warfare is not simply being stronger than the adversary but also knowing and taking advantage of where our enemy is weak. Both strength and skill are needed to prevail in any confrontation, but knowing how and when to apply our advantage(s) is imperative for victory.

For instance, broad strength trumps narrow strength as General William Tecumseh Sherman (1820 – 1891) demonstrated in 1864 during his infamous "March to the Sea." Even though he faced adversaries who held the advantage of fighting on their home terrain, Sherman's troops carried out a scorched earth policy that left virtually everything destroyed in their wake. Cleary this was a waste of resources, yet the Confederate resistance was overwhelmed by Sherman's battle-hardened army as they burned crops they did not consume, killed all the livestock they did not eat or appropriate, and destroyed military and civilian infrastructures alike.

For the Win: Bring your strength to the enemy's weakness, then peruse the win.

You Lose: Testing your strength against your enemy's strength is expensive. Even if you win, you lose.

5. Sun Tzu wrote:

"In all fighting the direct method may be used for joining battle but indirect methods will be needed in order to secure victory."

It's very difficult to win by doing the obvious. Obfuscation and trickery are necessary in warfare where deceptiveness delivers victory. For instance, Carthaginian general Hannibal Barca (247 – 181 BC) used duplicity to overcome a larger Roman army during the Battle of Cannae in 216 BC. The center of Hannibal's battle line allowed themselves to be driven back from the Roman's direct assault, bowing in the middle to form a crescent before stretching out to encircle their enemy.

The suddenly surrounded Romans found themselves unable to engage the Carthaginians, save only at the outer edges of their army where they could still fight. Before the day was over more than 70,000 Romans were killed or captured in a slaughter that still ranks as one of the bloodiest hand-to-hand battles in human history. The Carthaginians' superior strategy overwhelmed the misapplied brute strength of Rome's legions, reducing their adversaries to nothing, or *ad nihil* as it was said in Latin at the time. The French later adapted *ad nihil* into a new word, "annihilate." In other words, Hannibal literally invented the concept of annihilation.

For the Win: A major conflict will likely be strength on strength, but victory is secured by bringing your force against the enemy's weakness. This is the profession of the general. It is your calling and duty.

You Lose: Myopic, hyper-focused behavior that ignores alternate places and courses for action against the enemy sets you up to lose.

6. Sun Tzu wrote:

"Indirect tactics efficiently applied are inexhaustible as heaven and earth, unending as the flow of rivers and streams, like the sun and moon they end but to begin anew, and like the four seasons they pass away to return once more."

Indirect tactics can disappear, reappear, and reshape themselves as needed. Once our deception is discovered, we move on to the next, and the next, ever bewildering our adversary. Individual indirect tactics may not last long, but as skilled warriors, we can reach into our bag of tricks and pull out one after another until we prevail.

For example, the D-Day landing at Normandy in 1944 was arguably one of the greatest and most effective examples of deception in military history. Axis forces certainly knew that an Allied invasion of Europe was forthcoming, but they did not know exactly where it would be, hence could not defend effectively. Prior to the assault, British intelligence used double-agents to feed disinformation to the Germans while Allied generals reinforced their deception with false radio traffic, misleading messages, and legions of decoy tanks, trucks, and inflatable vehicles. Dubbed Operation Overlord, the successful landing included over 5,000 ships, 11,000 airplanes, and 150,000 servicemen and paved the way for the Allied defeat over Axis powers ending WWII.

For the Win: Great leaders reshape actions, remold and repurpose what brought success in previous campaigns to win new endeavors.

You Lose: Trying to create new actions for every eventuality is futile. At best it slows your response; at worst it leads to analysis paralysis and ultimate failure.

7, 8, 9. Sun Tzu wrote:

"There are not more than five musical notes, yet the combinations of these five give rise to more melodies than can ever be heard. There are not more than five primary colors (blue, yellow, red, white, and black) yet in combination they produce more hues than can ever been seen. There are not more than five cardinal tastes (sour, acrid, salt, sweet, and bitter) yet combinations of them yield more flavors than can ever be tasted."

The whole of our effort must be greater than the sum of its parts. The order in which we use our resources makes that vital difference. Will our efforts work in concert to create a song or merely generate noise through disharmony?

Good leadership helps make a team perform better than a random collection of individuals. It starts with clarity of vision, assuring that everyone is working toward the same end game. From there we must create an organizational structure wherein each team member can bring their strengths to bear in meeting that goal, is empowered to take measured risks, has the resources necessary to perform their role successfully, and where a healthy tension staves off groupthink to drive prudent decisions.

For the Win: The ability to mix and match tactics within a cohesive strategy is seen as genius, yet it may only be a slight adjustment.

You Lose: Being a "one trick pony" means that you know only one path toward victory. It may work in certain circumstances, but that does not mean that you are brilliant, merely lucky. Over the long run luck is no strategy for success.

10. Sun Tzu wrote:

"In battle there are not more than two methods of attack, the direct and the indirect, yet these two in combination give rise to an endless series of maneuvers."

Two forms of attack, direct and indirect, create an endless number of options from which to defeat our adversary. Combinations are valuable in both sport and combat. Consider boxing, a sport where the jab, hook, uppercut, and cross can be strung together in nearly limitless sequences.

The secret to skillful boxing is to avoid falling into a predictable rhythm by overusing the same combinations or over-focusing on the same area of the opponent's body over and over again. We must apply a natural flow of punches augmented by body positioning, range, and proxemics. In this fashion, we cause confusion, disrupt the other guy, and take advantage of openings as they are presented.

For the Win: Battle is a lot like cooking, you can emphasize or deemphasize individual ingredients and adjust recipes according to taste yet still deliver an exceptional result. Stay flexible within your strategy to prevail.

You Lose: Battle is not like baking. Change measurements even a little when baking and your recipe will fail. Overly rigid application in battle guarantees disaster much like mis-measurement of even a single ingredient can turn a delicious soufflé into an unpalatable hockey puck.

11. Sun Tzu wrote:

"The direct and the indirect lead on to each other in turn. It is like moving in a circle, you never come to an end. Who can exhaust the possibilities of their combination?"

Either the direct or the indirect can come to the top at any moment, yet neither stands alone. In concert, they confuse, confound, and compel conquest. Creative use of direct and indirect tactics wins battles. For example, in 1560 samurai warlord Oda Nobunaga (1534 – 1582) fielded a force of 2,000 retainers against rival daimyo Imagawa Yoshimoto's (1519 – 1560) army of 40,000 men. One would think this was a losing proposition, but history shows that was not the case.

When Yoshimoto arrived at Zenshoji, a temple fortress where Nobunaga's men had taken refuge, he allowed his troops to drink in celebration of their forthcoming victory over his enemy's much smaller force. Nobunaga, however, was undeterred. He took advantage of a thunderstorm to sneak out of the fortress, leaving mannequins behind to impersonate his troops. His retainers fell upon the drunken, unprepared enemy, causing Yoshimoto's men to flee in disarray. Yoshimoto, thinking the commotion was merely a drunken squabble amongst his men, was ambushed and slain before he could figure out what was going on. Despite facing odds of 20:1, the entire battle was over in less than two hours.

For the Win: Efforts in battle may appear to be separate and disassociated, but in your strategy they must all come together to support your overall goal.

You Lose: If your actions do not converge on the goal of victory, your strategy and tactics are incorrect. Without revision this will lead to failure.

12. Sun Tzu wrote:

"The onset of troops is like the rush of a torrent which will even roll stones along in its course."

Everything gets swept up in a strong attack. Even the most rigid and entrenched forces can be steamrolled. As a blitzkrieg is an all-out war, a marketing blitz is an intensive advertising campaign. Typically, short, concentrated, and highly focused, it is designed to spark consumer interest for a product or service. More often than not these short-burst campaigns drive a sales surge and then are abandoned in favor of the next advertising trend, but occasionally they go viral, transforming entire industries in a tidal wave of success.

For example, De Beers' diamond sales plummeted during the Great Depression. In 1948 the company was desperate to motivate more men to buy diamond rings, hence designed the "A Diamond is Forever" campaign which still exists to this very day. De Beers not only boosted sales but also created the concept of an engagement ring in the process. Prior to that time diamond rings were not associated with marriage proposals.

For the Win: The power of your onrushing forces must be so commanding that anything failing to get out of the way will be swept up like flood debris. Use the rushing force to your advantage.

You Lose: Trying to stifle or throttle a properly constructed force upon release is a waste of effort. Stand in the way and you'll be overrun.

13. Sun Tzu wrote:

"The quality of decision is like the well-timed swoop of a falcon which enables it to strike and destroy its victim."

Adroit, swift decision-making wins battles. The falcon may not be the most powerful avian, yet it stoops with speed and precision that overwhelms its prey. Likewise, well-designed, swift strikes are successful because they are unforeseen, hence extremely hard to defend. The adroit mind of the leader, informed by masterful strategy, moves from situation to decision with acute timing and velocity.

Analysis of the stock market can identify billions of data points moving at mind-numbing speeds, yet astute stock traders use software that can synthesize this information into understandable patterns that allow for informed decision-making. Clearly, no dashboard can determine buy or sell indicators for any given stock or portfolio with perfect confidence, yet the more noise one can eliminate the surer the trader can be about how to proceed. Much like warfare, this means building a strategy, setting triggers that drive action, and eliminating emotion (to the extent possible) from the equation. In this fashion informed individuals can create wealth by buying and selling stocks, bonds, and commodities.

For the Win: Timing is important, it goes hand-in-glove with the violence of action. Combining the two brings a multiplier of power for you to exploit.

You Lose: Separate timing from the violence of action and either becomes as ineffective as a falcon without talons.

14. Sun Tzu wrote:

"Therefore the good fighter will be terrible in his onset and prompt in his decision."

From the biblical book of Ecclesiastes, later memorialized in the Byrds song Turn, Turn, Turn written by Pete Seeger (1919 – 2014) there is, "A time to be born, a time to die. A time to plant, a time to reap. A time to kill, a time to heal..." When we know it is time for war, the proverbial time to kill, we must be fierce, be final in our decision, and bring the full might of our resources to bear on defeating the enemy. Any half-hearted attempt is folly, doomed to fail.

News stories often make it appear that violence is sudden, unexpected, that victims never know what hits them. Statistically, that's untrue, yet all too often those who are targeted waste precious seconds trying to make sense of "senseless" violence rather expeditiously acting to defend themselves. Aggression does not have to make sense at the time, and often won't. Whenever the face of violence is glaring at us with that cold, hard stare, however, we must deal with it promptly and effectively in order to survive. When it's "go time," we must fight now, contemplate later. We can sort out what happened afterward when we're safe.

For the Win: Self-defense guru Marc MacYoung (1960 –) has a saying, "It's all a negotiation until someone pulls the trigger." In other words, talking is talking and fighting is fighting. Once fighting starts, conversation has left the building. Know this!

You Lose: Fail to understand that once it comes to blows the enemy will be trying to kill, maim, or dismember you, and will use every means at his or her disposal to do so, guarantees your failure. Once the lead starts to fly, you cannot talk your way out of a gunfight.

15. Sun Tzu wrote:

"Energy may be likened to the bending of a crossbow, decision to the releasing of a trigger."

We must build what we need for battle long before we intend to use it, loading our forces with potential that can be released at the moment we desire. In this fashion we gather and store the energy necessary for physical or metaphorical battle long before we need to unleash it.

Consider the Cold War concept of "Mutually Assured Destruction," or MAD, where both the United States of America and the Soviet Union stockpiled enough nuclear missiles to annihilate each other (and pretty much all life on earth). This ability to near-instantly inflict unacceptable damage in retaliation to any preemptive strike helped stave off a major conflict between those nations. Likewise, good situational awareness augmented with a strong fitness and training regimen makes us a hard target that most threats will avoid in search of easier prey.

For the Win: Demonstrating the potential for violence to a threat who uses violence as a tool to get what he or she wants can stave off conflict.

You Lose: If you have no potential for violence, no resource, no skill, nor inclination, you're a victim.

16. Sun Tzu wrote:

"Amid the turmoil and tumult of battle there may be seeming disorder and yet no real disorder at all, amid confusion and chaos your array may be without head or tail yet it will be proof against defeat."

With a solid strategy, we are able to stick to our plans despite any chaos that may surround us. What appears disorderly at surface level is not necessarily loss or confusion upon deeper review. All battle is chaos, yet the shrewd warrior takes advantage of the pandemonium to prevail.

After years of terrorizing the Caucasus, one of Genghis Khan's (1162 – 1227) Mongol raiding parties managed to kill King George IV of Georgia (1191 – 1223) in 1223. In response, an army of some 80,000 Russians ambushed a small force of 20,000 of the Khan's raiders near the Kalka River (in modern-day Ukraine). At first, the battle seemed to be going as planned. The superior Russian troops charged forward, quickly forcing the Mongols into what appeared to be a panicked withdrawal. In fact, they were chasing after their enemy when they fell into the Mongol's trap. Genghis Khan's forces had not actually panicked, but rather feigned retreat, reassembling their forces in a narrow pass by the river where they surprised and butchered more than 75,000 Russians.

For the Win: A good plan will survive the layer of chaos that descends upon that plan.

You Lose: Becoming enticed by the trimmings of chaos is a fool's game. Feeding chaos brings pandemonium to your table. More often than not that makes you the dinner not the guest.

17. Sun Tzu wrote:

"Simulated disorder postulates perfect discipline, simulated fear postulates courage, simulated weakness postulates strength."

Clearly, the art of war is, at its heart, about deception. We can simulate disorder, fear, and weakness to catch an adversary off guard, but must consider that others use these same tricks as well. If our opponent looks confused, scared, or weak, we may have discovered a trap.

Unlike law enforcement officers or soldiers, civilians rarely take initiative during the opening stages of a criminal attack. After all, if we control the location, timing, and methods of attack we're likely the bad guy(s). This means that counter-ambush skills are vital for self-defense. At a high level, we use situational awareness to buy time, create options, and disrupt our adversary's design. From there we can evade and escape or counterattack with some chance of success.

For the Win: As the old saying goes, "All's fair in war." Lie, cheat, steal, and deceive as needed to earn victory.

You Lose: Fail to, lie, cheat, steal, and deceive and you hand victory to your adversary.

18. Sun Tzu wrote:

"Hiding order beneath the cloak of disorder is simply a question of subdivision, concealing courage under a show of timidity presupposes a fund of latent energy, masking strength with weakness is to be effected by tactical dispositions."

Using the deceptions of weakness and timidity are tactical decisions. We should only look weak to serve a specific purpose. Consider the battle of the Teutoburg Forrest in the year 9 AD, one of the most successful and consequential ambushes in military history. Arminius (18 BC – 21 AD), a 25-year-old chieftain of the Germanic Cherusci tribe, was taken as a hostage by the Romans, a common enough occurrence designed to keep conquered nations in line. While he received military training and eventually took command of an auxiliary cavalry troop under Publius Quinctilius Varus (46 BC – 9 AD), the Roman commander, he nonetheless plotted his revenge throughout his captivity.

Fabricating a revolt by the German tribes to lure Varus into a punitive expedition even though the season was late for campaigning, Arminius leveraged his knowledge of the terrain to string the Roman legions out across a swamp and forest, while his allies hemmed them in with improvised field works. Heavy rains rendered the Roman shields too heavy to use effectively and softened their sinew bowstrings making their bows all but useless, so when Arminius's men unleased their trap they were able to slaughter some 20,000 legionnaires and uncounted Roman camp-followers.

For the Win: Appearing weak when it suits your goal can be a good tactic. Weakness draws little attention.

You Lose: The tactic of false weakness requires discipline and immense patience; without these two elements failure is likely if not assured.

19. Sun Tzu wrote:

"Thus one who is skillful at keeping the enemy on the move maintains deceitful appearances according to which the enemy will act. He sacrifices something that the enemy may snatch at it."

Simply looking weak is not enough, we must appear helpless in a way that makes the bait irresistible to our enemy. This tactic not only works on the battlefield, it has also been leveraged for state spy craft, industrial espionage, blackmail, and other illicit purposes through the use of what's known as a "honey trap." This typically involves setting up a romantic relationship that can be leveraged to create influence over the victim, say threatening to expose an extramarital affair, unfashionable fetish, or another indulgence with photographs, videos, texts, venue appointment logs, or other substantiating artifacts.

One of the best-known honey traps in history involved Mata Hari (1876 – 1917), a beautiful Dutch woman who worked as an erotic dancer in Java where she obtained secrets for German intelligence by seducing French officers and politicians during World War I (WWI). After intercepting telegrams from the German military attaché in Spain, French authorities arrested her for spying. Although the evidence was somewhat circumstantial and she may have simply been the attaché's mistress, she was nevertheless convicted of spying and executed by firing squad on October 15, 1917.

For the Win: Your faux weakness must offer a solution to the enemy's desires. Bait your trap carefully while preparing to strike.

You Lose: Subservience without conclusion, with an end goal and strategy, this is a recipe for permanent captivity. If you build the cage by your own hand, don't be surprised when someone locks you in it.

20. Sun Tzu wrote:

> *"By holding out baits, he keeps him on the march, then with a body of picked men he lies in wait for him."*

The appearance of weakness is a bait; hence it must be used to spring a trap. The lure of weakness must end with a powerful strike that overwhelms and conquers the adversary. This doesn't necessarily need to be a military endeavor, however. There is a similar concept called "ambush marketing," where an enterprise takes advantage of the publicity provided by some major event, such as a World Cup, Super Bowl, or Olympic competiti0n, to create product awareness without actually making any financial sponsorship of the event.

Direct ambush marketing typically involves attacking rival event sponsors with counter-advertising, whereas indirect ambushing is designed to make the ambusher appear to be affiliated with an event even though they have not paid anything for the privilege of product association. Incidental ambushing involves saturating the area around an event without actually making any reference to it (or to rival sponsors). Sometimes ambush marketing doesn't even require an event. For example, when rival Fiat noticed a Google car updating street map views near Volkswagen's headquarters in Sweden, they strategically parked a Fiat 500 in the Volkswagen driveway.

For the Win: When the bait is taken by your enemy, you must have your best forces at hand to spring your trap. Ambushes only work once; consequently, they must be final and complete.

You Lose: By not establishing a place and a time for your ambush, or by acting before the bait is taken by your enemy, you lose your opportunity. Chances are good that once lost you will never find it again. Your enemy forewarned is forearmed.

21. Sun Tzu wrote:

"The clever combatant looks to the effect of combined energy and does not require too much from individuals. Hence his ability to pick out the right men and utilize combined energy."

The power of a group is undeniable. How we structure that group, however, is critical to the team's performance. No matter what the endeavor, we can do more of any given task when we leverage the combined resources and diverse talents of the group. This is the concept of synergy, a powerful dynamic where the whole becomes greater than the sum of its parts.

Teams work best when they have an emotional connection with objectives of the group, so as leaders we must paint a clear and compelling vision of what must be done, articulate each member's responsibility in achieving the desired objective, and then measure progress toward that goal to assure accountability. The right metrics hold team members accountable and make it easier for leaders to provide coaching and course corrections as needed to assure progress.

For the Win: Well-designed teams are stronger than individuals. Know that even the most heroic individuals must have backing and support from the group in order to be successful.

You Lose: The concept of a rogue warrior, out on a rampage extracting justice is a Hollywood creation. In real life lone wolves are put down.

22. Sun Tzu wrote:

"When he utilizes combined energy his fighting men become as it were like unto rolling logs or stones. For it is the nature of a log or stone to remain motionless on level ground and to move when on a slope if four-cornered to come to a standstill but if round-shaped to go rolling down."

We must set our forces in a way that allows them to gain momentum that is difficult for opposing forces to stop. Success breeds success, and early victories demotivate our adversaries while simultaneously inspiring our own troops. If we can earn a reputation for being unstoppable, it becomes a self-fulfilling prophecy.

Oftentimes fights are, for all intents and purposes, over before they begin simply because one party believes that they cannot win. Consider Captain Bill McDonald (1852 – 1918), a Texas Ranger who served from 1891 to 1907. Like his peers, McDonald took on challenging criminal cases such as riots, murders, and bank robberies, yet unlike his brethren, he earned a reputation for marksmanship that was unmatched. Legend states that he was so feared that he became the archetype of the famous saying, "One riot, one Ranger." Once he arrived, most of the bad guys surrendered without a fight.

For the Win: A victory, no matter how small, sets the tone for the next success. Leverage small wins to set your forces with an expectation for continued progress. In conquest, triumph begets triumph until victory becomes inevitable.

You Lose: Momentum from a win must be used or it will vanish like smoke. Failure to capitalize on victories is akin to failure.

23. Sun Tzu wrote:

"Thus the energy developed by good fighting men is as the momentum of a round stone rolled down a mountain thousands of feet in height. So much on the subject of energy."

Once the momentum of success gets started, it becomes a force unto itself. This is true for virtually any undertaking in any organization, which is why announcers focus on momentum in team sports, pundits focus on momentum in political endeavors, and journalists focus on momentum in military battles.

Consider the analogy of the enterprise as a giant cardboard box. Merely placing all the right people into the box and telling them to move it will not work. Well-meaning team members each push on a different wall, which not only assures that the box will go nowhere but also tends to damage the walls of the box. This dysfunctional dynamic accomplishes nothing and is no good for anyone. With good leadership, however, everyone aligns to push on the same wall. The box moves slowly, inching forward at first, but with the momentum the corners become rounded and it starts to move with ever increasing velocity.

For the Win: Momentum sustains only when it is fed the correct elements of strategy and tactics, this is the role of the leader.

You Lose: Momentum without direction is a storm that will eventually pass you by, leaving only waste and spent opportunity behind.

Chapter 6: Weak Points and Strong

In this chapter, we discover the "divine" art of subtlety and secrecy, through which we can hold any adversary's fate in our hands. We remain enigmatic while discovering our enemy's positions and disposition. We concentrate our forces while splitting the enemy into factions, force him to reveal his vulnerabilities, vary our tactics to remain unpredictable while holding true to our strategy, and leverage our strength to attack in ways that assure his defeat before we even begin to fight.

1. Sun Tzu wrote:

"Whoever is first in the field and awaits the coming of the enemy will be fresh for the fight, whoever is second in the field and has to hasten to battle will arrive exhausted."

As Italian Renaissance political philosopher and statesman Niccolò Machiavelli (1469 – 1527) once wrote, "Tardiness often robs us opportunity and the dispatch of our forces." Whenever we allow others to determine the time and place of our contest, we become subject to his or her devices. Not only will the resulting melee be fought under the adversary's rules, but we also succumb to his or her momentum. Whenever we can establish the field, however, we gain the upper hand.

To successfully own the field, we must not only lure the enemy to our location but also arrange our forces such that they are prepared to act the moment the adversary arrives. This means that everyone clearly knows their role, we assure the element of surprise via camouflage and noise discipline, and we have designated when and under what conditions we will initiate the attack. Finally, we must have a solid egress plan in case we have miscalculated and things go awry.

For the Win: Arrive first and all choices are yours.

You Lose: Arrive late and you must respond to what others have already done.

2. Sun Tzu wrote:

"Therefore the clever combatant imposes his will on the enemy but does not allow the enemy's will to be imposed on him."

We must never concede that which is valuable to the other side, but that the definition of value is not always clear cut. In any conflict, we must know what is of value, why it is valuable, and understand its relative worth for both sides. Oftentimes this affords us the opportunity to trade something of lower value to us for something we truly desire, the basis of negotiation.

As John Bolton (1948 –), an American diplomat, attorney, and former national security advisor once wrote, "Negotiation is not a policy. It's a technique. It's something you use when it's to your advantage, and something that you don't use when it's not to your advantage." The relative power of both parties, say a buyer and seller in a business endeavor, determine what strategy we must follow. For instance, consulting firm A. T. Kearney created a "Purchasing Chessboard" with 4 strategies, 16 levers, and 64 methods that are applied individually or in combination to set negotiations up for success. This approach leverages Sun Tzu's methods, making it extremely popular and commonly used by the procurement industry for over a decade.

For the Win: Forcing the enemy to help you is great; tricking the enemy into defeating themselves is even better.

You Lose: The moment you realize the enemy wants to you do exactly what you're doing is the moment you discover it's too late to prevail.

3. Sun Tzu wrote:

"By holding out advantages to him, he can cause the enemy to approach of his own accord, or by inflicting damage he can make it impossible for the enemy to draw near."

The proverbial "carrot and stick" is a metaphor for using a combination of rewards and punishments to induce desired behaviors. Historically a cart driver would often tie a carrot to a string and hold it above his or her pack animal's head, or tie it to a mule's bridle just out of reach. Attracted by the sight and smell, the mule stepped forward to bite, pulling the cart in its wake. If the animal pulled the cart as it was supposed to it would be given the carrot to eat at the end of the journey, yet if it rebelled it might be beaten by the stick to force it back in line.

We must know both the carrot and stick of any situation. It is imprudent to use either as a default action, yet by judiciously doling out rewards and punishments we can induce others to act as we desire. Many people are motivated by incentives, often overcoming instinctual fears in pursuit of rewards. As described in operant conditioning psychological theory, behaviors are learned by forming associations with outcomes. Reinforcement strengthens these behaviors, while punishment weakens them.

For the Win: The lure, the bait you cast to draw your enemy near, must appear to fulfill their desire.

You Lose: Let the enemy discover your craving, your deepest desire, and they will build a trap. Failing to recognize this trap is to become ensnared within it.

4. Sun Tzu wrote:

"If the enemy is taking his ease, he can harass him if well supplied with food, he can starve him out if quietly encamped, and he can force him to move."

Continuously harrying and harassing the adversary keeps him unsettled, disrupting his or her designs and casting doubt upon his or her aspirations. Every leader has preferences, game plans that they have grown comfortable with over long periods of success, yet the better we can scout and understand the other guy's tendencies the easier it is to flip their strengths and turn them into weaknesses. Whatever our opponent wants to do, we must make it hard for them to do it.

This isn't just a military thing, but also one that can be used in interpersonal conflict as well. For instance, it may also be possible to cause an adversary to make a mental twitch, providing a moment of opportunity to counterattack or escape by doing something unexpected. This is created by the dissonance between how the threat expects us to respond and what we actually say or do. A common tactic is asking a question. Try something bizarre like, "What was Pope Benedict's batting average?" During the adversary's momentary confusion, we create an opportunity to act.

For the Win: If the enemy wants to move, block them. If they want to rest stir them.

You Lose: When you let the enemy move freely answering their needs, you give them hope. This makes for a prolonged conflict.

5. Sun Tzu wrote:

"Appear at points which the enemy must hasten to defend, march swiftly to places where you are not expected."

Once the adversary is off-balance, we must keep him or her that way. This means repeatedly doing the unexpected. Every enemy has weak points. We must find them, close quickly, strike, and retreat. Harassment is illegal for a reason, it works… And, it goes both ways.

Consider harassment in the form of spam, robocalls, fake debt collectors, telemarketers, and other unscrupulous sales techniques. Over 100,000 people complain to the FTC about these tactics every month in the US, despite the fact that three-quarters of all Americans have listed their phone numbers with the federal Do Not Call Registry (at www.donotcall.gov). The scammers keep trying because their methods reliably work on gullible consumers, yet one of the simplest defenses is saying we're not interested and hang up on them. "No" is a complete sentence. It requires no explanation nor justification, and the other party's reaction to our rejection tells us everything we need to know about his or her motivation.

For the Win: Irritate the enemy; let his frustration divert his attention from the goal.

You Lose: Fail to recognize that harassment is a strategy, succumb to frustration, and you hand victory to your enemy.

6. Sun Tzu wrote:

"An army may march great distances without distress if it marches through country where the enemy is not."

If an opponent has a clear path, they can easily travel to their destination and arrive ready to fight. If we let our adversaries move with ease, life for them becomes easy, and we are not doing our job. When life is easy, we have little incentive to learn, grow, or reinvent ourselves, yet the speed of change today means that whatever makes us successful today may no longer work, or even exist, in a few short years.

Consider disruptive technologies like robotic process automation (RPA), artificial intelligence (AI), self-driving vehicles, factory automation, augmented reality (AR), industrial "internet of things" (IIoT), and additive manufacturing (3D printing), to name a few. These inventions impact companies and individuals alike, dramatically shifting jobs, cost structures, and capabilities. We need to understand and account for technological and societal evolutions in order to remain relevant, let alone be successful. Those who embrace valuable change can achieve their destination with ease whereas those who fall behind must fight their way through.

For the Win: Animals use of all their senses to identify a clear path, traveling with the herd for safety. Embrace this approach.

You Lose: Blindly moving without keenly observing your surroundings creates a false sense of comfort, one that invites predators to attack.

7. Sun Tzu wrote:

"You can be sure of succeeding in your attacks if you only attack places which are undefended. You can ensure the safety of your defense if you only hold positions that cannot be attacked."

Attack not the weakest points, but the undefended point. If we want 100% success in battle, we must attack the undefended. A common example of this is a cyber-threat, taking advantage of social engineering and flawed technology to infiltrate systems and steal, destroy, or adulterate valuable data. Examples of infamous data breaches include Target, Home Depot, Sony, Equifax, eBay, and Adult Friend Finder. One of the biggest cyber hacks in history, likely caused by a state-sponsored actor, impacted more than 3 billion Yahoo user accounts in 2014. This compromised customer names, emails, dates of birth, telephone numbers, and passwords, knocking an estimated $350M off Yahoo's sales price when Verizon bought their core internet business.

Common cyber risks include social engineered trojans, phishing attacks, unpatched software exploits, network traveling worms, malware, botnets, ransomware, malvertising, spyware, and advanced persistent threats. These threats are created by nation-states, industrial spies, organized crime groups, terrorists, hacktivists, and disgruntled insiders, to name a few, yet preventative measures such as strong user education, sophisticated software, vulnerability assessments, event monitoring, and robust change management discipline can stave off the danger. It's an investment that all businesses must make.

For the Win: Pick your battles, choosing weak adversaries over strong, and always prevail.

You Lose: Fall for the false chivalry of a head-to-head duel. The goal is not to fight, but rather to overcome. Seeking a fair fight is for losers.

8. Sun Tzu wrote:

"Hence that general is skillful in attack whose opponent does not know what to defend and he is skillful in defense whose opponent does not know what to attack."

In preparation for battle, it is important to confuse the adversary so that he or she cannot be sure of our point of attack. When an opponent tries to cover all options, they become lost. We must help them get lost and stay that way... In this fashion, our strength is nearly impossible to defend.

Those who play American football at a high level or intimately know the game understand that the better a quarterback can perform his pre-snap read the more his team gains an advantage over the opposing defense. He looks for the number of safeties, depth of corners, weak-side flat defender, and a number of run defenders to determine the defensive alignment, as there are fundamentally only seven coverage schemes the other team might utilize no matter how much they disguise their alignment. Likewise, receivers, tight ends, running backs, and offensive linemen also need to understand these coverages so that they can adjust accordingly. This insight lets the offense understand how best to elude the defense, knowing the safest throwing lanes, discovering what decoy routes to run, knowing who's the hot receiver (the person who must be prepared to receive the ball quickly on a passing play), etc. In this fashion, the offense is prepared to attack the weakest points of the other team's defense.

For the Win: Resources are always limited. In attacking or defending, force your enemy to place resources in places of no importance.

You Lose: Whenever you are unable to deduce your enemy's true place of battle you waste resources that could have been expended to help you win.

9. Sun Tzu wrote:

"O divine art of subtlety and secrecy! Through you we learn to be invisible, through you inaudible, and hence we can hold the enemy's fate in our hands."

Not being overt in intention or ability can be a great aid in winning. We need not be big, nor loud. Being smooth and secret creates one of our greatest advantages for victory. The game of poker is an excellent example where the best players routinely use subtlety and secrecy to win.

Integral to this winning poker strategy is the concept of a "bluff," action taken such as a call or raise that is designed to deceive the other players, persuading one or more of them to fold their cards despite holding a stronger hand than the person bluffing. To make this gambit work best, players must hide their emotions, sometimes even wearing hoodies and dark sunglasses so that others cannot read their expressions. While mathematically a player must have the strongest hand to win, astute players are often able to trick opponents into letting them prevail by giving up prematurely. In this fashion they play their competitors not their cards.

For the Win: The underlying bedrock of every predators' hunt is secrecy. Stealth is your friend.

You Lose: Whenever you fail to hide your intent, your plans are uncovered and schemes easily thwarted.

10. Sun Tzu wrote:

"You may advance and be absolutely irresistible if you make for the enemy's weak points, you may retire and be safe from pursuit if your movements are more rapid than those of the enemy."

The old adage "speed kills" is true in almost any physical competition. To go a step farther, athletes may be strong, fast, and well-conditioned, yet no matter their innate ability it takes more than physical attributes to win. Leveraging skill and experience, the superior practitioner can utilize precision and timing to overcome their foe, knocking them back on their heels. Disrupt the adversary's balance and he or she will have to focus on recovery and defense before even considering attacking back.

Speed has three components—physical capacity, technical development, and application. No matter what attributes we begin with, anyone can become faster with refined technique. We shave off reaction time both by making faster decisions, which requires experience and by eliminating nonproductive movements, which takes training. Refined, diligent practice allows for better application on the field, in the ring, or on the street. In this fashion, we evade swifter, attack faster, and more readily overcome our enemies.

For the Win: Hit a weak point of the enemy like a tsunami, and then retreat as swiftly. This makes retaliation difficult if not impossible.

You Lose: When you ploddingly engage the enemy, you become entangled. Constant and consistent use of resources will drain your reserves until victory becomes impossible.

11. Sun Tzu wrote:

"If we wish to fight the enemy can be forced to an engagement even though he be sheltered behind a high rampart and a deep ditch. All we need do is attack some other place that he will be obliged to relieve."

An entrenched adversary can be extremely difficult to overcome. Consequently, if the enemy is strong in one place, we should not attack there, but rather seek to draw him or her out to a location of our choosing where he will be weaker. Generally, this requires a feint, an indirect means of deceiving the adversary into doing our will.

Feints are common in boxing, for example, where skilled practitioners facing aggressive opponents often use subtleties such as a twitch, sharp exhalation, or weight shift to misdirect and draw in their adversary. Ineffective feints such as throwing a half-hearted punch are a waste of movement, whereas successful feints effectively simulate expected movements in order to trigger a conditioned response. In this fashion, the practitioner tricks his or her opponent into committing to a known movement that can skillfully be countered to control and win the fight.

For the Win: Make the enemy move to a place where they do not want to be.

You Lose: Engage on the enemy's terms, in a time and place of their choosing, and sow the seeds of disaster.

12. Sun Tzu wrote:

"If we do not wish to fight, we can prevent the enemy from engaging us even though the lines of our encampment be merely traced out on the ground. All we need do is to throw something odd and unaccountable in his way."

Whenever we do something out of the ordinary, something totally unexpected, we can make our adversary stop and wonder about the reasons for our actions. Whenever puzzlement causes our opponent to pause, we create an opportunity to counter, conquer, or escape. This can be thought of as "sleight of hand" for the battlefield, a misdirection that, much like stage-show prestidigitation, focuses the adversary's attention on one reality while concealing another.

Magicians layer multiple levels of misdirection and psychological manipulation to focus their audience's attention elsewhere while subtly maneuvering objects (such as coins, cards, rings, or ropes) to perform their "magic" tricks. In this fashion, they create illusions that convince bystanders that they have made something appear out of thin air, passed one solid object through another, defied gravity, caused an object to mysteriously vanish, or performed some other feat of magic. A well-known example is called the "French drop," where the illusionist fakes transferring a small object such as a coin from one hand to the other while secretly palming it in the original hand and then making it reappear with a flourish from a bystander's shirt pocket or from inside of an audience member's ear. Like maneuvers on the battlefield, all magic is deception.

For the Win: When it becomes difficult for the enemy's mind to grasp a pattern, this creates a pause. Create this moment. Use it wisely.

You Lose: Oddities must be examined quickly. Being fascinated with a potential threat is as productive as chimpanzees worshipping an obelisk.

13. Sun Tzu wrote:

"By discovering the enemy's dispositions and remaining invisible ourselves, we can keep our forces concentrated while the enemy's must be divided."

The better prepared we are, the more we increase our odds of success in any endeavor. Whenever we find out as much as we can about our opponent while simultaneously denying them information about us, we place ourselves in a better position to prevail. This is why politicians perform opposition research, sports teams scout their opponents, and generals study their counterparts. This inquiry uncovers tendencies that can be exploited.

Opposition research in politics, for example, involves collecting information on adversaries that can be used to weaken them. While this may involve dirty tricks that discredit the opposition through adverse press, more often than not it involves uncovering unflattering facts such as a person's voting record, financial acumen, college grades, social media profile, or criminal history. While a record of bankruptcies, arrests, racist media postings, or the like can directly be used against an adversary, anything that uncovers their disposition and predilections can create leverage to be used against them.

For the Win: Know your enemy, using their predilections against them.

You Lose: Sacrificing privacy for the illusion of fame cedes vital information to those who would move against you. Your social media friends and followers aren't truly your allies.

14. Sun Tzu wrote:

"We can form a single united body while the enemy must split up into fractions. Hence there will be a whole pitted against separate parts of a whole which means that we shall be many to the enemy's few."

Divide and conquer is a time-honored strategy, one that has proven successful in politics, on the battlefield, and in business. It is so intuitive that even small children often use it against their parents, for instance asking their father for something and then trying their mother if dad did not acquiesce to their desire. Without good information, the adversary will likely disperse his or her forces to cover a wide front while we can carefully select our targets and attack where we hold the advantage. A dispersed opponent is no match for concentrated force.

Napoleon Bonaparte's (1769 – 1821) campaign in Italy is an excellent example of this strategy. In 1796 French forces confronted a larger number of Allied troops, yet the opposing armies did not cooperate well and were quickly split into two smaller groups, some 25,000 Piedmontese troops in one army and another 35,000 Austrians in the other. Even though he had a smaller force of roughly 40,000 men, hence could not expect to prevail against the combined Allied forces, Napoleon was able to strike each opponent on relatively equal terms and outfight both of them one at a time. Napoleon later faced a series of Austrian armies sent across the Alps and reportedly took around 150,000 prisoners during the course of this campaign.

For the Win: Divide and conquer is a tried and true strategy as old as time itself. "Every kingdom divided against itself is brought to desolation…" — Matthew 12:25. Address discord quickly and appropriately.

You Lose: Let division grow. Like feeding cancer, discord will proliferate until it destroys you.

15. Sun Tzu wrote:

"And if we are able thus to attack an inferior force with a superior one our opponents will be in dire straits."

In battle we always seek a mismatch of force. While inequality in numbers may not always be enough to prevail, it certainly stacks the odds on our side. Combined with strong leadership, training, communication, and provisioning, a surplus of troops can become an insurmountable advantage.

Consider the battle of The Alamo, which raged for 13 days from Feb 23, 1836, to March 6, 1836, in the Texas Republic city of San Antonio de Bexar (now called San Antonio, Texas). A force of 189 Texans led by Colonel James Bowie (1796 – 1836) and Lieutenant Colonel William Travis (1809 – 1836) dug in at the Mission-turned-garrison where they faced roughly 6,000 Mexican troops led by General Santa Anna (1794 – 1876). Despite holding a strong defensive position and utilizing 24 captured cannons, the experienced American troops were able to kill 1,544 men and wound another 500, but ultimately succumbed to superior numbers of the Mexican forces. Santa Anna's men slaughtered nearly everyone, with Susannah Dickinson (1814 – 1883) one of the few survivors left to tell the tale. Their sacrifice eventually brought about independence for Texas, with "Remember the Alamo" becoming the battle cry of the American freedom fighters.

For the Win: Identify your enemy's weakest aspect. Hit it hard and without mercy.

You Lose: Fail to take advantage of an enemy's weakness and he grows strong.

16. Sun Tzu wrote:

"The spot where we intend to fight must not be made known for then the enemy will have to prepare against a possible attack at several different points and his forces being thus distributed in many directions, the numbers we shall have to face at any given point will be proportionately few."

Keeping our opponent wondering about where and when we will strike, and what manner our offensive will take is paramount. Clearly, we must keep our plans secret to leverage the value of surprise, yet to the extent that we can feint in multiple directions at once, the adversary will be forced to expend resources ineffectually. Consider the Merger and Acquisition (M&A) process in business by way of example.

When cash-rich enterprises cannot grow their way into meeting long-term goals such as market share, they may seek to acquire one or more companies to expedite the process. Other common reasons for M&A include access to technology, capacity, or diversification. The process typically begins with scanning the marketplace for suitable targets, making third-party brokered inquiries to anonymously gauge a target company's interests, and secretly gathering data to determine whether further pursuit may be warranted. By the time actual conversations occur, a confidentiality agreement is signed and a confidential information memorandum is solicited. Note the levels of secrecy here, if anyone prematurely discovers the buyer's interests that could materially affect the viability, price, and risk of the deal. Further steps include soliciting an indication of interest, conducting management meetings, submitting a letter of intent, conducting due diligence, negotiating an agreement, and then closing the deal.

For the Win: Coyote hunt in packs, ever circling their prey in search of weakness to attack. Follow this example.

You Lose: Fail to test multiple means, methods, and access to the enemy and you squander opportunity.

17. Sun Tzu wrote:

"For should the enemy strengthen his van he will weaken his rear, should he strengthen his rear he will weaken his van, should he strengthen his left he will weaken his right, should he strengthen his right he will weaken his left. If he sends reinforcements everywhere, he will everywhere be weak."

Organizational resources can be likened to balloons that never leak. Overall inflation is preserved such that when one side is pressed upon it forces air to flow to the other. The shape of the balloon may change through our manipulation, but the amount of air inside does not. This analogy demonstrates that wherever strength appears (like a bulging spot on the balloon) a corresponding weakness must be created, so we can look to the opposite to see what has been displaced. In other words, to the astute observer, an adversary can reveal their weakness merely by showing their strength.

Despite a myriad of play calling options in American football, fundamentally an offense may run the ball, pass the ball, or utilize some combination of the two in order to win the game. This choice is dictated in part by the coach's predilections along with his or her team's strengths and weaknesses, yet must also take into account the opponent's defensive strategy and capabilities. Furthermore, unless there is a massive disparity of talent, play calling cannot be easily predictable or it simultaneously becomes easy to stop. Consequently, coaches who prefer to run must call a pass from time-to-time and vice versa. Watching game film and analyzing historical play calling helps teams prepare for upcoming games, leveraging insight about strengths that were shown and tradeoffs that were made previously. In this fashion, astute coaches predict how their opposition will handle various scenarios throughout the game and prepare accordingly.

For the Win: Marshalling your forces is a zero-sum game; there are only so many resources to go around. Knowing this, place your forces strategically such that they may launch an assault or rebuff impending attack.

You Lose: Forgetting that focusing resources in one place weakens them in another, leaving openings for an enemy to leverage.

18. Sun Tzu wrote:

"Numerical weakness comes from having to prepare against possible attacks, numerical strength from compelling our adversary to make these preparations against us."

All things being equal, those who can compel an adversary to spread out his or her forces creates weaknesses that can be exploited. This is multiplied further whenever we have a numerical advantage to begin with. And, of course, it becomes paramount whenever we have a disadvantage in resources to overcome. In business, as in war, momentum is hard to overcome. Leaders who can predict trends and act ahead of the competition may develop an unbeatable lead. This includes discovering and exploiting approaching disruptions such as new technologies, markets, or societal norms.

While it's pervasive today, companies that adopted teleworking before their rivals were able to leverage the internet, audio- and videoconferencing, file-sharing, and similar innovations to create a happier, more productive workforce. Embracing virtual work reduced turnover, improved productivity, and even helped moderate greenhouse emissions associated with their employee's commute. As early as 1996, Merrill Lynch reported a 20% productivity increase, 3.5 fewer sick days per year, and a 6% decrease in turnover during the first year of their virtual worker program. Early adopters were also able to leverage crowdsourcing and the burgeoning "gig economy" to develop value-adding intellectual property their competitors simply could not match.

For the Win: Trick the enemy into expending their limited resources protecting things you do not care about.

You Lose: When the tables are turned you must secure your territory with forces that could have been used in combat.

19. Sun Tzu wrote:

"Knowing the place and the time of the coming battle, we may concentrate from the greatest distances in order to fight."

Location is important for any looming battle. We must assure that our troops arrive at the right place to confront the enemy. Likewise, timing is critical too, as without proper coordination we cannot deploy our resources very effectively. When both time and location are known to us ahead of time, we control our destiny. These circumstances create the best opportunity to consolidate our forces and deliver maximum strength with maximum surprise against our adversary.

Precision timing is vital for many industries. Consider telecom. We've all heard of 5G networks, but few non-IT professionals understand the precision timing and synchronization necessary to exploit their functionality. For example, beam-forming with New Radio Time-Division Duplex (NR-TDD) requires absolute time synchronization across an entire mobile network of approximately 1.5 microseconds (that's one-and-a-half millionths of a second). Without this the reliability of the network is diminished and advanced features like the Industrial Internet of Things (IIoT), which supports self-driving vehicles, robots, and factory automation, cannot be utilized. In other words, phones and other devices using 5G only work as we expect them too because of a complex, highly integrated, precision infrastructure that most of us never see. Without it, these devices become useless hunks of expensive plastic and circuitry.

For the Win: Choosing where and when the contest will take place is no a luxury; it is as essential as water.

You Lose: Fail to create initiative, to determine the time and place of battle, and you undermine victory.

20. Sun Tzu wrote:

"But if neither time nor place be known then the left wing will be impotent to succor the right, the right equally impotent to succor the left, the van unable to relieve the rear or the rear to support the van. How much more so if the furthest portions of the army are anything under a hundred li (~ 50 kilometers) apart and even the nearest are separated by several li (~500 meters)!"

It takes time to marshal and coordinate our forces. Communication and logistical challenges proportionately increase with distance. Lacking foreknowledge of the time and place of battle places us at a severe disadvantage even when we have well trained and provisioned resources, know the lay of the land, and have a well-thought-out strategy.

This challenge is nothing new. Any company that dispatches products to customers around the world has to orchestrate air freight, shipping, rail, and ground transportation. It's far more challenging than simply packaging things up and handing them to a post office or delivery company, requiring structure necessary to plan, execute, monitor, and measure where everything is at any point in time across the globe and communicate that information to customers and staff in a seamless, efficient way. This means contracting with logistics providers, dealing with import/export regulations, deploying management systems, optimizing the flow of goods, and managing deliveries and customer returns. Success requires a complex supplier ecosystem working in concert to support our business.

For the Win: Leverage alliances to accomplish more together than you can alone.

You Lose: Selfishly isolating yourself from potential allies feeds the ego while undermining your enterprise.

21. Sun Tzu wrote:

"Though the enemy be stronger in numbers we may prevent him from fighting. Scheme so as to discover his plans and the likelihood of their success."

Only a fool seeks a fight where he or she cannot prevail. If our adversary is powerful, we must understand his or her plans and take steps to counter them, staving off the battle until or unless we have a chance to win. We must do whatever we can to thwart or subvert his or her designs without simultaneously sacrificing our own. Sometimes this means that we must accept short term defeat in order to improve our chances in the larger conflict, but even when necessary this must be done judiciously. Welsh actor John Rhys-Davies (1944 –), who played Gimli in the Lord of the Rings trilogy, compared this to a game of chess, saying, "Sometimes you have to withdraw, sometimes you have to sacrifice one of your pieces to win—preferably a knight rather than a king or queen."

A certain level of risk is necessary with any battle, yet too much sacrifice risks creating a "pyrrhic victory." King Pyrrhus of Epirus (318 – 272 BC), was a Greek general and statesman who fought against Rome, Macedonia, and Sparta. He won numerous small victories, yet in doing so severely depleted his resources to the point that losses from minor skirmishes undid his ability to win the larger war. Eventually, he invaded Sparta where he was killed in the battle of Argos by a woman who threw a tile from a housetop that struck him in the head, an ignoble death for any great warlord. We must guard against following this example.

For the Win: Learn the enemy's plans, scrutinize their weakness, and you may yet prevail despite starting from an inferior position.

You Lose: Fail to understand, through every available avenue, the enemy's plans and you have failed as badly as arriving late for battle.

22. Sun Tzu wrote:

"Rouse him and learn the principle of his activity or inactivity. Force him to reveal himself, so as to find out his vulnerable spots."

To understand and best take advantage of our adversary's nature, we must trick him into acting in ways he is not naturally inclined to do. For instance, he may be happily entrenched behind fortifications only to be drawn out by our harrying attacks. Or, he may favor probing strikes to keep the offensive yet unable to carry them out if we fade into the distance. Spurring the opposite of his or her natural inclination provides vital insight into how our enemy thinks and acts, while simultaneously keeping him off-balance, guessing at our intent.

This is not all that different than hunting for sustenance. Throughout much of history, our ancestors could not purchase food or drink at a supermarket, relying on their stealth and skill to take down game animals to feed themselves and their families. This meant doing everything in their power to assure success, even when matched up against the most dangerous, elusive, or ferocious game. While horses were not tamed until sometime around 4,000 years BC, mankind domesticated canines roughly 20,000 years earlier, using dogs for hunting, herding, and personal protection. These dogs were used by hunters to locate, track, harass, flush out, and take down the animals they needed to eat.

For the Win: Poke, prod, tease, and tempt the enemy to discern their reaction. In this fashion you will know their tactics and reveal their intent.

You Lose: If you let the enemy blithely move as they wish, you cannot discern their intent.

23. Sun Tzu wrote:

"Carefully compare the opposing army with your own so that you may know where strength is superabundant and where it is deficient."

Statistics are used in statecraft, sports, business, and warfare to compare and contrast various factions, calculate odds, and formulate winning strategies. By measuring our assets, resources, threats, and opportunities and judging them against our foe's we may know before hostilities break out who will prevail in a fight. Look to Major League Baseball for an apt companion.

Differences amongst elite players who compete at the highest level are slight, so teams measure virtually everything to give themselves an edge, things like hitting, pitching, and base running statistics. These raw numbers are adjusted as necessary to account for variations that reliably impact player performance. For instance, some venues are considered "pitcher-friendly," like Dodger Stadium, whereas others at higher elevations may favor batters like Coors Field. Managers look at batting averages, stolen base percentages, earned run averages, on-base percentages, and the like to set their game plans. Who pitches, who bats, and in what order are all determined by with data augmented with the manager's experience.

For the Win: Measure weakness to strength, and strength to weakness. Ruthless assessment reveals truth.

You Lose: Spinning the data may make yourself feel good, yet you operate under delusion, hence cannot prevail.

24. Sun Tzu wrote:

"In making tactical dispositions the highest pitch you can attain is to conceal them, conceal your dispositions, and you will be safe from the prying of the subtlest spies, from the machinations of the wisest brains."

Even as we seek information about our adversaries, so too will they seek to understand us. The highest action in regard to our predilections, what we will instinctively do in battle, is to hide them. We must hide everything we can from our opponent, oftentimes withholding aspects of our plan even from our own men and women.

In Sun Tzu's time it took spy craft and subtlety to scout an adversary and discern his or her intentions, but with ubiquitous social media today it's almost too easy. Consider politics, which along with religion is one of the two "taboo" subjects at most workplaces. This is because roughly 40% of the population leans conservative, 40% has liberal inclinations, and 20% falls somewhere in between. While we are unlikely to change anyone else's mind with our political sentiment, we are quite likely to alienate anyone who disagrees with our dogma. Statistically, this means that we risk turning off half the population to the point that they may refuse to purchase our products or services because they disagree with our opinion. Not good odds. Consequently, unless we work in the political arena, we are far better off keeping our partisan beliefs to ourselves.

For the Win: Conceal your deepest, most important plans. Information to spies is like honey to bees, it draws them relentlessly.

You Lose: Fail to safeguard your data and reveal your intent to those who would do you harm.

25. Sun Tzu wrote:

"How victory may be produced for them out of the enemy's own tactics; that is what the multitude cannot comprehend."

While it is rarely a wise decision to directly play the other guy's game, especially when it comes to matters of warfare or interpersonal violence, the better we come to understand our adversary the more we can use his predilections against him. This goes far beyond merely mirroring an opponent's moves or adopting his or her style. Intimately knowing our adversary affords us opportunities to draw from his playbook, coopting his tactics and subverting his strategy to make it our own. We can intuit what he will do even before he puts his plans into action, and thwart them accordingly. It seems challenging, yet this principle is the foundation of an Olympic sport, judo.

Judo is a Japanese martial art which translates as "the gentle way" in English. Created by Jigoro Kano (1860 – 1938), judo emphasizes winning a fight by using an opponent's weight and strength against him or her while preserving one's own mental and physical energy. The art was designed to allow a smaller, weaker practitioner to overcome a stronger adversary with good technique, using minimum effort with maximum efficiency. This means that when attacked the judoka will not fight back, but rather yield, coopting the attacker's force and adding it to their own in order to defeat him.

For the Win: Tactics are obvious, grasped by the simplest of observations. Strategy, however, is what enables you to win.

You Lose: Confuse tactics for strategy and you set yourself up to fail.

26. Sun Tzu wrote:

"All men can see the tactics whereby I conquer but what none can see is the strategy out of which victory is evolved."

People see the apparent, the clear, the results. While tactics are easy to spot, the overarching strategy and skillful preparation that makes it work on the battlefield ordinarily remains unseen. This is because the strategy is a plan of action, a high level and oftentimes philosophical in nature. It is what we do ahead of time to prepare for contact with the enemy. Tactics, on the other hand, are what we do during contact with the adversary. They are expedient means of achieving an end, low level and immediate.

Ask a salesperson about his or her strategy for selling new vehicles and we will likely hear something about automobile selection, pricing, availability, and how to close a deal. This is a focus on the immediate, the tactics of a sale. While it may be how a salesperson earns his or her commissions, these things are easy to understand, yet not strategic. Ask the same question of the owner, however, and we will likely receive a different answer. Owners worry more about strategic things like building trusted relationships that drive referrals, methods of enticing potential buyers to visit the dealership, crafting the sales experience, and capturing the aftermarket for service revenue. Sales numbers are obvious, yet the infrastructure that turns visitors into customers is much harder to see.

For the Win: Most people see a strategy like a fish perceives a lure. The fish may be attracted by a shiny object in its path, but it cannot comprehend the predator who holds the fishing rod and hopes it'll take the bait. Further, it is pointless to try to explain this dynamic to the fish who cannot possibly understand. To succeed you must become the fisherman, not the fish.

You Lose: When you fail to see a strategy for what it is, an overarching environment created to employ tactics within.

27. Sun Tzu wrote:

> *"Do not repeat the tactics which have gained you one victory but let your methods be regulated by the infinite variety of circumstances."*

Every battlefield is unique, every army different. Consequently, each engagement requires a tailored approach. A fight in the desert is nothing like a fight in the jungle, yet even two battles that take place in the exact same terrain may require different tactics to yield our desired outcome. This is compounded by the fact that our adversaries continuously seek to understand and predict our behaviors just as we strive to confound and confuse them, so there's risk in trying the exact same thing twice.

During the American Revolutionary War period, it was rare to fight on Christmas, a holiday when armies usually held a temporary truce, yet that is exactly what George Washington (1732 – 1799) did when he braved frigid weather to cross the ice-choked Delaware river with 5,400 troops and surprise a Hessian force camped at Trenton, New Jersey. Short on supplies and desperate to recover from months of losses, Washington gambled on a treacherous Christmas night crossing to lead the unconventional attack at approximately 8:00 AM. While the original plan included three separate river crossings, only one was successful and that took longer than expected. Nevertheless, an hour-and-a-half later his troops had overwhelmed the German's defenses capturing a thousand enemies at the cost of only four lives. While the Hessians were forewarned by deserters, the bad weather and unbelievably audacious plan caught them by surprise. This victory was a key turning point by the Continental Army in their war for independence.

For the Win: Winning is wonderful, but it risks making you rigid in your strategy and tactics. To sustain the win you must be flexible, understanding that every battle is different.

You Lose: Show-up for a fight with the exact same plans you used in the previous contest and find yourself woefully unprepared. Everyone already knows what you did in the last battle so you've lost the element of surprise.

28. Sun Tzu wrote:

"Military tactics are like unto water, for water in its natural course runs away from high places and hastens downwards."

If given a choice or chance, it is preferable to fight from a high place downward. Good tactics flow downhill, with speed and velocity in our favor. Slogging uphill, on the other hand, runs against nature and takes excessive energy. Due to the inherent challenges, uphill battles should be avoided whenever possible. Consider the battle for Hill 937, named by military planners after its height in meters, by way of example. This location, nicknamed "Hamburger Hill," was one of the most intense and controversial battles of the entire Vietnam War. Its moniker came from 19-year-old Sergeant James Spears (1950 –), nicknamed "Grumpy" by his fellow soldiers, who told a reporter, "Have you ever been inside a hamburger machine? We just got cut to pieces by extremely accurate machine gun fire."

Although the hill itself had little strategic value, a protracted 10-day fight took place there as part of Operation Apache Snow, a US military sweep of the A Sau Valley designed to cut off North Vietnamese threats to the cities of Hue and Da Nang. It took the US troops 1o failed tries before they were finally able to storm up the hill and capture an enemy stronghold at its top, a battle in which some 630 North Vietnamese soldiers were killed while American forces suffered 72 losses and 372 wounded on their side. Nonetheless, that hard-won victory was fleeting. Two weeks later the hill was abandoned by US forces and re-occupied by the North Vietnamese a month later.

For the Win: From Roman fortifications, to motte and baileys, to stone keeps, to Victorian castles, to modern satellites, history demonstrates that the strategy of seizing the high ground is an immutable law of war.

You Lose: Fighting uphill sets your forces up for an expensive loss.

29. Sun Tzu wrote:

"So in war the way is to avoid what is strong and to strike at what is weak."

A "fair" fight is a child's idea of battle. Any violent encounter carries inherent risks, factors that we cannot control, so we must always seek to stack the odds on our side, leveraging strength against weakness to prevail. This may mean striking from concealment or straight-up battle, but either way, we must avoid attacking where the enemy has an advantage that will be difficult for us to overcome.

Consider the Maccabean rebellion against King Antiochus III (241 – 187 BC), an incident sparked by Hellenic overlords attempting to force their Jewish subjects to abandon their religion and conduct pagan worship. Jewish forces, led by Mattathias and his son Judah became known as the Maccabees, a term which translates as "hammers" into English, for their success in battle. They put together an army of some 7,000 insurgents and used superior knowledge of the area and innovative guerrilla tactics to take on forces more than five times their size and secure a seemingly impossible victory over the Seleucid Empire. After the Maccabees drove Antiochus out of Jerusalem, they not only regained their religious liberty but also rededicated the temple to God with festivities that continued for eight days. That ancient victory is still celebrated today as the festival of Hanukkah (which means "consecration" in English).

For the Win: Find and exploit the enemy's weakness.

You Lose: Foolishly matching force with force.

30. Sun Tzu wrote:

"Water shapes its course according to the nature of the ground over which it flows, the soldier works out his victory in relation to the foe whom he is facing."

There is a natural flow to all things in nature. So too, every conflict will ebb and flow in predictable ways. This means that we must let each situation and every adversary inform our strategy and determine our tactics. Different opponent, different means to prevail. In interpersonal conflict, this can be represented by the violence continuum.

Some violence can be staved off simply by our presence, looking and acting like we're more trouble than we are worth. Bad guys don't want to fight, they want to win. And they rarely mess with alert, prepared targets. We can use words to defuse many situations or apply a calming or directive touch to reach a resolution without fighting. But not always. Sometimes empty-hand restraint is required, particularly if we need to control a situation without seriously hurting anyone. Other times, less-lethal or even lethal force is necessary. These choices form a continuum, a set of options that may be drawn upon to resolve any situation we encounter. It is vital to enter this force continuum at the right level, if we use too much, we risk imprisonment, yet if we use too little, we may not survive the encounter. Consequently, we follow the "Goldilocks Rule" to get it just right.

For the Win: "Improvise, Adapt, Overcome," is an unofficial slogan of the US Marines popularized by Clint Eastwood's movie, Heartbreak Ridge. This is a good mantra to embrace.

You Lose: Treating all conflicts the same seals your downfall.

31. Sun Tzu wrote:

> *"Therefore, just as water retains no constant shape so in warfare there are no constant conditions."*

No plan survives contact with the enemy as he or she will not willingly comply with our designs. The shape of our plan must be flexible, continuously adjusting to account for evolving conditions we face on the battlefield. This requires both flexibility and innovation, attributes that are as important in business as they are in battle. Consider Amazon.com by way of example.

After surviving the dot-com bubble which destroyed most internet startups of that era, Amazon has grown into what is arguably the world's best business-model innovation organization. While most companies tend to focus on refining what they're already good at, branching out only in narrow ways, Amazon has succeeded in identifying and grasping onto opportunities that few others saw coming. Since setting out to change the way people buy books, they have subsequently created state-of-the-art e-readers, built a thriving internet marketplace, monetized social media, and used excess computing capacity to build their Amazon Web Services (AWS) cloud hosting service. Clearly, not every business has a culture that can embrace risk-taking to that degree, yet we all need to innovate. This goes beyond creating new products and services; we also need to learn how to identify opportunities to create and deploy new business models as Amazon has done.

For the Win: Sound strategy and flexible tactics win the day.

You Lose: Failure to exploit an enemy's error by dogmatically following your plan in the face of changing conditions is mindboggling stupidity.

32. Sun Tzu wrote:

"He who can modify his tactics in relation to his opponent and thereby succeed in winning may be called a heaven-born captain."

All leaders study strategy and tactics, yet few have the innate ability to asses, change, and secure victory time and time again. As German philosopher Arthur Schopenhauer (1788 – 1824) once wrote, "Talent hits a target no one else can hit. Genius hits a target no one else can see."

Whenever we earn a victory that others could not foresee, we become a hero. A challenge, however, is that to maintain our excellence we must not only be brilliant ourselves but also build a cadre of high performing leaders to carry out our plans. When it comes to significant endeavors, no one can go it alone. With a track record of success it's much easier to build an organization and spread the burden such that we can accomplish together what each individual only dreamed of themselves.

For the Win: Never sit on your laurels; continuously hone and refine your strategy.

You Lose: As the adage goes, "If as a coach you listen to the fans with respect to play-calling, you will soon be sitting in the stands watching the game with them."

33. Sun Tzu wrote:

> *"The five elements (water, fire, wood, metal, earth) are not always equally predominant, the four seasons make way for each other in turn. There are short days and long, the moon has its periods of waning and waxing."*

All factors in a fight are not created equal, they continuously ebb and flow with the tide of battle. We must be aware of when critical elements change, so that we may adapt and change with them. The five Taoist elements of water, fire, wood, metal, and earth are apt synonyms for aspects of the battlefield. Huo, or fire, for instance, is associated with passion, leadership, and heart. We may be impelled toward battle by our passions, but it takes heart to overcome the strain of war and prevail over the long run.

Even self-starters need encouragement to maintain morale during hard times. In order to set an environment that brings out the best in others, we must remember that organizations are fundamentally about relationships. Our men and women are people, not automatons. Leaders must set challenging yet realistic goals, listen to their teams, encourage innovative thinking, reward judicious risk-taking, diligently handle inadequate performance, develop transparent tracks toward promotion, and be generous yet genuine with praise. Celebrate success, learn from failure, and empower the team to find their own paths toward victory within our strategic framework.

For the Win: Certain elements in battle may be given emphasis while others recede, however these de-emphasized elements rarely go away completely. They may be recalled when it becomes their time to rise.

You Lose: Discarding what you don't need in the moment renders it unavailable for future imperative.

Chapter 7: Maneuvering

In this chapter, we discover the opportunities wrought by maneuvering our forces strategically. We may observe the enemy, determining his mettle and morale, and use this insight to position him to our advantage. We effectively communicate orders to our leaders, being understood above the chaos and fury of battle. In this fashion, we may concentrate or divide our forces and those of our adversaries, leveraging terrain, resources, and determination to overcome the enemy in both body and spirit.

1. Sun Tzu wrote:

"In war, the general receives his commands from the sovereign."

All advisors must be held accountable, from the highest to the lowest we serve at the pleasure of our leader, enacting policy rather than creating it. No matter how accomplished or lauded a general we may be, our role is to serve, carrying out the commands of our higher-ups. In other words, we do not determine whether or not to start a war, but once the order is given to unleash our forces, we must do everything in our power to create victory and in doing so hold our own subordinates accountable to their piece of the larger plan.

This is the way of every enterprise. In business, for instance, CEOs hold managers accountable for carrying out their strategies, yet are beholden to their board of directors. Boards, in turn, answer to shareholders. Control flows downward throughout the organization and, oftentimes, outward into the community it serves. As American psychologist Eugene Kennedy (1928 – 2015) once wrote, "As in the Divine Right of Kings, hierarchies invest those who preside at the top of their pyramidal structure with absolute power to rule over the lesser ranks that spread down like a marble staircase to the broad foundation stones of those with no power at all." Our goal, therefore, must be to judiciously advise our superiors, but once they understand our perspective, we are obligated to execute their lawful orders even when we disagree. If we cannot in good conscience do so, we must turn in our resignation and depart the endeavor with our honor intact.

For the Win: Know that while data alone is meaningless, and information can be useful, wisdom is invaluable.

You Lose: Confusing wisdom with information or data leads to false assurance.

2. Sun Tzu wrote:

> *"Having collected an army and concentrated his forces, he must blend and harmonize the different elements thereof before pitching his camp."*

Every army is comprised of many different elements, leadership, intelligence, logistics, infantry, cavalry, and force protection to name a few, each of which needs to clearly understand its unique role and mission within the larger endeavor. Before we can securely settle into our routine, this message must be in place. Done properly, each element understands their role, responsibilities, accountability, and integration with the rest of the troops.

Large endeavors must be broken into manageable components, yet simply creating numerous sub-teams is not enough. Without role clarity, these groups will step all over each other, driving confusion and rework. This is why defining who needs to be responsible, accountable, consulted, and informed (RACI) of each important decision is so important. If a person is responsible, he or she is assigned to the work, often in conjunction with a larger team. The accountable person makes the final decision and assumes the ultimate ownership of the group's deliverable(s). The people consulted are those with unique knowledge or perspective that the team must speak to before any important decision or action is taken. The people informed, are those who must know that a decision or action has taken place, often so that they can utilize the group's output. By using RACI, we make the complicated act of clear communication across a large endeavor more achievable and effective.

For the Win: Binding your disparate forces together under one single, motivating theme is essential to winning the battle.

You Lose: Allow competing agendas to arise within your team and you have lost the battle before you get started.

3. Sun Tzu wrote:

"After that, comes tactical maneuvering than which there is nothing more difficult. The difficulty of tactical maneuvering consists in turning the devious into the direct and misfortune into gain."

Driving our strategy into action not only requires clear communication, but also caution to assure that our orders are not intercepted or countermanded by the adversary. Leveraging our chain of command, officers must all come to understand the strategy, know their role within the larger endeavor, and have the flexibility to informed risks and implement tactics that help our undertaking succeed. In this fashion, we create velocity and agility in putting our plan to action.

This structure is much like navigating with a sailboat. While we cannot control the direction that the wind blows from, a skilled skipper can leverage whatever nature throws at him or her to trim the sails, tack the boat, and sail on virtually any bearing other than directly into the wind. "Heading up" means using the tiller to turn the bow of the vessel toward the wind direction whereas "falling off" means turning away from it. As we change our bearing relative to the wind, we alter the angle at which the wind pushes on the sail, simultaneously moving the sail in or out (a process called "sheeting") to optimize our speed. By judiciously tacking back and forth we can make progress against even the strongest headwinds.

For the Win: Position, both before and during contact with the enemy, is important. This is oftentimes difficult to achieve, yet it separates winners from losers.

You Lose: Engaging the enemy with only thoughts of battle demonstrates that you lack the vision necessary to win.

4. Sun Tzu wrote:

> *"Thus, to take a long and circuitous route after enticing the enemy out of the way and though starting after him to contrive to reach the goal before him shows knowledge of the artifice of deviation."*

In war, unlike most aspects of life, the destination is more important than the journey. We may maneuver directly or indirectly toward our target, making our determination based on shrewd insight into how the adversary will react to our movements. In this fashion, we control the location and timing of battle. This applies to virtually any enterprise, those who act confidently and arrive first control their destiny.

Paul Allen, (1953 – 2018), an American philanthropist who co-founded of Microsoft and owned both the Portland Trailblazers basketball team and the Seattle Seahawks football franchise, was the "idea man" who helped spark the computer revolution which has transformed the lives of billions of people throughout the world. He once wrote, "In my own work, I've tried to anticipate what's coming over the horizon, to hasten its arrival, and to apply it to people's lives in a meaningful way." To this end, he pledged over $100 million to combat Ebola in Africa and founded the Allen Institute for Cell Science to help fight cancer and other diseases. Those who likewise can anticipate trends and apply resources toward meaningful ventures create an enormous advantage over those who follow afterward.

For the Win: Every battlefield must have a purpose, an objective that furthers your goal. Move with determination and commitment to your plan.

You Lose: Waste energy by moving without bettering your position or weakening your enemy's.

5. Sun Tzu wrote:

"Maneuvering with an army is advantageous, with an undisciplined multitude most dangerous."

Disciplined armies can maneuver with precision, bringing necessary resources to fuel their journey, whereas ragtag, poorly assembled mobs not only stumble over themselves but also have a tendency to pillage and purloin whatever they desire along the way. Armies may be capable of horrific violence, yet undisciplined multitudes are in many ways far more dangerous and unruly. Consider the French Revolution, a decade of upheaval that wiped away that country's feudal system before degenerating into a chaotic bloodbath.

Following King Louis XVI's (1754 – 1793) execution in 1793, the Jacobins gained control of the National Convention and unleashed a "reign of terror" during which thousands of actual and conjectured "enemies of the revolution" were guillotined. Most of these executions were carried out by Maximilien de Robespierre (1758 – 1794), who lead the incongruously-named Committee of Public Safety until his own execution on July 28, 1794, proving that once the mob rules even its leaders are not safe. The order was not restored until general Napoleon Bonaparte (1769 – 1821) staged a coup d'état and declared himself France's first consul.

For the Win: Your agents must be disciplined, willing to maintain their restraint even at a high personal cost, thereby assuring the win.

You Lose: If your rank and file is weak, your whole enterprise becomes weak.

6. Sun Tzu wrote:

"If you set a fully equipped army on the march in order to snatch an advantage the chances are that you will be too late. On the other hand, to detach a flying column for the purpose involves the sacrifice of its baggage and stores."

While the army must remain fully intact and equipped in order to achieve its objectives over the long run, it is advantageous to set baggage aside and travel lightly whenever speed is of the essence. A vanguard may be dispatched to achieve each vital objective with the main force following after to secure what has been captured. Oftentimes this includes a contingent of outriders to scout the terrain, a group of engineers to build bridges and clear obstacles for those who follow, and a body of battle-hardened troops to seize each objective.

Consider the famous raid on Entebbe, Uganda, which took place on July 3rd and 4th, 1976, where an elite troop of Israeli commandos rescued 103 hostages from a hijacked jetliner. After stopping in Athens on route to France, an Airbus A300 was commandeered by members of the Popular Front for the Liberation of Palestine and their allies in the Red Army Faction, and flown to Uganda. In response the Israelis sent four Lockheed C-130 cargo planes loaded with commandoes and escorted by fighter jets to free their citizens. The raid took less than an hour, during which all 7 militants were killed. The Israelis lost one soldier, their team leader Yonatan Netanyahu (1946 – 1976), brother of Prime Minister Benjamin Netanyahu (1949 –), and 3 hostages during the fighting. They also destroyed 11 Ugandan Air Force MiG-17 and MiG-21 fighters stored at the airfield to prevent retaliation while making their escape.

For the Win: When the opportunity arises, seize the moment, even if that means engaging without your full compliment.

You Lose: Waiting for everything to be perfect before taking action means losing the moment.

7. Sun Tzu wrote:

"Thus, if you order your men to roll up their buff-coats and make forced marches without halting day or night, covering double the usual distance at a stretch, doing a hundred li *(~ 50 kilometers) in order to wrest an advantage, the leaders of all your three divisions will fall into the hands of the enemy."*

Speed is important in warfare, yet pushing overly hard to reach an objective is a strategy doomed to failure. Moving too quickly will exhaust our men, exposing our battle leaders to defeat, and undermine our plan. We must know how far and at what speed our troops can travel while retaining operational effectiveness, and issue achievable orders that assure they can arrive on the battlefield in good order. As French statesman and general Napoleon Bonaparte (1769 – 1821) once wrote, "The first virtue in a soldier is endurance of fatigue; courage is only the second virtue." If we exhaust their endurance through impudent strategy, we fail our men and women.

This principle is true not only for armies but also for individuals, even at the molecular level. Within each of us are billions of T-cells that protect us from bacteria, viruses, and harmful mutations. A single teaspoon of blood contains roughly 5 million T-cells. Among these are CD4 T-cells that act as "generals" to coordinate our immune response, and CD8 T-cells, that act as "soldiers" to battle unwanted invaders that may harm our bodies. In the face of a sustained or overwhelming attack, exhaustion can depress the effectiveness of these cells just like marching overlong without rest can harm the effectiveness of an army, allowing chronic infections, hepatitis, HIV, or cancer to persist. According to the University of Cambridge, new treatments for autoimmunity based on counteracting T-cell exhaustion funded by the National Institute of Health are currently underway, with hopes of eventually curing cancer and other horrific diseases.

For the Win: Move fast enough cover the distance, yet not so swiftly that you cannot arrive at full force. Never burn yourself out before the battle begins.

You Lose: Exhausted forces will be slaughtered at the battle. This is a triple loss, your time, your men, and your land.

8. Sun Tzu wrote:

"The stronger men will be in front, the jaded ones will fall behind and, on this plan, and only one-tenth of your army will reach its destination."

Setting too rigorous a pace means that many men and women will be unable to keep up. If only 1 in 10 in our army make it to the battlefield in fighting condition, we will be at a severe disadvantage during the struggle that follows. Moving too swiftly undermines morale, causing those of weaker spirit or stamina to be left behind.

Vince Lombardi (1913 – 1970) embodied the fighting spirit. He was a legendary American football player, NFL executive, and Green Bay Packers team coach whose organization won the first two Super Bowl games. A member of the "Seven Blocks of Granite," a nickname given to Fordham University's legendary offensive line, the NFL championship trophy was named after him in 1971. Lombardi once said, "Winning is a habit. Unfortunately, so is losing." Cleary this sentiment is true, yet as leaders, we can set our men and women up for success or failure based on our actions. Setting lofty yet achievable goals is good, but striving for the unachievable is disheartening. We must exercise caution to understand capabilities and push our team without breaking them.

For the Win: Let morale dictate your pace.

You Lose: Let the weakest slow progress in misplaced a desire to hold unity even at the cost of victory.

9. Sun Tzu wrote:

> *"If you march fifty li (~ 25 kilometers) in order to outmaneuver the enemy, you will lose the leader of your first division and only half your force will reach the goal."*

We must know our capabilities. When we weaken ourselves through folly, our hubris undermines our strategy. This loss will be expensive, running from top to bottom throughout the organization. This is the definition of "biting off more than we can chew."

Accepting too much responsibility can be stressful, especially when we are unable to negotiate deadlines and find ourselves attempting too much at once. Signs that we have overreached include feelings of irritability, exhaustion, distraction, or memory decline. We may also have trouble sleeping or experience sudden weight gain. Clearly, these are disturbing signals, and while they may or may not require outside intervention, they should be taken seriously. Turn things around by eliminating multitasking, working in 60 to 90-minute intervals, taking regular breaks, tracking and limiting time spent on low-value tasks, and giving up the illusion of perfection. By doing the best we can in the time allotted, focusing and finishing one thing at a time, and skipping the allure of social media, email, habitual snacking, and other distractions we give ourselves the best opportunity to be productive.

For the Win: Master Tzu used measurements appropriate to marching armies in ancient China. Identify the right measures for your endeavor and apply them shrewdly.

You Lose: Measuring the wrong things, or focusing on the wrong measures, leads you astray.

10. Sun Tzu wrote:

"If you march thirty li *(~ 15 kilometers) with the same object, two-thirds of your army will arrive."*

The difference between too far too fast and moving far enough and fast enough is measured by the resources we expend in route. On balance, we must know how to measure our resources and our expenditures judiciously. To carry too much or move too swiftly means that only part of what we need will actually arrive where it belongs when we need it to be there.

Anyone who has ever purchased something online understands the impact that deliveries have on customer experience. If the post office, parcel carrier, or Amazon delivery driver damages our package on the route, delivers it to the wrong place, or fails to show up on time, or if the package is stolen off our porch before we arrive home to claim it, we get irritated. Perhaps we'll become so upset that we'll stop using the site we purchased from. In fact, a recent survey demonstrated that 42% of customers and 66% of businesses stop buying from a seller after just one bad experience, with 95% of them sharing their feelings on social media in hopes of influencing others to follow their example. Additionally, 39% of customers shun a company for at least two years following a bad experience. The challenge, however, is that it's rarely the seller who causes the problem, but rather their logistics provider, even though most customers do not realize that. This means that businesspeople must focus on consistency and value rather than on cost-effectiveness when it comes to shipping.

For the Win: Know the pace of your endeavor.

You Lose: Set a pace without understanding the consequences and you can only win by accident.

11. Sun Tzu wrote:

"We may take it then that an army without its baggage-train is lost, without provisions it is lost, without bases of supply it is lost."

A constant supply is vital for the warfighter. We must have continuous access to resources, safeguarding supply lines to assure our mission's success. Should we lack for fuel, firepower, or food, any gains will soon be lost. The old adage, "An army marches on its stomach," has been attributed to both Napoleon Bonaparte (1769 – 1821) and Fredrick the Great (1712 – 1786). Regardless of who coined the term, this sentiment is absolutely true.

Consider the siege of Leningrad, which lasted for 872 days between 1941 and 1944. The German army and their Finnish auxiliaries surrounded the city, severed supply lines, and cut off escape the Soviet's escape. The effect was devastating, with the Soviet forces suffering the worst casualties of any siege in the history of modern warfare. Over 1 million Russian soldiers and more than 600,000 civilians were killed during the fighting, hospitals, water reservoirs, food stores, and critical infrastructure were utterly destroyed, and another 400,000 civilians perished soon after evacuation due to disease and starvation. Lack of food and water even drove many of the city's defenders to cannibalism.

For the Win: Never outrun your supply lines.

You Lose: Extending beyond your supply lines is like a maniac scampering blindly into the night… across a busy 8-lane highway. It tends to end badly.

12. Sun Tzu wrote:

"We cannot enter into alliances until we are acquainted with the designs of our neighbors."

Despite the old adage, "the enemy of our enemy" is not always our friend. We must know our prospective partners' true motivations before establishing any alliance. Consider not only the government or enterprise we may connect with but also the individual members as well. Feckless allies can easily cause more disruption to our plans than dynamic enemies. This is why we employ spies to gather information that helps us make prudent decisions.

Dusko Popov (1912 – 1981), a friend of British spy-turned-author Ian Fleming (1908 – 1964), was likely the real-life inspiration for Fleming's fictional character James Bond. A German-speaking Yugoslavian attorney and infamous playboy, Popov worked with British intelligence under the codename "Tricycle" to infiltrate the German Abwehr as a double-agent during WWII. In August 1941, Fleming was assigned to protect his country's financial investment in a money-laundering scheme when he observed Popov win an audacious baccarat bet at the Casino Estoril in Portugal, no doubt inspiration for Bond's debut in Casino Royale. Communicating via microdot codes, invisible ink, and various other tradecraft of the day, Popov worked to undermine the Germans and was even instrumental in convincing the Nazis that the D-Day invasion would take place at Dover, rather than Normandy, helping assure the success of the invasion.

For the Win: Know that an alliance built of convenience will only last as long as a common enemy exists.

You Lose: Believe that an ally of convenience will not turn on you at any moment and you'll be astounded when his knife slips between your ribs.

13. Sun Tzu wrote:

"We are not fit to lead an army on the march unless we are familiar with the face of the country—its mountains and forests, its pitfalls and precipices, its marshes and swamps."

Elements of the battlefield are final and uncompromising; it is our responsibility to understand this space, know its idiosyncrasies, and use them to our advantage. On defense, we naturally leverage the familiar for our benefit, yet even as invaders, the more we come to know the terrain, the better we can undermine our adversary's lead. The more we know, the wiser we are able to act. Like the United States, Marine General James "Mad Dog" Mattis (1950 –) once said, "The most important six inches on the battlefield is between your ears." To make the most of our brainpower we must be fully informed not only of the contest rules and strategy under which we plan to participate but also of the ground on which we will compete.

For example, playing football, lacrosse, rugby, or soccer on artificial turf is significantly different than playing the same game on natural grass. Turf emulates grass, is easier to maintain, and holds up better in wet conditions, but tends to run significantly hotter (by as much as 19 degrees Fahrenheit) in certain climates, which can adversely impact player performance. It is free of divots, ruts, and bumps yet are less forgiving than grass. Turf's rubber beads contain carcinogens, and beyond any inherent cancer risk, it has been known to cause "turf burn" abrasions, higher incidents of ACL damage, and other player injuries than natural grass.

For the Win: Know the lay of the land, be a marketplace, a regulatory environment, or physical battlefield, and use that knowledge to your advantage.

You Lose: If you have not reviewed the environment deeply before acting you cannot be certain where and how to tread. That's a lot like tiptoeing through a minefield blindfolded.

14. Sun Tzu wrote:

"We shall be unable to turn natural advantage to account unless we make use of local guides."

Maps are useful, but no one truly knows the terrain like those who were born and raised there. To best turn knowledge of the battlefield toward our advantage, we must acquire strategic insight from those who know it best. Whether we wish to know the best route, the best cover or concealment, or even the best food, we must ask the local populace for help.

As Iron Chef Masaharu Morimoto (1955 –) once wrote, "Just ask the local people for the best food. Don't rely on a guidebook." Every city has tourist attractions that are well known and hidden gems that only the residents know and frequent. Social media reviews, neighborhood guides, and the like may describe interesting places, but one cannot really know the local color and flavor without actually being there. And, if we get to know the chef and wait staff at our favorite restaurants, we often get access to "secret" menus and delicacies not offered to the general public. Better yet, from a self-defensive perspective, the more intimately we know locations where we live, work or attend school the safer we will be.

For the Win: Thoughtfully consider insight from those intimately familiar with the area to gain advantage.

You Lose: Ignoring insight from those who know the area best is an imprudent choice.

15. Sun Tzu wrote:

"In war, practice dissimulation and you will succeed."

The art of war is subterfuge, confusing and confounding our adversaries so that we may overcome them. We must practice deception, moving with stealth, striking with surprise, and fading into the distance. In this fashion, we keep the enemy guessing while we control the battlefield. Consider advertising by way of example.

Clearly, we must learn about products or services before we may choose to acquire or avoid them, yet the capitalist system is all about the exchange of value. The right merchandise all but sells itself, as its quality and usefulness fill a customer's unmet need. A challenge is that much of what is produced is truly not desirable for many, so advertising campaigns are created to convince us to covet and buy what we do not need. These campaigns use sex appeal, celebrity endorsement, positive association, peer pressure, laughter, reverse psychology, scare tactics, or promises of pleasure to trick us into parting with our hard-earned money. Like skilled generals, however, savvy consumers consider what to buy strategically on its merits, so these dissimulations do not sway us.

For the Win: Contrasts are important to observe and exploit. Be adroit in your observations.

You Lose: If all you own is a hammer, then everything becomes a proverbial nail. This fails to see the contrasts that may provide success. Losers believe that everything is exactly what it seems.

16. Sun Tzu wrote:

"Whether to concentrate or to divide your troops must be decided by circumstances."

If there is a reason to split our forces it must be done strategically, based on the facts of the moment, not on some whim. Concentrating our forces in one area weakens then in another, even as dividing our troops temporarily lessens our capabilities. Any decision that weakens our fighting strength must be thoughtfully considered and found beneficial before taking action lest we are deceived by enemy actions that play on our emotion or nefariously leverage our likings.

Tactical withdrawal is a common military operation, oftentimes used to simulate retreat while luring enemy forces into an ambush. Mongols hordes under the leadership of Genghis Kahn (1186 – 1241) used light cavalry to perfect this technique. In the heat of battle, they would pretend to become exhausted and confused, suddenly retreating in feigned defeat. The opposing force, thinking they had routed their adversary, would give chase only to discover that they had fallen into a trap. The Mongols used short recurve bows to accurately fire at pursuing forces without slowing, then suddenly turn and re-attack when pursuers tried to break away from the fatal counter-fire or slow their charge. In this fashion, the Mongols would break larger armies into smaller groups they could easily defeat.

For the Win: Since dividing your forces creates more contact with the enemy while simultaneously weakening your power, you must exercise caution to maintain advantage during such maneuvers.

You Lose: Allow yourself to be drawn into a division of power, one not of your own design, and you have fallen into the enemy's trap.

17. Sun Tzu wrote:

"Let your rapidity be that of the wind, your compactness that of the forest."

When engaging the enemy, we must move swiftly in close coordination so that each strike becomes a decisive blow against the adversary. This teamwork must be instilled from the newest recruit to the eldest veteran, each knowing his or her exact place in the larger formation. This is why armies throughout history have instilled discipline, teamwork, and attention to detail in their troops using various marches, drill formations, ceremonies, and parades. Individuals and units move together in orderly precision to carry out predesigned movements, be they at the squad, section, platoon, or company level, that simulate activities upon the battlefield.

What is trained in peacetime emulates what's done in combat, although with greater precision. This is because in the heat of battle adrenaline courses through our system. While it robs us of fine motor skills and a certain level of rational cognition, often causing tunnel vision and temporary hearing or memory loss, adrenaline helps us become temporarily stronger and more resilient. We can suffer significant damage without stopping, at least until the pain kicks in afterward. The more comprehensive and realistic our training is, the better we will perform in actual combat because conditioned responses can help us counteract, or at least work through, the negative effects of adrenaline.

For the Win: Swift, confident movement cannot be artificially created; it comes from holistic training and sound planning. Invest in this preparation.

You Lose: Cheerleaders falsely believe they are a part of the game because of their emotional investment in their team, yet they face away from the action. If you're nothing more than cheerleader you will have virtually no impact on the outcome.

18. Sun Tzu wrote:

"In raiding and plundering be like fire, in immovability like a mountain."

Raids must be quick and violent, tearing through the enemy like a windswept inferno. Our goal is shock and awe, disruption and fear. This is the role of light, swift forces. Holding ground, on the other hand, is the role of an entrenched and fortified army that refuses to bend. Consider the Dardanelles, the only waterway between the Black Sea and the Mediterranean Sea, which was the site of a pivotal campaign during WWI.

On March 18, 1915, British First Lord of the Admiralty Winston Churchill (1874 – 1965) ordered six English and four French battleships to steam toward the Dardanelles with a goal of taking it away from Turkish and German forces led by Mustafa Kemal (1881-1938). Despite a heavy bombardment campaign that preceded the attack, half the Allied ships were sunk or taken out of commission due to mines that blocked the channel. A second attack, which combined sea power with a ground invasion of the Gallipoli Peninsula which bordered the northern side of the strait, followed. It was a disaster. Allied forces fought for eight months without taking much more than the beachhead where they initially landed. Approximately 205,000 Brits and 47,000 Frenchmen were killed, and Churchill was forced to resign his role in the Admiralty over the debacle. He later headed to the Western Front to command an army battalion as a Lieutenant Colonel in the 6th Royal Scots Fusiliers.

For the Win: Raids lack mass, so surprise, speed, and violence of action, always critical in warfare, are accentuated.

You Lose: Executing a raid in the same manner as advancing an entire army makes your movement ponderous. You will fail from lack of momentum.

19. Sun Tzu wrote:

"Let your plans be dark and impenetrable as night and when you move fall like a thunderbolt."

We must never reveal our intent until the last moment. When our adversary knows what is coming he or she can prepare and counter our victory. When caught completely by surprise, however, the enemy is at our mercy. This is as true for armies as it is for individuals. Consider the pre-attack indicator, or "tell."

Poker players coined this term, which refers to some movement or gesture that lets them figure out when an opponent is bluffing. In the self-defense communities, this tale has been called many things such as the adrenal dump or the twitch. Whatever we call it, there is virtually always a tell that precedes a threat's attack. If we fail to spot this tell, often a subtle change of energy, we are bound to lose. This is because even if we are exceptionally fast, the action is always faster than reaction. In other words, missing the tell is what gets us sucker punched. Recovery after a successful first strike is challenging.

For the Win: Disguise your intentions, obfuscating what others may observe and use against you.

You Lose: Fail to recognize that your enemy's observations have greater intensity than your own and you give away your intentions.

20. Sun Tzu wrote:

"When you plunder a countryside let the spoil be divided amongst your men, when you capture new territory cut it up into allotments for the benefit of the soldiery."

Leaders may design the strategy, but the men and women under our command are the ones who carry it out. With this risk should come reward, and loot in all its forms is one of the greatest rewards we can grant to our forces. To maintain morale, the spoils of victory must be shared amongst all who play a role in acquiring it. Consider stock options as an example.

A stock option grants an individual the right, but not the obligation, to buy or sell a stock at an agreed-upon price and date. They are a popular form of executive compensation because if a company does well and its stock price increases those who helped bring about that success can become rich. To stave off short-term behaviors that may temporarily increase the stock but damage the enterprise over the long run these options typically vest over a period of 3 to 5 years. The most senior executives tend to get more shares with lower-level employees earning fewer, but with a well-thought-out compensation program, everyone can share in a publicly-traded company's success.

For the Win: Resources earned through victory make low-cost rewards to those who helped you win. Share generously.

You Lose: Greedily keeping everything for yourself undermines not only your victory, but also your entire endeavor.

21. Sun Tzu wrote:

"Ponder and deliberate before you make a move."

Our plans must be thoughtfully designed and thoroughly communicated to those who are tasked with carrying them out. To do this we must analyze and evaluate, not just list the critical elements of our design but deeply understand them. In this fashion we know why, not just what, determine where and when, and let our commanders determine how to put our plans into fruition. We cannot expect that our entire leadership chain will survive the battle, hence safeguard our designs by distributing responsibilities.

British Field Marshal Bernard Law Montgomery (1887 – 1976) was among the most decorated military leaders of WWII, instrumental to designing the Allied victories at El Alamein, Egypt in 1942 and Normandy, France (D-Day) in 1944. Montgomery wrote, "Every soldier must know, before he goes into battle, how the little battle he is to fight fits into the larger picture, and how the success of his fighting will influence the battle as a whole." In this fashion, troops on the ground can react to unforeseen circumstances, improvising where necessary, while firmly keeping the greater strategy and objectives in mind.

For the Win: Winners have a propensity for action, yet hold their base instincts in check, advancing only after careful evaluation.

You Lose: Jumping in without thoughtful consideration accelerates failure.

22. Sun Tzu wrote:

"He will conquer who has learnt the artifice of deviation. Such is the art of maneuvering."

A movement must never give away our intent. The shortest distance between two objectives may be fastest, yet sometimes a more indirect, lengthier path is strategically preferable. We must be flexible within our strategy, making nimble adjustments as the tactical situation dictates. Team leaders, therefore, must develop and drill hand gestures to facilitate swift, silent communication with their men and women to coordinate responses in the most effective way.

Our patrols must be prepared to make contact with the adversary's forces, especially during operations where the enemy is disguised, dispersed, or otherwise more elusive than in conventional operations. Unit size, speed, terrain, transport, and munitions all play a role in our response once the enemy is encountered, yet immediate action must be undertaken to gain control of each encounter.

For the Win: Know that the enemy will adapt to your measures, so you must vary your approach with each adaptation.

You Lose: Assuming that your enemy is foolish, that he cannot counter your designs, is flawed thinking that leads to recklessness. This undermines you long term prospects for survival.

23. Sun Tzu wrote:

> *"The Book of Army Management says, 'On the field of battle the spoken word does not carry far enough, hence the institution of gongs and drums. Nor can ordinary objects be seen clearly enough, hence the institution of banners and flags.'"*

Communication amongst our troops must be bold, loud and clear, designed to be perceived over the chaos of battle. We must use the clearest means to communicate commands such that where we cannot be heard our men and women nonetheless know and immediately react to our intent. In Sun Tzu's time this often meant the use of gongs or drums whose resonance reverberates far beyond the spoken word, and banners or flags which could be seen above the fray.

No matter how good our ideas may be, if we cannot convince others to listen, we are lost. American motivational speaker Emanuel James (Jim) Rohn (1930 – 2009) once said, "Take advantage of every opportunity to practice your communication skills so that when important occasions arise, you will have the gift, the style, the sharpness, the clarity, and the emotions to affect other people." People rarely recall what we say to the same degree they remember how they feel about the conversation. This means that the best communicators draw upon both logic and emotion to bring listeners around to their point of view, yet it is rare to be able to do this naturally. Communication is a skill that must be practiced.

For the Win: Hand signs, semaphore, smoke signals, searchlights, and flags, these all serve as examples of situational means of communication. As a leader, you must establish layers of communication such that your message can be always received.

You Lose: Whenever you fail to implement back-ups for your backup plans Murphy will strike, rendering you mute when communication is imperative.

24. Sun Tzu wrote:

"Gongs and drums, banners and flags, are means whereby the ears and eyes of the host may be focused on one particular point."

Our men and women must always know where to look for guidance as the course of the battle unfolds. This means that we need an observable place where we can communicate from throughout each battle such that all our people know where to look for our message. With modern technology this may be a location far removed from the battlefield whereas in Sun Tzu's time it had to be a site nearby. Nevertheless, clear signaling is instrumental for clear communication in any game. Consider American football as an example.

It is impossible for players on the field to hear their coach's instructions over the roar of the crowd, so quarterbacks routinely wear an armband containing numerous color-coded offensive plays grouped into various categories. Before each play coaches and select players, such as the backup quarterback, send instructions to their men on the field with hand signals, placards, or similar means. Some of these indicators are fake, designed to mislead the other team, while others are commands that tell the offense what primary play to run and what alternative to check down to as needed. By comparing these instructions to the sheet on his arm, the quarterback knows what to do in any given situation and can quickly communicate the coach's selected play to the offense.

For the Win: Set standards for communication and assure they are diligently followed. In this fashion your plans are carried out as expected.

You Lose: Making up your protocols and methods as you go along assures miscommunication.

25. Sun Tzu wrote:

"The host thus forming a single united body is it impossible either for the brave to advance alone or for the cowardly to retreat alone. This is the art of handling large masses of men."

In unity there is strength. When our troops move together in harmony, we encourage the strong while fortifying the weak. In this fashion, brother spurs brother, the multitude emboldening each other toward heroism that individuals may not be capable of when facing the adversary alone. This hearkens back to the fable of the master and his quarreling disciples.

A certain master had disciples who were always quarreling with one another. Try as he might he could not get them to live together in harmony, so he determined a plan with which to convince them of their folly. Bidding them go into the woods and fetch back a bundle of sticks, he stacked the branches and tied them tightly together. The master then invited each disciple, in turn, to break the bundle in twain by striking it with their foot or fist. All tried and all failed despite their utmost determination and vigor. When the master then undid the bundle and handed each disciple the sticks one-by-one they had no difficulty in breaking them whatsoever. "There, my disciples," said he, "united you will be more than a match for your enemies, yet if you quarrel and separate your weakness will put you at the mercy of those who wish you harm." Thus chastened, the quarreling disciples pledged to argue no more.

For the Win: Create a unifying purpose that spurs action greater than anyone on the team's personal agenda.

You Lose: Allow self-aggrandizement, bickering, and pettiness to divide your forces and you have done the enemy's job for him.

26. Sun Tzu wrote:

"In night-fighting then, make much use of signal-fires and drums and in fighting by day of flags and banners as a means of influencing the ears and eyes of your army."

Battles may take place night or day, in the rain, fog, snow, or storm, and throughout all these environs we must clearly communicate to our men and women on the field. To make our intentions seen we must use contrast, bright against the dark, dark against the light. In this fashion, our signals become known with no confusion.

To communicate unambiguously, we must hone our message, knowing with certainty what we wish listeners to understand, remember, or do based on our conversation and then deliver that core substance in the simplest, most concise manner possible. While fewer words may mean more messages, the structure in which we deliver our message is critical too. For best results we begin by building rapport, gathering and sharing information in an affable way, and then use story-telling to draw in and convince our audience of our perspective, closing with a call to action. This structure helps assure the greatest impact in the shortest amount of time.

For the Win: Every environment has its best communication format. Be attuned to this, taking best advantage to spur your success.

You Lose: Building a lighthouse in the desert makes no sense when a flashing pocket mirror will suffice.

27. Sun Tzu wrote:

"A whole army may be robbed of its spirit; a commander-in-chief may be robbed of his presence of mind."

In warfare the victor rarely annihilates his foe, but rather he overcomes his adversary's will to continue the fight. During the ebb and flow of battle, there will come instances when either or even both sides may consider themselves beaten, yet those who persevere through those moments of doubt while creating uncertainty for the other side will ultimately prevail. A well-struck blow can steal the spirit from our opponent, causing him to doubt his plans and prowess. The more pressure a leader feels the greater the likelihood that he or she will lose attendance to the plan.

Morale is critical for virtually any undertaking, and nothing undermines it faster than whining, negativity, and tolerance of abusive, disrespectful, or subversive behavior. We must hold ourselves and our team accountable for putting forth our best effort, celebrating successes, and learning from mistakes as we progress toward our goals. Never let self-inflicted wounds sabotage our endeavor.

For the Win: Seeing the battle for what it is, in all its ebbs and flows, while holding fast to the goal is the mark of a great leader.

You Lose: Letting your spirit collapse from the enemy's first blow turns a setback into a loss.

28. Sun Tzu wrote:

"Now a soldier's spirit is keenest in the morning, by noonday it has begun to flag, and in the evening his mind is bent only on returning to camp."

The natural cycle is to rise with the sun and set with the sun. The promise of each new day brings a fresh renewal, yet our stamina often flags under the weight of what we are tasked to do throughout our waking hours. The strain of warfare brings mental and physical exhaustion in its wake.

Biorhythms are natural fluctuations that govern our physical, emotional, and intellectual pursuits. Physical cycles impact our strength, endurance, vitality, and resistance to disease, whereas emotional cycles our passions, sense of optimism, and positive or negative feelings. Intellectual cycles impact memory, alertness, and reasoning. Knowing, monitoring, and leveraging these patterns can be a boon to our creativity, productivity, and success.

For the Win: Understand the natural rhythms and use them to your advantage.

You Lose: Break the rhythm, counter the natural pattern, and pay the price in chaos.

29. Sun Tzu wrote:

"A clever general, therefore, avoids an army when its spirit is keen but attacks it when it is sluggish and inclined to return. This is the art of studying moods."

The cycles of the hour, day, week, month, and years serve as signposts articulating when we are to attack. We improve our odds by striking the enemy when he or she is exhausted, despondent, or listless, capitalizing on periods of lethargy and low morale to further crush their fighting spirit. In this fashion, we fight not just the adversary's body, but also their hearts and minds.

As traditional war assaults the enemy's men, machines, and infrastructure, psychological warfare attacks their will to enter into or continue the fight. Oftentimes this is performed through various forms of propaganda aimed not only at combatants but also at civilians. Propaganda relies on the perception of credibility in order to be successful, falling into three categories: white, grey, and black. White information is real, cited, and sourced, albeit moderately biased in some instances. Grey information is also largely truthful but contains no cites or sources. Black information is wholly deceitful, and when attributed the referenced sources are counterfeit. While black information can have the most impact, such as with false flag events, it simultaneously carries the greatest risk as sooner or later the target population will discover that it is deceitful. After all, Hitchens's Razor states, "That which can be claimed without evidence can be dismissed without evidence."

For the Win: Aim to unleash your forces when they are at the height of their mental prowess and physical strength, harnessing their fighting spirit.

You Lose: Break the cycle of rest and recuperation, fighting as whim and will dictate, and place yourself at grave disadvantage.

30. Sun Tzu wrote:

"Disciplined and calm, to await the appearance of disorder and hubbub amongst the enemy, this is the art of retaining self-possession."

As leaders, we must be self-possessed. Our strategy is formidable, our tactics strong. Buttressed by our mastery of the art of war we portray discipline and calm, no matter what uncertainty we may feel about our plans, despite any nagging fear of our enemy's designs, notwithstanding any anxiety about our capabilities that seek to contaminate our thoughts. A clear, orderly mind and calm demeanor not only boosts our troops' morale but also enables us to experience and react to what is real, ignoring what is imagined.

The Japanese term mushin or "no-mind" comes from the Zen expression "mushin no shen" which translates into English as "the mind without mind." It sounds confusing, but this concept merely relates to the absence of thought. With mushin, the warrior's mind is open and not fixed on anything in particular. It is the opposite of daydreaming, a higher state of mental clarity, awareness, and perception without contamination by emotions such as fear or anxiety. When all of these extraneous thoughts are brushed aside, warriors can perceive what is real and react instantly to any threat as it appears.

For the Win: Make every effort to maintain discipline and focus, even in harsh conditions, and you will prevail.

You Lose: Allow the conditions of the moment to undermine your discipline and suffer for your inattention.

31. Sun Tzu wrote:

"To be near the goal while the enemy is still far from it, to wait at ease while the enemy is toiling and struggling, to be well-fed while the enemy is famished, this is the art of husbanding one's strength."

Energy ebbs and flows during battle. Where we are able to conserve our strength, building toward greater stores while sapping the enemy's reserves before we meet upon the field, we set victory in place before the first blow is struck. Leading our adversary astray, we move ever closer to our goal while setting our enemy upon an arduous path such that he arrives in disarray.

Exhaustion can be mental or physical. To guard against mental fatigue we must begin by prioritizing, realistically determining what can and cannot be accomplished during any given day. Next, we must take micro-breaks (every 45 minutes to 1 ½ hours) during which we get up, do something physical (preferably strenuous, but even walking around for a couple of minutes can work), and give our minds a respite. During this exercise, we pay attention to physical sensations such as the movement of our muscles, inhalations, and exhalations of breath, rather than on the task we were performing. And, we must give ourselves permission to relax. In this fashion, we are most productive, even when faced with seemingly overwhelming responsibilities.

For the Win: Assure that the basic needs of your forces are provided, keeping them strong even in hardship, as they will have few concerns beyond the order of battle.

You Lose: Failing to meet fundamental needs of food, fuel, rest, and supplies undermines discipline, sparking defiance and rebellion within the ranks.

32. Sun Tzu wrote:

"To refrain from intercepting an enemy whose banners are in perfect order, to refrain from attacking an army drawn up in calm and confident array, this is the art of studying circumstances."

If the adversary appears calm, prepared, and confident, we must exercise caution in executing our plans. Scout, appraise and determine the true state of enemy forces before acting. By measuring and managing our circumstances we press forward or slink away with informed intent.

Nikola Tesla (1856 – 1943) was a Serbian-American inventor, engineer, and futurist who invented the induction coil, developed modern methods of electric power transmission, and patented the rotating magnetic field, the basis for most alternating-current machinery today. He once wrote, "Today's scientists have substituted mathematics for experiments, and they wander off through equation after equation and eventually build a structure which has no relation to reality." As Tesla states, leaders must ferret out the truth through experimentation and data rather than relying on unsubstantiated models that may seem impressive yet fail to reflect reality.

For the Win: The day-to-day actions of the enemy will tell you their order. See what's shown, looking behind the obvious to discern their weakness and strength.

You Lose: Fail to observe overt acts by your opponent and you cannot even begin to perceive vital clues that may flip the outcome of battle.

33. Sun Tzu wrote:

"It is a military axiom not to advance uphill against the enemy nor to oppose him when he comes downhill."

The terrain is immutable, it gives and it takes advantage with no favor. Fighting uphill battles taxes our strength and will. Conversely, a downhill charge by the enemy is problematic as it may be countered but only through enormous sacrifice. Rather than face an enemy's strengths augmented by his or her mastery of terrain we must set the field in our favor, hence prevail.

On August 24, 1942, at Hill 213, 5 near Isbuschenskij in what was then the Soviet Union, a group of 600 Italian horsemen led by Colonel Alessandro Bettoni di Cazzago (1892 – 1951) carried out the last known cavalry charge of the modern era. Armed with sabers, hand grenades, and a few rifles, they charged down the hill and across open ground to attack a dug-in infantry troop backed by machineguns and mortars. While this assault should have been suicidal, it worked. Stunned by the anachronistic maneuver, the 812th Siberian Rifle Regiment forces fell before the fury of the Italian assault. By the end of the day, 150 Soviet soldiers died, 300 were wounded, and another 600 captured at a cost of 32 dead Italian cavalrymen, with another 52 wounded. A hundred cavalry horses were also killed in the battle.

For the Win: An uphill battle is a Sisyphean task best avoided.

You Lose: Forget that charging uphill is folly, meeting a downhill charge foolhardiness, and your battle lust will be your undoing.

34. Sun Tzu wrote:

"Do not pursue an enemy who simulates flight, do not attack soldiers whose temper is keen."

There is a tremendous difference between a routed foe and one simulating flight. If we choose to pursue a professional, battle-tested adversary, we risk running into a trap. A feigned retreat is a common method of stretching out a pursuer's forces, to make them susceptible to ambush. Before taking action, we must keenly observe our adversary and determine whether the enemy truly is in disarray or if they are merely attempting to lure us into a position of vulnerability.

Physical conflict is time-bound, whereas emotional and spiritual battles may extend over very long periods of time. Consequently, while we may capture enemy territory, we must guard against losing control as insurgents strike back over a period of months, years, or even decades. Consider the Revolutionary Armed Forces of Colombia (FARC), which carried out a guerrilla war with Columbian government forces for more than 50 years by way of example. Without extensive negotiations, reintegration plans, and political reconciliation we may "control" territory yet periods of unrest and counterinsurgency may carry on indefinitely.

For the Win: If engagement is too easy, if you appear to be winning on all fronts, beware the enemy's duplicitous trap.

You Lose: Pursue a false battle, chase after an early retreat, and find yourself right where the enemy wants you to be.

35. Sun Tzu wrote:

"Do not swallow bait offered by the enemy. Do not interfere with an army that is returning home."

The only guarantee of victory is to avoid fighting altogether. If the adversary's spirit is broken such that they do not wish to fight, best to not seek that fight. Let him slink back to his home unhindered. In this fashion, we win double-victory.

Rule number of self-defense is, "Don't get hit." Sounds simple at first blush but it is really more complicated than that. At best, it's about avoiding situations or locations where violence is most likely to occur. In circumstances where fighting is inevitable, however, it is about avoiding damage while staving off the threat until he or she is no longer a danger or we can escape. As the Indian proverb states, however, "Dead tigers kill the most hunters." We must remain vigilant during any pause in a fight. Once we have removed ourselves from danger and reached a location out of harm's way, we may we begin to safely relax our guard.

For the Win: Break the enemy's spirit to secure your victory.

You Lose: Refusing to let the enemy quit, even after he has given up the fight, compounds risk and prolongs the conflict unnecessarily.

36, 37. Sun Tzu wrote:

> *"When you surround an army leave an outlet free. Do not press a desperate foe too hard. Such is the art of warfare."*

An army may fight or flee, yet when cornered such that there is no option but to fight a desperate foe will harden their hearts against inevitable, striking out with the utmost ferocity. Leaving and giving choices for the enemy, therefore, will lead to a less expensive resolution for the conflict.

When an otherwise gentle soul is backed into a corner, he or she will virtually always fight back. Consider then, how someone inclined toward violence may react to finding him or herself trapped. The book Bad Intentions: The Mike Tyson Story (by Peter Heller) contains the passage, "He didn't know what to do, but his instincts, his blind rage, the surge of revulsion at what this bully had done, his fear, his pent-up emotions, all spilled over, and he attacked like a cornered animal, gouging, pulling, kicking, punching." Offering some escape, a face-saving way out deescalates most conflicts.

For the Win: When an enemy is defeated, accept the easy victory.

You Lose: Giving a conquered foe no option but to continue the fight often pulls defeat from the jaws of victory.

Chapter 8: Variation in Tactics

In this chapter, we discover that a wise leader's plans blend considerations of advantage and disadvantage together, assuring that we can always wrest the advantage from the enemy or extricate ourselves from misfortune. We understand the five dangerous faults that may affect a general, recklessness, cowardice, intemperateness, delicate honor, and over-solicitude, and meditate upon them as the underpinnings of defeat. Through this examination, we thoroughly understand the opportunities that arise from varying our tactics such that we can confidently face any situation and prevail.

1. Sun Tzu wrote:

"In war, the general receives his commands from the sovereign, collects his army and concentrates his forces."

War is expensive, risky, and destructive, yet at times necessary. Nonetheless, declarations of war must come from the sovereign before any military leader may launch an offensive. This chain-of-command is essential, not only to the general order but also for assuring that necessary resources and support are gathered to make the war effort successful. In this fashion, everyone knows why they fight, understands their role in the war effort, and may carry out their part in the plan of battle.

A military coup is the violent overthrow of a legitimate government by revolutionary forces or members of the country's military. A relatively recent example took place in the West African nation of Mali, resulting in the overthrow of President Amadou Toumani Touré's (1948 –) regime on March 22nd, 2012. Prior to this event, Mali has been one of the most politically and socially stable countries in Africa, yet afterword it quickly became one of the world's fastest failing states. Soldiers led by Captain Amadou Hoya Sanogo (1972 –), ostensibly displeased with their government's handling of the Tuareg rebellion revolted, suspending the constitution, closing the country's borders, and targeting military barracks, the presidential palace, international airport, and the state television center. Members of the international community, including the United States, immediately condemned the revolution and cut off foreign aid.

For the Win: Follow the chain of command.

You Lose: Act outside the chain of command and you become an outlaw.

2. Sun Tzu wrote:

"When in difficult country do not encamp. In country where high roads intersect, join hands with your allies. Do not linger in dangerously isolated positions. In hemmed-in situations you must resort to stratagem. In desperate position you must fight."

Never rest in a vulnerable position, this invites ambush. When we find ourselves in the difficult county, we must find friends where feasible, yet never delay moving clear of the area lest we find ourselves in a desperate position where we must fight on the enemy's terms.

Street predators are crafty, yet it doesn't take a genius to know that if he or she attacks a victim in a public place he is likely to get caught. While the bad guy(s) might want privacy to commit his assault, rape, murder, or robbery, he is not likely to find too many victims in remote, secluded locations. Consequently, fringe areas adjacent to heavily traveled public places are where the majority of violent crimes occur. That is where we need to pay the most attention to our surroundings. This includes areas such as parking lots, public parks, bike paths, alleyways, bathrooms, stairwells, ATM kiosks, bus terminals, train platforms and the like, particularly at night when few bystanders are hanging around.

For the Win: Notorious bank robber Willie Sutton (1901 – 1980) once told reporters, "I rob banks because that's where the money is." Know what resources are coveted by your enemy and deny them access.

You Lose: Falsely assuming something bad cannot happen leaves you unprepared when it does.

3. Sun Tzu wrote:

> *"There are roads which must not be followed, armies which must be not attacked, towns which must be besieged, positions which must not be contested, commands of the sovereign which must not be obeyed."*

Knowledge is liberating, yet the experience is invaluable. The astute commander knows that some things should not be acted upon, some opportunities left untaken. Our decisions must be tempered with wisdom, knowing that which must or must not be pursued to carry out our strategy.

The term "wisdom" can be challenging to define as it is it goes both broad and deep, encompassing knowledge, experience, and intelligence, along with a deep understanding of how seemingly unrelated phenomena may or may not work together. An experience by itself does not confer wisdom, as there are cognitive, emotional, and social factors that play an essential role too. Consequently, balance is the key to wisdom, the ability to understand and thoughtfully judge multiple factors that can result in good decisions for ourselves and our teams.

For the Win: Understand the context in which information is presented; this is the first step toward wisdom.

You Lose: "Black and white" worlds devoid of nuance are the demesne of fools and second-rate fiction writers.

4. Sun Tzu wrote:

"The general who thoroughly understands the advantages that accompany variation of tactics knows how to handle his troops."

The best leaders understand their forces' strengths and weaknesses, know their organization's opportunities and threats, and with this insight become able to harness their men and women most effectively. Those who can grow not only the individuals within their command but also the enterprise itself create an unstoppable advantage.

Peter Senge (1947 –), founding chairman of the Society for Organizational Learning, defined a learning organization as the one "where people continually expand their capacity to create the results they truly desire, where new and expansive patterns of thinking are nurtured, where collective aspiration is set free, and where people are continually learning to see the whole together." This is accomplished by understanding that people learn best by doing so we must incorporate learning into management processes, invest in the team, leverage technology that accelerates development, get lower-level members involved in key decisions, allow measured risk-taking, and measure results. In this fashion, we continuously improve competence and capabilities.

For the Win: Continuously learn and grow from experience.

You Lose: When you stop learning, or place the responsibility of your education in the hands of others, the world passes you by.

5. Sun Tzu wrote:

> *"The general who does not understand these may be well acquainted with the configuration of the country yet he will not be able to turn his knowledge to practical account."*

Those who turn data into information may practically apply what they know. The wise leader understands the lay of the land, its resources, and how to leverage what is available in support of his or her team. The greater the familiarity the greater the advantage.

In most team sports, the hosting team gains an advantage over the visitors due to a variety of factors like crowd involvement, travel, time zone differences, facility layout, environmental considerations, and the like. In American football, for instance, the home-field advantage tends to run anywhere from 2 ½ to 3 ½ points as reflected in sports betting odds. Due to this benefit, important games such as playoff or elimination matches have special rules for determining which game is played where. For example, Major League Baseball used to determine home-field advantage using the score of the All-Star Game, but after a 7 to 7 tie after 11 innings in 2002 they reconsidered and in 2017 changed their rules as part of the Collective Bargaining Agreement to favor whichever pennant winner had the better regular-season record.

For the Win: The home crowd that cheers you on is irrational. In fact, the word "fan" is a shortened version of the Latin *fanaticus*, which refers to people driven frantic, frenzied, or mad. Enjoy your fans, but do not take your lead from them.

You Lose: A home-field advantage, be it in sport or combat, is nice, but counting on it to deliver victory is a fool's wager.

6. Sun Tzu wrote:

"So, the student of war who is unversed in the art of war of varying his plans, even though he be acquainted with the Five Advantages, will fail to make the best use of his men."

It is insufficient to memorize the principles of warfare, to commit oneself to study the strategy and tactics of war, without also understanding how to apply them. The relevance lies solely in the application. With a flexible mind and discerning insight, a meritorious leader varies his or her plans to best meet each situation as it arises and thereby prevails.

For thousands of years, the art of warfare evolved slowly yet WWI (1914 – 1918), a global conflict amongst 32 nations fought over five theatres which led to the death of roughly 15 million soldiers and 40 million civilians, created monumental shifts in technology which in turn sparked revolutionary change in how generals conducted war. For example, it was the first-time that airplanes were used in battle, first to observe and report on enemy troops and later to drop bombs and shoot down other planes. Land ships (later renamed "tanks" for their shape) were also introduced during this period, allowing soldiers to cross the "no man's land" between trenches in the relative safety of their armored vehicles. Dreadnaughts (armored battleships) ruled the surface of the sea, while submarines patrolled under the water. Newly invented chemical weapons such as chlorine and mustard gas, flamethrowers, mobile artillery, and machineguns all brought new levels of lethality into play, altering strategies and rendering tactics of the past obsolete.

For the Win: Do you know the name of the most successful jewel thief of all time? Of course you don't, no one does, because that person knows how to break the rules and get away with it.

You Lose: Petulantly breaking the rules is juvenile behavior, irrational, and reckless. Break the rules without reason, without strategy, and you're a child.

7. Sun Tzu wrote:

"Hence in the wise leader's plans, considerations of advantage and of disadvantage will be blended together."

It is often said that leaders must be circumspect, perceiving all aspects of their forces as well as those of their adversaries. To not thoughtfully observe all parts of one's own army is a failure at the outset. A thorough understanding of strengths, as well as weaknesses of all sides in a conflict, leads to optimal decision-making.

Coach Vince Lombardi (1913 – 1970) once wrote, "Character is just another word for having a perfectly disciplined and educated will. A person can make his own character by blending these elements with an intense desire to achieve excellence. Everyone is different in what I will call magnitude, but the capacity to achieve character is still the same." Mentally strong individuals are self-aware, and in objectively understanding their attributes able to be confident, tenacious, and optimistic. Relentless in pursuit of goals, we are nevertheless flexible in approach to solving problems that may block our way. This adaptability sets leaders apart from the norm.

For the Win: Set a path toward your goal but remain flexible in the tools and methods you use to get there.

You Lose: Confuse rigidness with discipline at your peril. One is brittle, easily broken, while the other is flexible and strong.

8. Sun Tzu wrote:

"If our expectation of advantage be tempered in this way, we may succeed in accomplishing the essential part of our schemes."

No matter how thoughtfully we have prepared, we cannot in good conscience assume that all aspects of our strategy will go as planned when it is implemented. All elements of the plan must be taken into account, the good, the bad, and the just plain inconvenient. In holistic appraisal, we may account for contingencies with the flexibility to face any challenge that arrives.

Carl Philipp Gottfried von Clausewitz (1780 – 1831) was a Prussian general and military theorist who defined the nature of war as, "The realm of uncertainty; three-quarters of the factors on which action in war is based are wrapped in a fog of greater or lesser uncertainty." This means that the flexibility to change our plans based on the nature of any battle as it unfolds is paramount. Freedom of action through adaption, planned flexibility, creates a competitive advantage for our forces.

For the Win: Feed your endeavor with attention, energy, and adjustments to keep it on track.

You Lose: Divert your attention to other things while assuming your tactics have been set in motion and everything is moving forward according to your plan.

9. Sun Tzu wrote:

"If, on the other hand, in the midst of difficulties we are always ready to seize an advantage we may extricate ourselves from misfortune."

Open minds and flexible plans afford us the advantage of opportunities that lessor leaders neither notice nor pursue. By keeping the broadest vision possible, we may well identify fleeting opportunities that can turn the tide of battle, yet must simultaneously be prepared to take advantage of them before they disappear.

Even as Starbucks revolutionized the coffee business, so too can our endeavors set us apart from others if we firmly keep this principle in mind. American Billionaire Howard Schultz (1953 –), the former CEO of Starbucks, once said, "I believe life is a series of near-misses. A lot of what we ascribe to luck is not luck at all. It's seizing the day and accepting responsibility for your future. It's seeing what other people don't see and pursuing that vision." It doesn't matter if we can see beyond what others notice if we fail to act on what we discover.

For the Win: Here is the way to orient your vision, from an exchange in the movie Apollo 13: NASA Director (actor Joe Spano) pronounced, "This could be the worst disaster NASA's ever experienced!" Gene Kranz (actor Ed Harris) responded, "With all due respect sir, I believe this is going to be our finest hour."

You Lose: When you collapse under adversity you can no longer find a way out. Small, yet transformational changes, still await discovery.

10. Sun Tzu wrote:

"Reduce the hostile chiefs by inflicting damage on them and make trouble for them and keep them constantly engaged, hold out specious allurements and make them rush to any given point."

The adversary's most aggressive generals need to be abridged. Offer them traps, deceptions, and distractions that take advantage of their belligerent tendencies. This will bog them down in extended conflicts. Such attacks will degrade their resources and damage their spirit. In this fashion we distract, degrade, and ultimately destroy the enemy, using his own nature against him.

Aggression is used for a variety of purposes, some good such as to compete with others and achieve challenging goals and some bad, such as to inappropriately assert dominance and threaten others to get one's way. Psychologists distinguish between two types of dysfunctional aggression: affective and instrumental. Affective aggression is characterized by strong, impulsive emotions such as rage whereas instrumental aggression is more predatory in nature. Compare flipping someone off for driving erratically versus hijacking their car, stealing their wallet, and shooting them in the head for the same perceived offense. While aggression can stem from biological, physical, or environmental factors, anyone whose emotions can be manipulated by others will find themselves easily controlled.

For the Win: When an enemy is tested on many fronts their discipline will show. Test, badger, poke, and prod, forcing them to expend energy and patience.

You Lose: Overreacting to harassment makes you the tail not the dog.

11. Sun Tzu wrote:

> *"The art of war teaches us to rely not on the likelihood of the enemy's not coming but on our own readiness to receive him, not on the chance of his not attacking but rather on the fact that we have made our position unassailable."*

While we cannot know with certainty our enemy's intentions, nor control his or her actions, we can be prepared for any eventuality. As we cannot control the precise moment a dinner guest will arrive, we certainly can control the reception they receive once they get here. In this fashion, we may sleep comfortably, secure in the knowledge that we have prepared for everything within our control.

William "Bobby" Unser (1934 –) is a legend in American racing. With 35 career Indy car wins and 49 Indy car pole positions under his belt, he was the first to record a 200-MPH average qualifying speed at any Indy car competition. Eldest of the famed "First Family" of auto racing, he along with his younger brother Al and nephew Al Jr. have won nine Indianapolis 500 races, a record unmatched by any other racing family. He is also famous for the quote, "Success is where preparation and opportunity meet." While one cannot control all contingencies of the battlefield any more than one can control all eventualities of the racetrack, the Unser family is an example of where those who are most prepared most often prevail.

For the Win: Hope for the best, but prepare for the worst.

You Lose: Trusting to luck without any fallback plan is delusional.

12. Sun Tzu wrote:

"There are five dangerous faults which may affect a general: (1) recklessness, which leads to destruction, (2) cowardice, which leads to capture, (3) a hasty temper, which can be provoked by insults, (4) a delicacy of honor which is sensitive to shame, and (5) over-solicitude for his men, which exposes him to worry and trouble."

Thoughtlessness, spinelessness, rage, oversensitivity, over-attentiveness are all elements of a poor leader. Think of the opposites to find value. In this fashion recklessness becomes caution, cowardice becomes courage, irritation becomes calm, fear of shame becomes resiliency, and excessive courtesy seeks the balance of care and concentration.

Emotional intelligence is defined as the ability to identify and manage one's own emotions, as well as influence the emotions of others. While there is no validated psychometric test or scale for emotional intelligence, leading many psychologists to argue that it is not an actual construct, it is a valuable way of describing interpersonal skills and the ability to work well with others. Clearly, this is valuable for leaders in any capacity. When we are able to both recognize and regulate our emotions as well as help others to do the same, we are able to respond to challenging situations rather than reacting to them. In this fashion, we are better able to recognize opportunities and improve our control over any adversities we face.

For the Win: Never forget that leadership is not about you. It's about offering your best to others so that they can find the best in themselves in furtherance of your common goal.

You Lose: Dress yourself in finery, demand the best of everything, and expect others to kowtow to your whims—these are the marks of a commander who only leads on paper.

13. Sun Tzu wrote:

"These are the five besetting sins of a general, ruinous to the conduct of war."

An immature leader's recklessness, cowardice, hasty temper, oversensitivity, or solicitousness exposes him or her to worry and trouble. These turpitudes, when known, will be used against him, proliferating their destructive impact.

Socialized power is used by leaders to get things done for their team, whereas personalized power is used to benefit themselves. When immature leaders delude themselves into thinking they are acting for the greater good when in reality they are working toward self-aggrandizement, believing for instance that they may break the law because they serve a higher purpose, they forfeit moral authority. In pursuit of their egocentric desires, they become intoxicated by power. Leaders who make such gains at their follower's expense tend to discover that this behavior rarely ends well.

For the Win: As a leader enforce the rules lightly and at suitable times.

You Lose: If you find yourself issuing constant, omnipresent threats, our using overt force to maintain control, you are not a leader. You're a dictator.

14. Sun Tzu wrote:

"When an army is overthrown and its leader slain, the cause will surely be found among these five dangerous faults. Let them be a subject of meditation."

Inferior leaders rarely stay in control overlong, yet when one's art is warfare his or her demise may be swift and fatal. When such a general is deposed or slain, we discover the root cause in one or more of the five dangerous faults. This merits study and contemplation, lest we ourselves fall victim to one of these deficiencies. Consider the case of former Sudanese President Omar al-Bashir (1944 –) by way of example.

Al-Bashir came to power when he led a coup that toppled the elected government of Prime Minister Sadiq al-Mahdi (1935 –) in 1989. He ruled Sudan until he was similarly deposed in a coup d'état in 2019. Although he was indicted by the International Criminal Court over allegations of genocide when roughly 300,000 people were killed in his country's Darfur region during an insurgency that began in 2003, his demise was likely sealed in 2011 when South Sudan became an independent state, taking with it many of the oil-rich fields that kept the northeast African nation afloat. The loss of oil revenue led to currency devaluation which, in turn, combined with international sanctions, led to draconian austerity measures. When food and fuel subsidies were also cut, the people decided they'd had enough. What began as widespread protests ended with a military coup. Al-Bashir was convicted of corruption in December 2019 and sentenced to prison.

For the Win: Dictators who die comfortably in their own bed at an advanced, old age are exceedingly rare.

You Lose: Succumbing to these five faults will undermine your leadership and tear your enterprise apart.

Chapter 9: The Army on the March

In this chapter, we discover the art and science of moving troops about the battlefield, strategically leveraging the terrain, flora, and fauna to intuit where the adversary's forces are positioned and what they are planning. We are able to interpret our men and women's determination and morale by their actions, discerning where we may be lenient and when we must exercise discipline to assure appropriate control of our forces.

1. Sun Tzu wrote:

> *"We come now to the question of encamping the army and observing signs of the enemy. Pass quickly over mountains and keep in the neighborhood of valleys."*

Holding an entrenched defensive position on a mountaintop may be desirable, yet on the high ground is virtually impossible to hide the movement of troops and equipment. Thus, on the move, we seek to stealthily progress through valleys where resources are plentiful and our passing discrete, crossing high passes with haste to disguise our operations. An army on the move is at risk, especially when encamped in enemy territory. Consider the battle of Stamford Bridge, which took place on September 25, 1066.

Anglo Saxon King Harold Godwinson (1022 – 1066) had positioned an army of 15,000 men in southern England, ready to drive off an expected invasion from William of Normandy (1028 – 1087), when his scouts reported the arrival of 300 Norse long-ships some 200 miles further north. Taking advantage of his knowledge of the terrain, Harold raced to the landing site in just four days, arriving at the Viking camp without warning. The Norsemen, dozing lazily in the autumn sun, were caught completely by surprise and slaughtered by the thousands. The few survivors fled the scene, sailing home in disgrace aboard their 24 remaining ships while Harold's army celebrated their victory. Ironically, Harold was defeated and killed a mere two weeks later by William, who seized the English throne, becoming the country's first Norman king. History remembers him by his moniker, William the Conqueror.

For the Win: Let the terrain aid you and your forces.

You Lose: Expend time and energy fighting uncooperative environments and you've lost valuable resources that should have been used to further your cause.

2. Sun Tzu wrote:

"Camp in high places, facing the sun. Do not climb heights in order to fight. So much for mountain warfare."

We may camp in high places, when necessary, but fighting in high places is treacherous and undesirable. It takes special skill to overcome the mountains themselves, let alone to successfully win any battles there. This should be avoided whenever possible.

Mountain warfare is extremely challenging as we fight not only the enemy but also the weather and the terrain. According to the US Army Infantry Mountain Operations Manual (ATTP 3-21.50), "Small mistakes can lead to catastrophic events, while technological supremacy can be negated by even the crudest and non-technical enemy actions." To succeed we must clearly have specialized training, but even that is not enough. "Extreme physical fitness, mental toughness, endurance, and the utmost in tactical and technical proficiency" are required as well. Without proper preparation, the physical characteristics of the mountains themselves will undermine our operations.

For the Win: It's hard enough to win, don't make things worse by fighting the terrain along with your adversary.

You Lose: Engaging on difficult terrain, whether material or metaphorical, is expensive for you and your enterprise.

3. Sun Tzu wrote:

"After crossing a river you should get far away from it."

Riverine warfare is the term for the projection of sea power onto inland waters, including rivers that may open out into the sea. It is challenging when compared to fighting on the open ocean, as the flow of current through swamps, deltas, and tributaries control our actions and those of our enemy. Navigation and tactics may be compromised, and ground troops may reinforce or intervene from the sides. Consequently, when crossing any river, we must swiftly move toward better ground lest we become trapped and have to fight.

Before he famously switched sides, Benedict Arnold (1741 – 1801) was a Brigadier General in the American Revolutionary Army. On October 11, 1776, his small naval force was tasked with holding off the British advance from Canada at the Battle of Valcour Island on Lake Champlain so that his compatriots would have enough time to prepare a proper defense of New York. This holding action lasted for two days during which all 15 of Arnold's gunboats were sunk, yet it proved to be enough, a small loss that was instrumental to the larger war. In 1997 the Lake Champlain Maritime Museum's Lake Survey team discovered Arnold's ship Spitfire, a 1776 gondola, intact and upright on the bottom of the lake, declaring it an American Treasure.

For the Win: Barriers are often barren. This means exposure, which is bad. Seek cover immediately after any barrier is crossed.

You Lose: Stopping to gaze upon your achievements before seeking cover causes needless exposure.

4. Sun Tzu wrote:

> *"When an invading force crosses a river in its onward march do not advance to meet it in midstream. It will be best to let half the army get across and then deliver your attack."*

If we meet an enemy in the water we fight as equals, both beholden to the currents, whereas if we wait until half of the adversary's forces have crossed and then attack while they are bogged down, we gain an advantage. Catching an enemy force during their river crossing is a boon.

The Battle of Stirling Bridge took place on September 11, 1297, when the invading forces of King Edward I (1239 – 1307) clashed with Scottish rebels under the command of William Wallace (1270 – 1305) and Andrew de Moray (? – 1297). The English knights outnumbered the Scots by roughly 5 to 1, yet when Edward's men attempted to cross the River Forth, the Scots used their elevated position upslope to shoot arrows and hurl spears and rocks down onto the advancing troops. Abandoning the narrow Stirling Bridge, the English forces soon floundered in the marshy ground where nearly half of them, some 5,000 men, were killed and the rest fled in one of England's most humiliating defeats.

For the Win: Crossing any barrier is difficult. Use the challenge your enemy faces to divide their forces and strike when they are imperiled by the barrier.

You Lose: Let the enemy strike during a transition where you cross a barrier and you give him the upper hand.

5. Sun Tzu wrote:

"If you are anxious to fight you should not go to meet the invader near a river which he has to cross."

Crossing a river without a bridge takes enormous effort, we must let the enemy expend their resources and tire their men overcoming this obstacle before engaging. In this fashion, we let the river do much of our work for us. When the adversary's men and women are soaked, exhausted, and embittered, this is when we fight.

Ralph Marston (1907 – 1967) was a professional American football player who sagely said, "There are plenty of difficult obstacles in your path. Don't allow yourself to become one of them." What we believe and expect for ourselves tends to become a self-fulfilling prophecy. If we think we can we will, whereas if we believe we cannot we won't. Consequently, we must guard against self-defeating beliefs and focus on those things that advance our cause. Simple phraseology differences like saying and thinking "challenge" instead of "problem" helps us develop a mindset that can overcome.

For the Win: Don't become the obstacle in your own path.

You Lose: If you let emotions control your choice of action, you fail on multiple levels.

6. Sun Tzu wrote:

"Moor your craft higher up than the enemy and facing the sun. Do not move up-stream to meet the enemy. So much for river warfare."

Like fighting up-hill, fighting up-stream compounds our challenge. We must guard against fighting the current, the tide, or the terrain in addition to combatting our adversary. To prevail we make the enemy tire themselves against the tide, squint into the sun, and fight the environs as much as they strive against our forces.

WWI German Ace Hauptmann Oswald (1891 – 1916), considered the godfather of air fighting tactics, documented his rules for success in combat in The Dicta Boelcke, a compendium which was used by pilots around the world throughout WWII and the Korean war until technology began to make dogfighting obsolete. In it, Hauptmann wrote, "Secure the benefits of aerial combat (speed, altitude, numerical superiority, position) before attacking. Always attack from the sun." It matters not whether we fight on land, sea, or air, in all environs we must leverage the environment to our advantage.

For the Win: Know that fighting upstream is akin to fighting uphill.

You Lose: The world evolves even though the fundamentals of conflict do not. Your circumstances aren't so different than what has come before, so you ignore these warnings at your peril.

7. Sun Tzu wrote:

"In crossing salt-marshes your sole concern should be to get over them quickly without any delay."

Salt marshes are coastal wetlands that are flooded and drained by salt water brought in by the tides. They are marshy, comprised of deep mud and peat, and very challenging to navigate. If we find ourselves caught in the marshes, we cannot maneuver quickly enough to mount a defense. Whenever we cannot avoid marshlands altogether, we must traverse them quickly as it is a death trap to be caught in a salt marsh. The term "bogged down" comes from this environment.

In 1945 British soldiers invaded Ramree Island, near the Burmese coast, in order to drive out Imperial forces and establish airbases to support the mainland campaign against Japan. After heaving fighting, the Japanese army was routed, but rather than surrendering chose to fade into a dense mangrove swamp nearby. While retreating soldiers knew they would be facing mosquitoes, poisonous snakes, spiders, and scorpions in the saltwater marsh, they were shocked to discover 20-foot-long, 2,000-pound saltwater crocodiles, reptiles massive enough to easily consume an Indian water buffalo let alone a full-grown human, which thrived there as well. Of the thousand soldiers who entered the Ramree swamps, only 520 survived, many so sick with malaria and injured from the dangerous wildlife that they were easily recaptured by the British forces later on.

For the Win: Adjust your strategy to account for the terrain you face.

You Lose: Treating all terrain as equal means you cannot arise to the unique challenges that will undermine your endeavor.

8. Sun Tzu wrote:

"If forced to fight in a salt-marsh you should have water and grass near you and get your back to a clump of trees. So much for operations in salt-marshes."

If we must traverse a marsh, we find a firmer ground where trees grow in open water. This is a good place to fight when forced to, as it presents better footing, cover, and maneuverability. In this fashion we make the most of an unfortunate situation, overcoming ill-timing or luck with sound strategy.

The Iran-Iraq war began on September 22, 1980, when Iraqi forces invaded western Iran along the counties' joint border. The fighting lasted for 8 years, before ending with a United Nations-brokered ceasefire. In 1983, a pivotal battle took place when Iran changed tactics to launch an amphibious assault in the Hawizeh Marshes along with the Tigris-Euphrates river system in Iraq. Although the Iranians suffered heavy casualties from the Iraqi gunboats, artillery, and airstrikes, they leveraged chemical weapons, primarily mustard gas, to turn the tide of battle. In this fashion, the Iranian forces were able to invade the oil-rich Majnoon Islands, nearly breaking past Iraq's defensive lines before ultimately being driven back into the marshes once again.

For the Win: When entering into a marsh, real or metaphorical, you must seek a protected area to exit.

You Lose: If you leap into a marsh with no entrance plan, no crossing plan, and no exit plan, you have already lost before the crossing is undertaken.

9. Sun Tzu wrote:

"In dry level country take up an easily accessible position with rising ground to your right and on your rear so that the danger may be in front and safety lie behind. So much for campaigning in flat country."

Dry, arid plains offer little in the way of cover or concealment, yet we must become adept at using terrain to our advantage. Natural and manmade hills and depressions in the land can be used to channel the adversary's forces, hence concentrate the field of battle where we wish to fight. In this fashion, the landscape becomes our ally. Many Native American tribes, for example, were adept at operating in the prarie, steppe, and grassland of the North American plains.

When gold was discovered in Montana in 1863, John Bozeman (1835 – 1867) blazed a trail through land that had been promised to Native American Sioux, Cheyenne, and Arapahoe Indians a mere 12 years earlier. When white soldiers upped the ante by murdering more than 200 Cheyenne civilians, an attack known as the Sand Creek Massacre in 1864, they sparked an insurgency. While the Battle of Little Bighorn was the most famous retaliatory battle, the Fetterman Massacre in 1866 was a close second. Under the leadership of Red Cloud (1822 – 1909) and Crazy Horse (1841 – 1877), an army of 2,000 natives set a trap for Colonel William Fetterman (1833 – 1866) and a company of 80 troopers near Fort Phil Kearney. Crazy Horse and a handful of decoy warriors first rode into view of the fort and then pretended to flee when shot at. When Fetterman and his men gave chase, they rode into an ambush. There were no survivors. All but one of the Americans were found beheaded, disemboweled, scalped, and castrated, save for a bugler, whom the natives respectfully covered with a buffalo robe after his valiant attempt to fend off their attack with his instrument.

For the Win: Protect your flank.

You Lose: Leaving an open access point for the enemy's attack is supreme negligence.

10. Sun Tzu:

"These are the four useful branches of military knowledge which enabled the Yellow Emperor to vanquish four several sovereigns."

Legend states that Huangdi, the Yellow Emperor, was the first Chinese ruler to institute a feudal system of vassal princes sometime around 2697 BC. All four of his subordinates originally bore the title of Emperor before swearing allegiance to him, hence Sun Tzu's reference here. The four terrains he refers to are those that affect our armies when on the move, including high ground, rivers, salt marshes, and dry, level ground. It is invaluable to recognize the ground over which we travel, discerning the advantages and disadvantages that each confers upon ourselves and our adversaries.

Much like leveraging the four terrains in warfare, analysis of our competitive landscape in business helps us categorize strengths, weaknesses, opportunities, and threats in contrast with our competitors. This is known as a SWOT analysis. Strengths describe what separates us from our competition such as unique technology, brand loyalty, or innovative culture. Weaknesses keep us from performing at our best, areas we must improve such as weak capitalization, inefficient supply chain, or rising employee turnover. Opportunities examine favorable factors that might improve our competitive edges such as acquisitions that might infuse needed technologies or market share. Threats are unfavorable outside factors that may cause us harm, such as a tightening labor market, rising material costs, or looming trade war. With thorough analysis we develop strategy to deal with all eventualities.

For the Win: Know the environment you operate within. If the environment is unknown, seek counsel from those who live there and know it best.

You Lose: Assume a new setting is the same as the old setting and you'll find yourself wandering aimlessly.

11. Sun Tzu wrote:

"All armies prefer high ground to low and sunny places to dark."

Whenever we design a plan that plays into our strengths while shoring up our weaknesses, the odds improve in our favor. The challenge is that every adversary will attempt to do exactly the same thing. Consequently, the higher our mastery of strategy, the more flexibility we allow in our plan, the better off we will be. This works the same in business as it does in war.

There are three methods for separating ourselves from our competition, operational excellence, customer intimacy, and product differentiation. Most companies can focus on one of these three, a few enterprises are able to achieve two out of three, but no business can do everything well. Operational excellence means providing customers with reliable products or services at competitive prices that are delivered with minimal inconvenience. To succeed with this strategy, we must become world-class in continuously improving efficiencies in order to drive profit margins since we are primarily competing on price. Customer intimacy means precisely segmenting and targeting markets, then tailoring offerings that exactly match the demands of customers in each niche. To succeed with this strategy, we must be brilliant at combining detailed customer knowledge with the flexibility to respond quickly to almost any need. Product differentiation means offering customers leading-edge products or services that consistently enhance their use of the merchandise. To succeed with this strategy, we must be exceptional at understanding what our customers value most and then boosting the level they come to expect beyond what any competitors can provide.

For the Win: Dispassionately view your opponent, observing from a good vantage point for comprehensive appraisal, all while knowing he will be doing the same thing to you.

You Lose: Assuming you know your adversary with only a casual glance.

12. Sun Tzu wrote:

> *"If you are careful of your men and camp on hard ground the army will be free from disease of every kind and this will spell victory."*

For centuries more soldiers perished from malnutrition, disease, and infection than from mechanizations of the enemy. This means that we must choose encampments wisely, maintaining hygienic conditions which are conducive to our men and women's welfare. For instance, settling too close to the water means besiegement by biting insects, whereas damp ground brings rot and disease. The dry, hard ground may prove uncomfortable, yet it is safe from everything but the enemy who we already know how to defeat.

A healthy lifestyle is easier to maintain than many realize. To begin, we must drink plenty of water and eat "real" food, avoiding highly-processed and sugar-laden items. We must prioritize exercise, preferably by lifting weights for about an hour 3 days a week, get enough sleep, and avoid sitting for long periods of time. And, we must regularly bathe, wash our hands, and exercise good hygiene. There's more to mastery, clearly, but it really is as simple as that.

For the Win: It takes a combination of simple protocols to keep your forces healthy. Prioritize these mundane acts to preserve your enterprise.

You Lose: Ignore the fundamentals and you will pay a high price for your error.

13. Sun Tzu wrote:

"When you come to a hill or a bank occupy the sunny side, with the slope on your right rear. Thus, you will at once act for the benefit of your soldiers and utilize the natural advantages of the ground."

The sun is a natural disinfectant, not the best, nor the fastest, but it does work. Utilizing the sun, the hillside, and the natural advantages of the terrain make our men feel warm and safe. With sound minds and healthy bodies, our troops will remain ready for anything. This is but one method of using the land to one's advantage.

Land is a critical factor in economic production, encompassing natural resources like fisheries, forests, farming, mineral deposits, rainfall, hydroelectric power, wind turbines, etc. Countries and corporations rich in resources have an inherent advantage over their adversaries. To manage the land successfully we must know that it is bountiful but immovable, comprising a limited in area. Consider farming where industrialized economies can invest large amounts of capital into the land leading to huge farms where agriculture is carried out scientifically with significant production. Emerging economies, on the other hand, tend to have small-scale farming with comparatively anemic output after accounting for natural factors like soil, rainfall, climate, and topography. In farming, as in most things in life, better investments lead to better outcomes.

For the Win: Make prudent investments to assure the success of your endeavor.

You Lose: Cut corners out of laziness or greed, rather than inevitable necessity, and that underinvestment will undermine your whole enterprise.

14. Sun Tzu wrote:

"When in consequence of heavy rains up-country a river which you wish to ford is swollen and flecked with foam you must wait until it subsides."

Fording a river at high water is foolhardy. Even if a river appears calm on the surface, it may have deceptively fast currents, be clogged with dangerous debris, or be frigid enough to shock a person's system and cause him or her to drown. Current only compounds this risk. Whitewater denotes danger, the more churning foam the faster the river's flow. We faced with whitewater we must either look up- or down-stream for a safer location, build a bridge, or wait until the current subsides to cross.

If we fall into a raging river and are taken by the current it is best to float on our back with feet pointed downstream. It is easier to breathe this way, our head is best protected, and our legs may soak up damage from rocks, logs, and other debris. Once we find ourselves in a location where the flow has calmed enough to fight we may flip over and swim diagonally toward shore using the current to assist our progress.

For the Win: You may be ready, your forces may be ready, but the terrain may not be ready. Respect the terrain lest it swallow you.

You Lose: Ignore the terrain and you battle far more than your opponent.

15. Sun Tzu wrote:

"Country in which there are precipitous cliffs with torrents running between, deep natural hollows, confined places, tangled thickets, quagmires and crevasses, should be left with all possible speed and not approached."

Some terrain is all but impassable; we cannot deplete our resources fighting the landscape when we should be focusing our attention on our enemy. We must never willingly seek to pass through difficult terrain. The coming battle will be challenging enough to overcome, so we must never add an immutable force of nature into our calculations.

While many historians account Hannibal Barca (247 – 181 BC) crossing the Alps in 218 BC as one of the most celebrated military achievements in history, it is important to point out that he lost roughly 60% of his Carthaginian army, many of whom simply stumbled into crevasses or lost their footing and fell to their deaths, in the process. His elephants, men, and mules faced avalanches, altitude sickness, frostbite, starvation, and disease making the hazardous five-month journey, descending into Italy with some 25,000 infantry and 6,000 cavalrymen to catch the Romans by surprise. In the ensuing Battle of Lake Trasimene, Hannibal's troops crushed the Roman army, killing at least 15,000 soldiers and capturing an equal number, many of whom were driven into the lake to drown. Imagine what a brilliant strategist like Hannibal could have accomplished if he had not lost more than half of his resources fighting the terrain.

For the Win: When the environment is bad, get away from it. You cannot negotiate with the environment.

You Lose: Press forward with inflexible, rigid plans into territory that sets the environment against from every side.

16. Sun Tzu wrote:

> *"While we keep away from such places, we should get the enemy to approach them, while we face them, we should let the enemy have them on his rear."*

The lay of the land, be it precipitous cliffs with torrents running between, deep natural hollows, confined places, tangled thickets, quagmires, or crevasses, will not change no matter any desire we may have to the contrary, yet we may determine how we may best use these entanglements against our adversaries. Forcing the enemy to make poor choices regarding the terrain affords us a distinct advantage.

When the Carthaginians spent four days traversing the Arno marshes to reach the Lake Trasimene in 217 BC, many of Hannibal's men became sick during the journey. Hannibal Barca (247 – 181 BC) himself lost his right eye to infection. Nevertheless, it was there that the Carthaginians concealed themselves in heavy fog that rolled off the lake and ambushed Gaius Flaminius's Roman army in central Italy. Carthaginian cavalry swept down from the hills, forcing the Roman infantry into the lake where many drowned in their heavy armor. Those who did not surrender fast enough were massacred. At a cost of only 1,500 soldiers killed in battle, Hannibal pulled off one of the greatest ambushes in history, slaughtering 15,000 Romans, capturing another 15,000, and crushing the Roman's morale.

For the Win: Draw the enemy into hostile terrain.

You Lose: Taking the enemy's bait such that the land fights you.

17. Sun Tzu wrote:

"If in the neighborhood of your camp there should be any hilly country, ponds surrounded by aquatic grass, hollow basins filled with reeds, or woods with thick undergrowth, they must be carefully routed out and searched for these are places where men in ambush or insidious spies are likely to be lurking."

We must guard against any adversary exploiting the terrain around our camp to our detriment, clearing brush, felling trees, removing rubble, and placing pickets so that there is nowhere for spies or ambushers to lurk unseen. In this fashion, we are forearmed and forewarned if trouble approaches. Clearly modern technology aids this process, but fundamentals have changed little since Sun Tzu's time.

We must train pickets to keep a vigilant watch over our encampment, keeping a close eye on enemy movements while preventing unauthorized persons from passing in or out of their lines. This safeguards against spies or ambushers sneaking in, or deserters slipping out, leading to the capture or killing of any suspicious individuals. In case of an attack, this advanced guard acts as a skirmish line, giving us early warning while holding their ground. If forced to retire, these men and women close their intervals and fall back to the main camp for support.

For the Win: Anyplace nearby that may provide cover for an enemy must be thoroughly searched and vetted.

You Lose: Assuming adjacent lands are uninhabited without thoroughly checking, not once but regularly.

18. Sun Tzu wrote:

"When the enemy is close at hand and remains quiet, he is relying on the natural strength of his position."

If our enemy believes he is in a strong position, he is likely to stay there awaiting our movement. When he or she knows we are coming and fails to take action we must expect a well-entrenched foe. Like a medieval lord in his castle, the adversary believes his position is unassailable. There are corollaries to this even in modern times, such as the "castle doctrine" which, in certain circumstances, permits the use of deadly force against someone invading our home.

Self-defense is an affirmative plea (in the United States). That means that it shifts the burden of proof from the prosecutor to the defense. In essence, we are telling a judge that we did it, the homicide, assault, or whatever we're charged with, but had an excellent excuse for doing so, hence should not be held responsible for our otherwise illegal behavior. This justification starts with four factors: intent, means, opportunity, and preclusion. To be a legitimate threat in most jurisdictions the bad guy(s) must have intent (desire), means (ability), and opportunity (access) to hurt us, and we must also (in most circumstances) also be able to show that we had no safe alternatives other than countervailing force before engaging. Oftentimes this means a "duty" to retreat, save where castle doctrines apply. Under this legal theory, a homeowner is not required to retreat but may stand his ground to defend himself, his family, his home, or his property.

For the Win: An entrenched enemy believes he has a superior position. Account for this before making your move.

You Lose: Playing the enemy's game, engaging against his strength without a viable plan.

19. Sun Tzu wrote:

"When he keeps aloof and tries to provoke a battle, he is anxious for the other side to advance."

If an adversary attempts to draw us out, he or she wants to fight. He is prepared, primed, ready and willing to go. And, he believes he will prevail. Now may be the enemy's time, but we must ask ourselves if it is our time before engaging.

Fedor Emelianenko (1976 –) is a Russian MMA champion, considered by many the greatest heavyweight fighter ever. He wrote, "A fighter, a real strong fighter, should always look dignified and calm, and I believe that any expression of aggression is an expression of weakness. A strong person will not be nervous and will not express aggression towards his opponent. He will be confident in his abilities and his training; then he will face the fight calm and balanced." Violence professionals, such as bodyguards, bouncers, muggers, and MMA fighters often appear calm before suddenly attacking. To see it coming we must look for a change in energy, such as when a person who was glaring at us suddenly looks away (checking for witnesses and/or clearing the shoulders and spine to strike), or a person who was looking away abruptly makes eye contact (targeting where to hit). Any sudden change in the other person's posture, breathing, voice, or skin pallor in a conflict situation is a danger signal, a moment when we must immediately be prepared to defend ourselves.

For the Win: If the enemy draws you to battle, he already has a plan.
Do not react to his enticement; respond to the situation.

You Lose: Reacting to the enemy's provocation means ceding initiative.
In this fashion you let an adversary dictate your moves.

20. Sun Tzu wrote:

"If his place of encampment is easy of access, he is tendering a bait."

We can never safely assume our adversary is stupid. If he or she offers us an easy avenue, we must surmise that it is bait for a trap. Fish instinctively take the bait when it is placed in front of them, yet as students of the art of war, we can step above our instincts for a more measured response.

American actor and director Paul Newman (1925 – 2008) once said, "If you're playing a poker game and you look around the table and can't tell who the sucker is, it's you." If something looks too good to be true, it probably is. Con artists use a variety of ploys to defraud millions of victims every year, so we must constantly be on guard against these scams. Criminals may impersonate charities, banks, government agencies, or creditors, so whenever we receive unexpected requests from these types of agencies, we must double-check to know with certainty who we're dealing with. Caller ID is not enough, it can be spoofed, so if in doubt hang up and call the organization directly before giving out any personal or financial information. And, report any scamming attempts to the authorities.

For the Win: As the old adage states, if it looks too good to be true it almost certainly is. The enemy will make nothing easy for you.

You Lose: Ignore your intuition, take the bait, and suffer the consequences.

21. Sun Tzu wrote:

"Movement amongst the trees of a forest shows that the enemy is advancing. The appearance of a number of screens in the midst of thick grass means that the enemy wants to make us suspicious."

When the enemy moves his or her actions will disrupt the environment, causing the surrounding area to move as well. In the wilds, flora may shift in ways that counter the direction of the wind, fauna may unexpectedly startle and flee. Oftentimes the adversary will attempt to advance with stealth, hence catch us by surprise, so when an enemy makes their actions obvious, we must be extra wary.

Humans are natural predators, difficult to catch unawares when alert. Our eyes naturally seek unexpected movements, shapes, and colors, focusing our attention when encountering anything unusual. This means that to trick an adversary's eyes, we must remain still, avoiding direct eye contact, whenever he or she looks our way. Many people can intuitively "feel" other people's eyes on them when under observation. Moving stealthily, masking our footfalls with natural noises, blending with the elements that an enemy expects to observe, and wearing colors that that do not stand out unnaturally gives us a chance to reach our objective unobserved.

For the Win: Disturbances result from action. Observe the effect, recognize the cause, and thereby remain safe.

You Lose: When clear signs of threat are ignored, or laughed off as meaningless, you walk blindfolded through a minefield.

22. Sun Tzu wrote:

"The rising of birds in their flight is the sign of an ambuscade. Startled beasts indicate that a sudden attack is coming."

Game animals are easily startled, frightened by any disruption to their natural rhythm that may indicate the presence of a predator. Clearly, the movement of any large body of troops and equipment, no matter how stealthy, will spook any animals that cross their path. While we may not spot the enemy's movements directly, we may intuit their location by the reaction of the environment around them.

Security professionals, especially those who work at concerts or sporting events, often identify altercations not by the person who causes the confrontation but rather by the reaction of the crowd around the incident. Knowing this, we can often dispatch officers to control the situation before it escalates into a full-fledged fight. Similarly, anyone with good situational awareness can get a feel for what is "normal" where they live, work, attend school, or otherwise frequent, and take action to protect themselves if anything unusual happens. In this fashion, we will usually have sufficient warning to get away before anything bad happens, a chance to verbally de-escalate where possible, or time to prepare to fight when faced with the unavoidable.

For the Win: Leaders keenly observe, interpret, and act, knowing that an ounce of prevention is worth far more than a pound of cure.

You Lose: Just because something bad hasn't happened yet does not mean that it never will. Pass off irregularities as if they are nothing and sooner or later one will become something… to your regret.

23. Sun Tzu wrote:

"When there is dust rising in a high column it is the sign of chariots advancing, when the dust is low but spread over a wide area it betokens the approach of infantry. When it branches out in different directions it shows that parties have been sent to collect firewood. A few clouds of dust moving to and fro signify that the army is encamping."

Like ripples from a pebble dropped in water, actions of the adversary create signs of his or her passing. These disturbances, fast or slow, narrow or wide, allow us to intuit what the enemy is doing even when we cannot directly observe their activities. We must pay attention to the sights, sounds, and smells of the adversary to inform our strategy and tactical plans. Intuiting actions of the enemy may be used defensively to best prepare for what's coming or offensively to engage with long-range artillery.

Artillery and mortars use indirect fire, lobbing munitions at targets long distances away that are rarely in their gunner's line of sight. Consequently, artillery teams rely on spotters to designate targets and correct their aim as necessary to accurately strike and destroy what they are hoping to hit. These forward observers conceal themselves in locations where they can spot intended targets with binoculars or scopes and provide critical data and feedback to gunners using a pre-defined coordinate system. Forward observers not only assure accurate indirect fire, but also may make tactical decisions like calling in smoke to aid in concealment, movement, or deception.

For the Win: Dispersed military activity is much like herd animals seeking food and water. You are not primarily on their list of needs.

You Lose: As a herd beginning a stampede, when forces coalesce, they become ready for action. Failing to see joining activity leaves you unprepared for what follows.

24. Sun Tzu wrote:

"Humble words and increased preparations are signs that the enemy is about to advance. Violent language and driving forward as if to the attack are signs that he will retreat."

War is deception, so when the adversary does something overly obvious it must be a ruse. The opposite of what he or she appears to be planning is their likely course of action. What goes for leaders of armies applies equally to all soldiers, if an enemy combatant suddenly looks away be prepared, he or she is likely about to turn and strike.

In one of the most infamous acts of deception in the art world, Leonardo da Vinci's painting Mona Lisa was stolen off the wall of the Louvre Museum where it had been hung behind a protective pane of glass on August 21, 1911, missing some 26 hours before anyone even noticed that it was gone. It took two years to discover exactly what had happened when the thief, Vincenzo Peruggia (1881 – 1925) attempted to sell it to an antique dealer in Florence, Italy and was subsequently arrested. Like a scene from a heist movie, Peruggia and his two accomplices had entered the museum on Sunday and hidden in a storeroom. The next day, while the Louvre was closed, they dressed in stolen workman's smocks, removed the protective glass and the frame, and simply walked out the front door with the painting hidden under their clothes. After recovery, Mona Lisa was displayed at the Uffizi Museum in Italy for a few months before it was returned to France. Peruggia and his accomplices spent 7 months in jail for the theft.

For the Win: The maxim, "Actions speak louder than words," was first spoken in 1628, during the English Civil War, by parliamentarian John Pym (1854 – 1643). When an adage lasts nearly 400 years it's well worth remembering and acting upon.

You Lose: Only a fool believes an enemy's words while ignoring their acts.

25. Sun Tzu wrote:

"When the light chariots come out first and take up a position on the wings it is a sign that the enemy is forming for battle."

The formations needed for fighting are obvious, used by every army, yet the timing of the enemy's plan may cause uncertainty. We must watch for movements from the swiftest elements of our adversary's forces; this will tell us when he or she is about attack. Focusing on this crucial element allows us to cut through the confusion and see with clarity.

Khalil Gibran (1833 – 1931) was a Lebanese artist, poet, and writer who said, "The obvious is that which is never seen until someone expresses it simply." The ability to describe complex subjects in simple terms is a sign of mastery, denoting a deep understanding of a subject, yet it can also be a learned skill. This is how great speeches are made. Begin by starting with the right question, the more targeted and precise we can be, the easier it is to simplify. Often it helps to create an image, a picture that vividly demonstrates exactly what we are trying to describe. Next, we must shave off any corollary elements not germane to the topic, logically organize our thoughts, and boil things down to the bare essentials. In this fashion, we may communicate the most complex subjects clearly and compellingly.

For the Win: Look for preparation from the swiftest elements of an enemy's forces, this tells you that he is about attack.

You Lose: Admiring the chaos rather than discerning its meaning is like a lot like falling for a charlatan's Three-Card Monte.

26. Sun Tzu wrote:

"Peace proposals unaccompanied by a sworn covenant indicate a plot."

Most people act in their own self-interests. If a peace proposal does not have something valuable attached to guarantee the deal, chances are good that it is not real. Exchanges of hostages and arranged marriages amongst nobles are examples of covenants commonly used throughout history to assure peace treaties. This incentive puts a price on breaking the truce, helping assure that it will hold.

As the adage dictates, there's no such thing as a free lunch. Whenever a service is "free," we are the product. Consider Facebook, Google, LinkedIn, TikTok, Instagram, Twitter, WhatsApp, and other social media platforms. These companies capture user data and sell it to enterprises that wish to create tailored ads to sell their products and services to us. Facebook, for instance, made 98% of its 2019 revenue from advertising. Our likes, shares, searches, logins, demographic information, and the like provide insight into our interests and desires. In this fashion, our freely given information is used by the platform to create value. It's not just way we do, but correlations of behavior patterns including what we don't do that creates deep insight into our psyche. Consequently, we must determine whether or not the value we receive from using these services offsets the invasion of our privacy necessary for access.

For the Win: If the enemy is serious about peace, they will arrive at the table with a reasonable proposal and prepared agenda. This is the beginning of a true negotiation.

You Lose: Attempting to negotiate with an enemy who brings nothing of value to the table.

27. Sun Tzu wrote:

"When there is much running about and the soldiers fall into rank it means that the critical moment has come."

The last formation of battle is the infantry. When they come to order, the battle is on. We cannot allow the adversary to set up faster than we are prepared to counter. Identifying these trends faster than our enemy affords us the opportunity to turn the tide of battle in our favor.

A turning point is a time where a decisive change has happened, usually for the better. It takes practice and experience to know when you are seeing a turning point because they are most often recognized in retrospect. When the proverbial seas have calmed it is possible to look back over a series of events and point to the moment, or cluster of moments, where something significant occurred and label that the turning point. Take the American Civil War (1861 – 1865), for example. Historians widely consider the turning point in that conflict the Battle of Gettysburg Pennsylvania which took place from July 1st through 3rd, 1863. That period was the bloodiest battle of the entire war, a decisive victory by Union troops over the Confederate forces' greatest military leader, General Robert E. Lee (1807 – 1870).

For the Win: Recognize that a sudden flurry of activity is preparation for battle.

You Lose: Dismiss preparation as busywork.

28. Sun Tzu wrote:

"When some are seen advancing and some retreating it is a lure."

Half a fight is not a true fight. If the enemy does not bring all his or her forces to bear then they have a different agenda then straight-up battle. We must be wary of falling into this trap. This takes a flexible mind and keen appraisal to look beyond the obvious and ascertain what's truly going on behind all the noise and confusion.

The more educated and experienced we get the less creative we oftentimes become as we gravitate again and again toward the "right" answer, even if it's the same answer we have used countless times before. Innovation is not always necessary, but developing a mindset that allows us to think beyond the obvious can help set ourselves and our teams apart from your competition. Nevertheless, some people are so locked into a certain way of thinking that they need to fail in order to learn and grow. As a leader, it is our responsibility to limit the damage and, without saying "I told you so," move forward to a better plan while keeping the end goal in mind.

For the Win: Partial commitment indicates a trap, the enemy is probing to gauge your reaction. In these moments take caution to fend him off without revealing your full design.

You Lose: In responding to a feint as if it is a committed attack you let the enemy test your capabilities and identify the weaknesses that can be your undoing.

29. Sun Tzu wrote:

"When the soldiers stand leaning on their spears, they are faint from want of food."

We may measure the disposition of an enemy by their soldier's stance as they prepare for battle. In this fashion, we discern their health and readiness. Weakened warriors look for help in the simple things, food, water, shelter, and safety, whereas vigorous troops set themselves toward girding their armor and honing their blades for the fight that is about to come. While weapons, armor, and provisions today are technologically superior to those of Sun Tzu's time, the nature of men and women remains much the same.

Fatigue is a common complaint, especially for folks who chain themselves to a desk, working long hours without break. Much of this can be countered with coffee or other caffeinated beverages but moderate physical activity has a far greater and more beneficial impact. Take yoga, for instance. Studies show that it only takes a half dozen classes for practitioners to feel improvements in energy, confidence, and clear-mindedness.

For the Win: Nature is demanding and final. It is impossible for an exhausted force to hide the fact they are tired.

You Lose: Failure to address your team's fatigue or take advantage of the enemy's exhaustion.

30. Sun Tzu wrote:

"If those who are sent to draw water begin by drinking themselves, the army is suffering from thirst."

The basic elements of health must be addressed before troops can excel in battle. We cannot survive long in combat conditions without replacing fluids lost to sweat and urination. To intuit an adversary's state of readiness, we may examine how they satisfy their fundamental needs. The thirsty rush to the water, the hungry toward food.

Roughly 60% of our body weight is comprised of water and we cannot survive overlong without replenishing vital fluids we sweat away. Environmental conditions, activity levels, age, and general health all play a role in how much we need and at what frequency we must consume, but most adults should drink 8 to 12 glasses of water or other hydrating fluids a day. Without enough, our ability to regulate our body temperature is lowered, our electrolytes become unbalanced, and our physical and mental performance is degraded. Untreated dehydration can lead to brain swelling, seizures, organ failure, or death.

For the Win: People will preserve themselves first. See how they use the resources and opportunities around them. This will tell you what is happening in the enemy's camp.

You Lose: An enemy's scouts, emissaries, and gatherers are the vines of the enemy, they seek the need. Failing to observe their actions is lost opportunity.

31. Sun Tzu wrote:

"If the enemy sees an advantage to be gained and makes no effort to secure it their soldiers are exhausted."

Subterfuge aside, if a clear advantage is presented to the enemy and he or she does not act, they are too tired to fight. An exhausted adversary can neither attack, retreat, nor take advantage of opportunities.

The war of the Triple Alliance began in May of 1865 when Paraguay, under the leadership of megalomaniac dictator Francisco Solano Lopez (1827 – 1870), declared war on Brazil, Argentina, and Uruguay simultaneously. It was a failure of epic proportions. In the battle of Tuyuti, for instance, the Paraguayans attempted to surprise an allied encampment, but in failing to properly reconnoiter the terrain failed to account for thorny underbrush which slowed their attack. The poorly coordinated effort began at noon, rather than at dawn, and 20,000 of Lopez's best men were exhausted and ultimately wiped out during the fighting. Unhinged by a series of subsequent losses, Lopez ordered the executions of hundreds of his officers, including his own brothers and relatives. Finally, on March 1, 1870, his remaining forces were overrun and Lopez was killed in the combat. Ultimately, 70% of the adult male population of Paraguay perished during the five years of strife.

For the Win: When an opportunity becomes available and the enemy cannot act upon it, they are too weak, in resources or ability, to fight. That's your giftwrapped opening to prevail.

You Lose: Let yourself or your team become exhausted such that you can no longer project your force.

32. Sun Tzu wrote:

"If birds gather on any spot it is unoccupied. Clamor by night betokens nervousness."

Nature reacts instantly to incursion. Pay attention to where game animals and birds congregate, this is a safe place, where the enemy is not. So too, note the sounds (or lack thereof) of creatures made nervous by the passing of troops. In this fashion, we know where to look for danger.

Publilius Syrus (85 – 43 BC) was a Syrian slave brought to Rome who earned his freedom by wit and talent, eventually becoming a famous writer in the ancient world. In the Sententiae he wrote, "One is not exposed to danger who, even when in safety is always on their guard." The French term "en garde," literally "on guard" in English, is used by referees to call fencers to action at the beginning of a match. At this signal contestants take their positions, unsheathe their swords, and prepare to act. Constant vigilance in the face of danger means that we are similarly prepared to act to defend ourselves when called upon to do so.

For the Win: Civilians avoid war. Identify where people who have no power in the conflict gather; this is where the enemy is not.

You Lose: If you confuse guerrilla warfare and traditional conflict, irregular combatants will hide amongst the civilians.

33. Sun Tzu wrote:

> *"If there is disturbance in the camp the general's authority is weak. If the banners and flags are shifted about sedition is afoot. If the officers are angry it means that the men are weary."*

If the ranks are in turmoil, large or small, the authority of the leader will be called into question. Disorganization indicates an internal weakness, one that can be exploited. We must keep pulse upon the fitness of our officers lest they undermine our authority, weaken our men and women's morale, or spark sedition.

Jose Rizal (1861 – 1896) was a nationalist hero of the Philippines who was executed by firing squad while agitating for freedom from Spanish rule. He wrote, "The government that governs from afar absolutely requires that the truth and the facts reach its knowledge by every possible channel, so that it may weigh and estimate them better, and this need increases when a country like the Philippines is concerned, where the inhabitants speak and complain in a language unknown to the authorities." In order to manage any team, leaders must understand what is actually happing throughout their organization. We cannot isolate ourselves, relying solely on the institutional hierarchy for this insight, but rather must get to know and interact with our men and women directly. This dynamic is what sparked the 80s business trend of "management by walking around."

For the Win: Watch for any aberration within the enemy's camp, errant movement, undisciplined acts, or rumblings of dissatisfaction. These are easily exploited.

You Lose: Failure to keep a close eye on the enemy's leadership is dereliction of your position.

34. Sun Tzu wrote:

"When an army feeds its horses with grain and kills its cattle for food and when the men do not hang their cooking-pots over the campfires showing that they will not return to their tents you may know that they are determined to fight to the death."

There is nothing more dangerous than a foe who's determined to fight to the last man to achieve their aims. Beware of any acts that reveal an enemy has no intention of returning home, this is perilous. After all, a cornered rat will fight a lion, even if the rat has chosen its own corner.

The Battle of the Aegates Islands was the final naval battle of the 23-year long First Punic War, which took place in 241 BC when a Roman armada of 200 quinqueremes sailed to Carthage to lay siege to the North African city-state. Before the melee, Roman commander Quintus Lutatius Catulus (149 – 87 BC) reduced his vessels' weight by ordering his men to strip everything unessential to combat and throw it into the sea. The lighter weight Roman ships were thus able to outmaneuver the Carthaginians' heavier vessels, using their bronze rams and wooden boarding ramps to sink 50 ships and capture 70, taking half of Carthage's entire fleet out of commission during the conflict. Faced with no choice but to surrender, Carthage agreed to a treaty that ended the war.

For the Win: An adversary who intends to fight to the last person will make their position clear. Thoughtless use of resources is one indicator of their aims.

You Lose: Engaging with an adversary who intends to die and take you with him is a dangerous proposition.

35. Sun Tzu wrote:

"The sight of men whispering together in small knots or speaking in subdued tones points to disaffection amongst the rank-and-file."

Dissatisfaction does not begin with the bang of an explosion; it has a slow-burning fuse. We must attend the whispers of our men and women, for in these quiet conversations lies the truth that points toward the heart of our forces. So too do the whispers of our enemies point toward their determination and willingness to prevail against us.

Gossip is poisonous, undermining morale, damaging interpersonal relationships, and disrupting the productivity of the workplace, yet more often than not it is a failing of leadership rather than the fault of the employees. If we find ourselves spending too much time addressing gossip it is likely that we are not communicating effectively with our team. Whenever folks do not have enough information they speculate, filling in the blanks with suspicions and suppositions. It is vital to counter this before it creates a toxic culture that is difficult to overcome.

For the Win: Quickly address anything that undermines morale.

You Lose: Only fools let rumors grow unhindered.

36. Sun Tzu wrote:

"Too frequent rewards signify that the enemy is at the end of his resources, too many punishments betray a condition of dire distress."

Leaders acting in desperation take actions of great reward or excessive punishment when resources become scarce. We must observe how the adversary remunerates their men and women, these actions provide insight into their condition.

Praise is good, but even the sincerest recognition can seem disingenuous if we do not do it right. Leaders must be specific about the behaviors or results that we value rather than offering generalized platitudes. We explain what was done, why it matters, and how much it means to us that the person did it. To be relevant and meaningful any reward that accompanies this recognition must be appropriate for the size of the achievement and presented in a manner that the person being recognized will appreciate.

For the Win: Indications of extreme rewards or punishments by your enemy is a sign of desperation that may be exploited.

You Lose: Attempting to keep order with disingenuous, unearned awards or broad-reaching punishments demonstrates that you have lost control.

37. Sun Tzu wrote:

"To begin by bluster but afterwards to take fright at the enemy's numbers shows a supreme lack of intelligence."

To rage at the enemy and then flee rather than fight demonstrates a lack of preparedness, a lack of intelligence, or both. Name-calling is childish bluster. Juvenile behavior is no match for military capability. When any dispute turns to name-calling it is no longer about the disagreement but rather has turned personal. This is a distraction from the main issue, clearly, but it also means that the adversary is unable to win on the merits of his or her argument.

With little substance to stand upon, yet unwilling to concede defeat, the small-minded eventually resort to bluster and insult. This may make them feel better about themselves but it also demonstrates their lack of intellect to everyone around them. As leaders, we must never give in to this temptation. When wrong we must admit it and move forward.

For the Win: Look beyond your enemy's outer shell to know their inner fortitude. Is the armor strong, or merely a cover for weakness and fear?

You Lose: If your bark is worse than your bite, sooner or later someone will call your bluff. A peacock may appear large, multi-eyed, and frightening, yet it stands no chance against a large housecat.

38. Sun Tzu wrote:

"When envoys are sent with compliments in their mouths, it is a sign that the enemy wishes for a truce."

Emissaries who carry pleasant words, no matter their form, indicate some possibility of peace. Wise leaders listen guardedly to these words as they reveal an adversary's intent to pause or pursue the battle. Under a flag of truce, ambassadors have historically passed messages back and forth amongst warring parties. Killing these messengers meant that there would be no opportunity for peace short of total annihilation, so the custom evolved to grant free passage for those who wished to parlay in good faith, hence the origination of the term, "Don't shoot the messenger."

In the modern world, leaders who punish those who transmit messages we do not wish to hear undermine our own success. No one in our organization should ever fear to give us an honest answer. After all, if we cannot handle the truth, we do not deserve to be in a leadership position.

For the Win: If your enemy speaks with respect and admiration, he may be seeking an agreement short of violence.

You Lose: Fail to observe an enemy's tone and you will miss vital clues to their intent.

39. Sun Tzu wrote:

> *"If the enemy's troops march up angrily and remain facing ours for a long time without either joining battle or taking themselves off again, the situation is one that demands great vigilance and circumspection."*

If the enemy is on guard, we must be as well. We need not act, but we must be ready. Standoffs between armed camps are perilous. If our adversaries appear coiled to strike we must be extra vigilant. The term "Cold War" was coined by English writer George Orwell (1903 – 1950) in 1945, referring to a rivalry between nations waged with politics, economic machinations, and disinformation rather than with bullets, bombs, or other weapons. At that time the United States of American (USA) and its North Atlantic Treaty Organization (NATO) allies were embroiled in a cold war (often referred to as "the" Cold War) with the Union of Soviet Socialist Republics (USSR).

This Cold War was the ultimate stalemate, one where armed conflict amongst ideologies could easily have sparked worldwide conflagration and nuclear war. Incidents such as the Cuban Missile Crisis in 1962 demonstrated how perilous that standoff could be, and thousands of minor skirmishes ebbed and flowed over the years, yet the collapse of the Soviet economy in 1991 led the USSR to break into 15 independent nations, innocuously ending the nearly five-decade Cold War. The whole world breathed a little easier after that stalemate was resolved peacefully.

For the Win: A showdown can tip to battle in an instant. This is an anxious time, one that requires acute leadership. Remain flexible to craft a constructive solution.

You Lose: When you believe that violence is the only option to end a standoff, everything short of war is off the table.

40. Sun Tzu wrote:

> *"If our troops are no more in number than the enemy that is amply sufficient, it only means that no direct attack can be made. What we can do is simply to concentrate all our available strength, keep a close watch on the enemy, and obtain reinforcements."*

When students of the art of war come to blows, numbers will usually decide the outcome. When we find ourselves equal in resources to our adversary, the disadvantage is unlikely to be found on either side. Thus, we may safeguard our position, but not take the offensive directly without moving up reinforcements to augment our capabilities.

As with clashes amongst nations, interpersonal battles are also impacted by numbers. A lone individual dealing with multiple attackers is placed at a great disadvantage as we can only really engage one adversary at a time. Despite what we see in kung fu movies, bad guys do not line up and wait their turn to attack, they swarm and overrun. This means that defense against a group must be handled strategically, engaging one person at a time in a manner that confounds the other's ability to strike. Once the first opponent has been defeated, we may have a chance to flee or may be forced to move on to the next attacker before making our escape.

For the Win: When faced with a standoff, strengthen your forces quickly.

You Lose: Remaining in a protracted standoff is unsustainable. Failure to craft resolution exhausts your resources.

41. Sun Tzu wrote:

> *"He who exercises no forethought but makes light of his opponents is sure to be captured by them."*

To miscalculate an adversary's capabilities is to court disaster. It is folly to underestimate our opponent, overestimate our prowess, or trust to Providence to determine the outcome of any forthcoming battle. We must realistically appraise our changes, moving forward with forethought and strategy.

Lieutenant General Lewis Burwell "Chesty" Puller (1898 – 1971) was a barrel-chested Marine veteran with extensive combat experience, who invaded the island of Peleliu with 3,000 men to take on 11,000 entrenched Japanese soldiers and seize control of an Imperial airbase in 1944. Compounding his numerical disadvantage, Puller ignored intelligence descriptions of the enemy's extensive fortifications, reports of the coral promontories and rugged terrain that would hamper his men's advance, and even rejected subordinates' pleas to ask for reinforcements from the Army 81st Infantry Division waiting on a nearby ship to deploy. After six days of intense battle and 70% casualties, Puller and his men were ordered to give up the battle and retreat.

For the Win: Unleashing the full force of all you can muster in combat is the only course once the path for war has been laid. If you must fight, always fight to win.

You Lose: Underestimating your opponent is for braggarts and fools. Going in halfheartedly is a recipe for disaster.

42. Sun Tzu wrote:

"If soldiers are punished before they have grown attached to you, they will not prove submissive and unless submissive they will be practically useless. If, when the soldiers have become attached to you, punishments are not enforced the men will still be useless."

While we cannot be too hard on our men and women without causing resentment, we must also not be too soft lest we undermine discipline. Soldiers are aggressive by nature, particularly those who pursue the military as their profession, so taking a hardline prematurely risks belligerence and subterfuge. We must, therefore, establish reasonable rules of conduct and earn our troops respect by modeling these behaviors before they will willingly accept punishment for not living up to our standards. Conscripts, who fight not out of patriotic duty nor pursuit of glory, but rather out of necessity require more oversight.

Leaders create codes of conduct for their organizations that identify social norms, rules, and responsibilities that everyone on the team should follow. These need not be complicated, merely common sense, yet by writing them down and referring to them regularly we clarify expectations in a meaningful way. Everyone, from the highest executive to the lowest intern, must be held accountable for following the code for it to remain viable and enforceable, however. If tempted to allow exceptions we must examine our principles and, should we discover divergence, consider rewriting the code.

For the Win: To earn respect you must have your force's hearts; to have their hearts you must be worthy of respect.

You Lose: If your leadership style is one of unforgiving force, it will only be successful in the short term.

43. Sun Tzu wrote:

> *"Therefore soldiers must be treated in the first instance with humanity but kept under control by means of iron discipline. This is a certain road to victory."*

Leadership is a balance of concern and resolve. We must be concerned about our men and women's needs, attentive to their welfare, yet resolved to keep our forces strong. Undisciplined they cannot prevail. As the proverb states, "Spare the rod, spoil the child." This holds true for adults as well. While we give warning for a single violation, contempt for our command or blatant disregard for our instructions must be punished.

Military discipline is vital in any conflict. In times of war, breaches of the protocol were often judged by a courts-marshal on the battlefield with justice swiftly following, though deserters were often summarily executed without any trial. For example, between the Union and Confederate armies, approximately 500 men were shot for violations of their army's codes of behavior during the American Civil War (1861 – 1865), two-thirds of that number for desertion. Colonel Samuel Bassett French (1820 – 1898), an aid to Lieutenant General "Stonewall" Jackson (1824 – 1863), wrote about this stating, "The preservation of the army itself was dependent on the maintenance of discipline, and discipline could not be had if desertions were longer to go unpunished."

For the Win: Firm but fair is the best policy.

You Lose: Choose favorites and give them special treatment. This poisons the water your forces drink from.

44. Sun Tzu wrote:

"If in training soldiers commands are habitually enforced the army will be well-disciplined, if not its discipline will be bad."

Erratic leaders destabilize their forces. Men and women will not willingly follow an undisciplined general, so we must be consistent when dealing with our forces. This improves accountability, morale, and performance. Different leaders have different styles, some more desirable than others, yet research demonstrates that underlings can adapt to virtually any approach as long as their supervisor is consistent.

Predictability in leadership is key; when folks come to know what to expect they will naturally adjust and accommodate. If we value first time quality, for example, people will double-check their work. If we embrace gossip, we create a culture of backstabbing; it's dysfunctional but people will know how to succeed. Similarly, if we're late for meetings, they will rarely start on time. However, if we exhibit moodiness, irritability, or inconsistency we create stress for our team as they cannot know what they will face at any given moment. This leads to costly productivity loss and unnecessary turnover.

For the Win: Demonstrate firm and fair leadership, in big and small moments alike. This will help bind your forces together.

You Lose: Favoritism demonstrates erratic, emotional thinking. Behave this way and lost the trust and respect of your team.

45. Sun Tzu wrote:

"If a general shows confidence in his men but always insists on his orders being obeyed, the gain will be mutual."

Generals not only formulate winning strategies but also build and enable a winning team. As leaders, we assign underlings to roles and responsibilities based on their ability to execute our plan. Having positioned our men and women, therefore, we must show confidence in their expertise, secure in the knowledge that they will faithfully carry out our orders.

Most people grow into challenges. They will step up or down to our expectations. To create a high-performance team, we need to help those around us acquire the knowledge, skills, and abilities they need for success and give them a chance to practice such that they can hone their capabilities. Showing confidence means understanding people's potential, placing them in roles where they have a chance to succeed, setting guiderails, and getting out of the way. Micromanagement, even when we feel it's necessary, demonstrates distrust. Our team cannot grow if they never have the opportunity to fail.

For the Win: Clear and direct orders assure your instructions will be carried out by well-intended people aiming to do the right things to further your enterprise.

You Lose: Continually second guessing your team demonstrates a lack of trust, drying up necessary creativity and proactivity.

Chapter 10: Terrain

In this chapter, we learn to leverage the strengths of each type of earth, distinguishing amongst the accessible ground, entangling ground, temporizing ground, narrow passes, precipitous heights, and positions at a great distance from our adversaries to impel our forces toward victory. With keen insight, we examine six calamities that may befall us—flight, insubordination, collapse, ruin, disorganization, and route—knowing that armed with this understanding, once put in motion our plans can never be confounded.

1. Sun Tzu wrote:

"We may distinguish six kinds of terrain, to wit: (1) accessible ground, (2) entangling ground, (3) temporizing ground, (4) narrow passes, (5) precipitous heights, and (6) positions at a great distance from the enemy."

A wise general classifies the six types of ground his or her forces may encounter, the better to intuit the optimal strategy for meeting an enemy in each one. In this manner, we know ahead of time what to do in any confrontation. For example, the Swiss Confederation is a country situated in the mountainous region at the confluence of western, central, and southern Europe. It is characterized by the Swiss Alps to the south, a Central Plateau, and the Jura Mountains to the west.

In 1315, Duke Leopold II (1797 – 1870) led an army of heavily armored knights to put down a Swiss rebellion. Ascending the mountains to the Morgarten Pass near Lake Aegeri, Leopold and his men abruptly found their route blocked by a troop of peasant infantry. Strung out along a narrow trail, the Austrians were unable to use cavalry to their advantage, yet the Swiss found the steep terrain more to their liking. They rolled logs and boulders down the hillside onto the Austrian forces, knocking men and horses off the cliff, then charged into their flank driving more into the lake. In an extraordinary victory of commoners over mounted knights, more than 1,500 Austrian knights perished in the fight, marking the establishment of the Eidgenossen, or "oath brothers," who soon earned a reputation as the most ferocious shock troops in Europe.

For the Win: Classify territory to know in advance how to handle whatever you'll face.

You Lose: Failure to recognize and deal with terrain effectively will undermine your endeavor.

2. Sun Tzu wrote:

"Ground which can be freely traversed by both sides is called accessible."

If we can come and go freely through an area, so can our adversaries. This accessible ground is open to both sides, hence may be seized as easily by the enemy as by our own forces. In accessible ground, either side is able to take the initiative. Napoleon Bonaparte (1769 – 1821) wrote that "Two armies are two bodies that clash and attempt to frighten each other. At impact, there is a moment of panic and it is that moment that the superior commander turns to his advantage." When two opposing forces contest the same ground, the one that seizes the offensive is likely to prevail. This is why accessible ground may be either a blessing or a curse, depending on what we do with it.

Consider new marketplaces. There is a predictable lifecycle starting with the creation and introduction of an innovative product or technology where whoever is first to market has an inherent advantage. With the right offering, they will experience a period of rapid growth. As other competitors discover this money-making opportunity, they are likely to join in, especially whenever barriers to entry are low. This is followed by a maturity stage, where products are optimized, profits are lowered, competition becomes fierce, and weaker enterprises are forced to drop out of the market. Eventually, as the product nears the end of its lifecycle, market opportunities rapidly decline as customers become picker, seek value pricing, and margins are at their smallest. Only the development of a new value-adding product or service will restart this lifecycle.

For the Win: Free ground is "free" for a reason. Only contest this space when it adds value to your overall plan.

You Lose: Spending resources trying to create value where there is inherently little wastes your time and energy.

3. Sun Tzu wrote:

"With regard to ground of this nature be before the enemy in occupying the raised and sunny spots and carefully guard your line of supplies. Then you will be able to fight with advantage."

Should we be the first to capture accessible ground, we must position our forces strategically such that it cannot be pried away from us easily. It's not just the location we occupy that matters, but also the routes through which we transport our supplies there, for without our baggage we cannot hold the field overlong.

The battle of Huai-Hai, which took place between November 6, 1948, and January 10, 1949, was the pivotal fight for control of China, a contest between the Chinese Communist Party led by Mao Zedong (1893 – 1976) and Nationalist Party of Kuomintang (KMT) under the leadership of Chiang Kai-Shek (1887 – 1975). Their civil war began in earnest in 1927, but the two sides temporarily combined forces to defend against invasion by Japan. After WWII, the Communists re-launched their offensive, ultimately dividing Nationalist-held territories into three areas and then methodically conquering each one. By the end of the battle of Huai-Hai, more than half a million KMT soldiers were dead, captured, or converted to the other side, placing China firmly in the hands of the Communists. Over the next two decades, Mao ruthlessly crushed dissent to solidify his rule, killing more than 20,000,000 of his own people in the process.

For the Win: If you seize the high ground without supplies you cannot stay long. If you spend too much time securing your supply lines, however, you will be late for the fight. These must balance.

You Lose: Fail to take the high ground and secure your supply lines.

4. Sun Tzu wrote:

"Ground which can be abandoned but is hard to reoccupy is called entangling."

We cannot afford to become entangled in battle. Each engagement has a clear purpose, victory, yet if a conflict is drawn out our anticipated triumph can become hard to achieve. When faced with entanglement we must set ourselves toward unraveling our bonds before we can prevail.

The city of Kuldhara is a ghost town in western Rajasthan, India. Sometime in the early 19th century its inhabitants, the Paliwal Brahmins, suddenly decided to abandon their city and 83 nearby villages after having thrived there for more than seven centuries. According to legend a local warlord lusted after the most beautiful girl in the community, the chieftain's daughter. While he wished to marry her, she refused his advances so he gave the villagers an ultimatum, they were given a single day to accept his proposal or face his wrath. That evening chiefs of all 84 villages gathered together and, as a sign of respect to their friend, decided to leave their birthplaces in the dark of the night. It is rumored that they cursed their old homes never to be inhabited again, bringing death and devastation to anyone who moved there. Those who later tried to reoccupy the area reportedly experienced frightening paranormal activities that drove them away, solidifying Kuldhara's reputation. The city has become a tourist destination today.

For the Win: It is expensive to return to a place you once won and vacated. This consideration must be part of your movement of forces decisions.

You Lose: Moving from battle to battle without concern for the territory seized along the way squanders both resources and opportunity.

5. Sun Tzu wrote:

"From a position of this sort if the enemy is unprepared you may sally forth and defeat him. But if the enemy is prepared for your coming and you fail to defeat him then return being impossible, disaster will ensue."

Because the entangling ground is fraught with dangers, we must engage the adversaries only when they are unprepared for our strike. If the enemy is ready, dug-in with anticipation of our strike, we will fail.

The Tet Offensive, which began with the observance of the lunar New Year in 1968, was a pivotal turning point in the Vietnam War. Just as the New Year's festivities began, Viet Cong forces attacked 13 cities in central South Vietnam in a well-coordinated action. In one key battle, broadcast on live television by American and international press observers, insurgents overran and destroyed the US Embassy in Saigon. While United States and South Vietnamese forces inflicted heavy damages killing over 5,000 Viet Cong in response, anti-war sentiment ballooned to the point where US President Johnson announced that he would not run for re-election. On March 31, 1968, he further limited bombing to areas below the 20th parallel, sparing 90% of Communist-held territory from the US strikes. While peace talks took another five years to conclude, Johnson's decision to halt escalation after the Tet Offensive was the beginning of the end of the Vietnam War.

For the Win: When you strike at a king, you only get one chance. Best kill him lest you fail and suffer his wrath.

You Lose: There is more than one way to kill the king, failure to see the alternative methods narrows your chances of success.

6. Sun Tzu wrote:

"When the position is such that neither side will gain by making the first move, it is called temporizing ground."

The definition of temporizing is to be indecisive or irresolute in order to gain time or delay taking action. When both sides of a conflict hesitate to act, we find ourselves on temporizing ground. Sensing the lack of a path toward clear victory we vacillate, searching for better alternatives, knowing that premature action will prove regrettable.

In late 1917 British Field Marshal Douglas Haig (1861 – 1928) launched an offensive against German lines at Passchendaele in Flanders. While before the war this region had been an open plain, a combination of heavy autumn storms and millions of shells flung back and forth over months of fighting combined to overwhelm the drainage system and turn the area into a lake of waist-deep mud. Conditions were horrific for both men and their equipment, as troops became mired in the mud, drown in their sleep, and fought from waterlogged mud holes left by exploded ordinance. By the time it was over, more than 4,250,000 shells were fired between both sides and 275,000 Allied forces, including some 38,000 Australians, 15,600 Canadians, and 5,300 New Zealanders, were killed along with roughly 220,000 Germans. In what became a symbol of the futility of trench warfare, some 90,000 bodies from this 105-day battle were never identified and another 42,000 never recovered.

For the Win: When delays created by the terrain affect both parties; the resulting ponderous movements must be recognized and understood. Never take hasty or impulsive action in these circumstances.

You Lose: Acting rashly is always a poor choice. Trying to get the ground to bend to your will is an injudicious act.

7. Sun Tzu wrote:

"In a position of this sort even though the enemy should offer us an attractive bait it will be advisable not to stir forth but rather to retreat thus enticing the enemy in his turn, then when part of his army has come out we may deliver our attack with advantage."

If temporizing ground causes hesitation and our enemy makes a poor first move, we may safely hold fast. This false move is not threatening, yet if we react impulsively it will draw us into a poor position. Best to retreat and entice the adversary to act such that we may strategically counter and seize the advantage. The temporizing ground is all about temptation. Billy Sunday (1862 – 1935) was an American baseball player turned preacher who once said, "Temptation is the devil looking through the keyhole. Yielding is opening the door and inviting him in."

In order to avoid temptation, it is advisable to stop and think before we act. We must reflect on what we gain by proceeding, the opportunity cost of delay, and whether or not we believe that we will come to regret our actions later on. While it is wise to sleep on critical decisions, letting our subconscious mind consider and weigh in overnight, for most things we can make sensible decisions using the "15-Minute Rule." In this way, we consider for fifteen minutes before deciding. This is enough time to keep from acting hastily but not so much that it is likely to harm our position by waiting overlong on something time-critical. This small delay helps us respond rather than react to the risky situations we face.

For the Win: Heed the Admiral Akbar moment… When you know it's a trap, don't rush in.

You Lose: Let the enemy bait your frustration to lure you onto temporizing ground.

8. Sun Tzu wrote:

"With regard to narrow passes, if you can occupy them first let them be strongly garrisoned and await the advent of the enemy."

A narrow pass is one of the easiest environments to defend. Using a narrow pass to focus our forces and keep an adversary from attacking in mass makes any defensive force formidable. This was the lesson of Thermopylae, of course, yet if we adequately fortify the area it need not become a famous last stand. Well-positioned and supplied troops entrenched in a narrow pass are extremely hard to displace. Leveraging narrow ground, a small force can overcome a much larger one.

Led by Raymond le Gros (1185 – 1198), the second Anglo-Norman invasion of Ireland took place in 1170 at Baginbun beach. While le Gros only had 80 men in his company, his cunning made that small force quite formidable. Faced with a nearly 3,000 Irish adversaries, his men made a brief probing attack and then quickly retreated, feigning panic. The Irishmen chased after them along a narrow promontory where they were caught completely off guard when the Normans stampeded a herd of cattle across their path. As the Irish forces were crushed by the massive stampede, survivors scattering in pandemonium, le Gros's men reengaged, capturing and killing thousands of men. In this fashion, a small group of raiders defeated a force more than 37 times their size.

For the Win: Control a narrow space and you multiply your capabilities.

You Lose: Attack a narrow space secured by your adversary and you must waste powerful resources against a weaker foe.

9. Sun Tzu wrote:

"Should the army forestall you in occupying a pass, do not go after him if the pass is fully-garrisoned, but only if it is weakly garrisoned."

If we cannot keep an adversary out of a narrow pass, we're ill-advised to pursue him, particularly if he or she is well-entrenched inside. Our advantage is either to draw him out onto the better ground or, if necessary, to strike before he is fully-garrisoned inside.

The battle of Dien Bien Phu, a deep valley surrounded by foothills in northwest Vietnam, took place between March 13th and May 7th, 1954. French General Henri Navarre (1898 – 1983) led his troops deep into enemy territory where he engaged Viet Minh commander Vo Nguyen Giap (1911 – 2013) in battle. It was just about the worst location Navarre could have selected. Caught in the lowland, surrounded by enemies on higher ground, Navarre discovered that the thick underbrush hindered the progress of his tanks and foiled his design. He quickly found his troops besieged and cut off from supplies, for even airdrops proved ineffectual due to the terrain. Monsoon rains made matters even worse. By the time the battle was over 2,293 Frenchmen were killed, 5,195 wounded, and 10,998 captured. This disaster marked the end of the First Indochina War, leading to the 1954 Geneva Accords which partitioned Vietnam at the 17th Parallel, creating a Communist state in the north and a democratic state in the south.

For the Win: If you cannot keep the enemy out of a narrow pass, do not pursue. Find a way to draw him into a fight you are better prepared to win.

You Lose: Believe that your forces are special, that you can swim against the tide of history by defeating a force in a narrow valley head-to-head, and you will go into the history books a buffoon.

10. Sun Tzu wrote:

"With regard to precipitous heights if you are beforehand with your adversary you should occupy the raised and sunny spots and there wait for him to come up."

To succeed in mountainous regions, we must arrive before the enemy and seize the high ground. Forcing our adversaries to fight an uphill battle saps their strength. When arrive first, we create the opportunity to make our position unassailable.

Portrayed with the battle on Mustafar between Anakin Skywalker (actor Hayden Christensen) and Obi-wan Kenobi (actor Ewan McGregor) in the movie Revenge of the Sith, the strategy of taking the high ground has been commonplace throughout most of human history. Marcus Vitruvius Pollio (90 – 20 BC), a Roman author, architect, and military engineer wrote in De Architectura, "In setting out the walls of a city the choice of a healthy situation is of the first importance: it should be on high ground." This term applies to much more than terrain, however; it can be defined as, "Acting morally, especially in times of disagreement or tension." This is important for all our endeavors, for without setting our compass with a certain moral authority we are apt to act out in selfish, narcissistic, and self-indulgent ways. We should aspire for a legacy much greater than that.

For the Win: Take the high ground before your enemy, making him fight uphill.

You Lose: Let the enemy take the high ground, metaphorical or physical, and you cede valuable advantage.

11. Sun Tzu wrote:

"If the enemy has occupied them before you, do not follow him but retreat and try to entice him away."

If we chase an enemy into a high place they occupy, we must be ready to accept heavy losses. As the adage states, if we're late to the party, we don't chase the party. Create interest to lure it toward us instead. Uphill battles rarely lead to victory.

Paul Wolfowitz (1943 –) is an American diplomat who served as the President of the World Bank. He once said, "You can't win if you're chasing the wrong problem." This is absolutely true, especially when it turns out that we're the cause of the issue. People generally prefer to avoid conflict, so it takes courage for someone to come to us when they believe that we have caused them harm. While it is easy to be offended, we must do our best not to take such things personally. Consider it a hallmark of good leadership that our teammate found us approachable enough to express their concern in the first place, then focus on what can be done to resolve the issue.

For the Win: Lure your opponent away from the high ground.

You Lose: Stubbornly fight uphill despite the enemy's advantage.

12. Sun Tzu wrote:

"If you are situated at a great distance from the enemy and the strength of the two armies is equal it is not easy to provoke a battle and fighting will be to your disadvantage."

To wage a battle across great distances with a comparable enemy is expensive in every way. The greater the distance from our enemy, the less likelihood of making a successful war. Historically it was challenging to carry out warfare over great distances due to the logistics of command, control, and communication, though technology has changed that dynamic to large degree. Innovations in communication technology have proven as imperative for successful warfare as advances in offensive and defensive weaponry.

Nicknamed the "walkie-talkie," the SCR-300 backpack radio was the first technological breakthrough that helped armies fight at great distances. First field-tested in the spring of 1942, this battery-powered FM radio weighed 35 pounds and was rugged enough to be carried into combat. The SCR-300 was designed to handle rain, sleet, snow, and mud, but required fungicide treatments for the circuit boards to withstand the heat and humidity encountered in the Pacific Theater during WWII. It had an operational distance of about eight miles, using noise-canceling circuitry to help facilitate clear reception on the battlefield. This radio proved invaluable not only to communicate between commanders and their troops but also for forward observers to direct artillery and call in airstrikes.

For the Win: When you fight over a long distance every logistic is stretched, so communication becomes paramount.

You Lose: Place other aspects of long-distance warfare above communications and your orders will not be carried out effectively, undermining you plan.

13. Sun Tzu wrote:

> *"These six are the principles connected with earth. The general who has attained a responsible post must be careful to study them."*

The six principles of terrain are associated with earth, which comprises distances, great and small, danger and security, open ground and narrow passes, and the chances of life and death. They are of great importance, meritorious of study and analysis for any leader. Without this understanding we cannot formulate a sound strategy. Anyone in a position of responsibility must prepare for their role and continuously hone their skills for the benefit of both themselves and their team.

Many consider it unfair that the average CEO makes roughly 361 times more than the average worker earns, yet their impact on their enterprise is immeasurably higher than that of other employees. Think about why Bill Gates, Steve Jobs, Jeff Bezos, Jack MA, Satya Nadella, and Jack Welch have become household names. Would their companies be anywhere near as successful without their leadership? Likely not. For example, Steve Jobs was removed from the company he co-founded by Apple's board in 1985 only to be brought back to save the company in 1997 after it nearly collapsed under CEOs John Scully, Michael Spindler, and Gilbert Amelio. With the right person is in charge, an enterprise thrives. The reverse is also true.

For the Win: Thoughtfully prepare for leadership, continuously honing your skills for the benefit of your team.

You Lose: Failing to learn how each element of warfare can be woven together to your advantage renders you unfit to lead.

14. Sun Tzu wrote:

"Now an army is exposed to six several calamities not arising from natural causes but from faults for which the general is responsible. These are (1) flight, (2) insubordination, (3) collapse, (4) ruin, (5) disorganization, and (6) rout."

While anyone may be at risk from natural disasters, an astute leader controls his or her own fate. Nevertheless, we must guard against shortcomings that may undermine our strategy, leading our forces to prematurely flee from battle, disregard sensible orders, shut down mentally, act recklessly rather than strategically, fall into disarray, or otherwise be defeated by the enemy. Mistakes are not necessarily problematic, so long as we learn from them, though some are worse than others.

There are four kinds of mistakes leaders can make, foolish, simple, involved, or complex. Foolish mistakes are silly errors like stubbing one's toe that does not matter all that much. Simple mistakes are those that are easily avoidable like forgetting to pay a bill and acquiring a late fee, which may be prevented with a little forethought. Involved mistakes are also preventable, like gaining weight due to bad diet and insufficient exercise, but take more effort to stave off or recover from. Complex mistakes, on the other hand, are not so obvious, hence much harder to avoid. They take some form of retrospective, like performing a root cause analysis, to understand what actually happened and learn from what we did wrong or did not do right.

For the Win: Govern the space between your ears; it is the most important arena to control if you wish to conquer your enemy.

You Lose: Fail to learn from your mistakes and they will compound them again and again until you fail utterly.

15. Sun Tzu wrote:

"Other conditions being equal, if one force is hurled against another ten times its size, the result will be the flight of the former."

The adage attributed to Mark Twain, a pen name of American writer Samuel Langhorne Clemens (1835 – 1910), states, "It's not the size of the dog in the fight, it's the size of the fight in the dog that matters." This is largely true, yet bluster, bravery, words, and insults are no substitute for brute force. Small combatants are small, no matter how big their words. When faced with a clearly superior adversary we must withdraw.

Attributed to the Athenian orator and statesman Demosthenes (384 – 322 BC), who fled from a battle with the Macedonians in which Athens was soundly beaten in 338 BC is the maxim, "He who fights and runs away may live to fight another day." Without superior skill, weapons, or ferocity, and a certain amount of luck, it is extremely challenging to overcome a larger, stronger adversary. This is as true on the street as it is in the ring. We must know our capabilities and do our best to avoid situations and actions where we are unlikely to win.

For the Win: When faced with a superior adversary, withdraw.

You Lose: If you fail to retreat when outmatched your downfall may be epic, but you won't be around to see your enemy celebrate it.

16. Sun Tzu wrote:

"When the common soldiers are too strong and their officers too weak the result is insubordination. When the officers are too strong and the common soldiers too weak the result is collapse."

A balance must be maintained between a leader and his or her subordinates, between subordinate and superior. Officers may be friendly with their troops, but cannot be friends with them. This undermines authority. It cannot be taken too far in the other direction either, however, as overly strict oversight will crush the spirit of our underlings, impeding their effectiveness and capabilities. We must, therefore, act much like a parent raising children. It is a balance between compassion and assertiveness that assures the best outcome.

We cannot concurrently be mentor, counselor, friend, spiritual guru, financial advisor, dog-walker, and savior of everyone around us no matter how talented we are or how much we may feel inclined to try. We must know our limits. Good leaders are empathetic to those around them, but they can only do so much. We are responsible for fostering an environment where individuals on our team can learn and grow, where talents are effectively utilized to further our enterprise goals, and where everyone has access to the resources that they need in order to be successful. We can assure communication, break down barriers, handle politics, acquire funding, train, and mentor, all things that help set folks up for success, but after that, it's up to them. At that point, we must learn to let go.

For the Win: Balance is important in all things, especially your leadership structure. Your venture depends on it.

You Lose: Overemphasize one aspect of your role, leading to a distortion that ultimately fails your entire endeavor.

17. Sun Tzu wrote:

"When the higher officers are angry and insubordinate and on meeting the enemy give battle on their own account from a feeling of resentment before the commander-in-chief can tell whether or not he is in a position to fight, the result is ruin."

Our captains earn their role through merit, each fully capable of carrying out our plans, yet none has the knowledge, skill, or ability to build and execute a winning strategy in our stead. When officers are not aligned with the leader, they will fight, but fight at the wrong time, in the wrong place, and for the wrong reasons. This is disastrous.

One of the fundamental human emotions, anger is a response of our sympathetic nervous system that helps prepare us to fight. Anger can motivate us to perform great feats, yet it can just as easily undermine our plans if it boils over in inappropriate ways. Like all emotions, it should be self-monitored and managed. Should we discover that excessive hostility interferes with our relationships or work performance, or causes us legal troubles, it is time to get help. Likewise, if those on our team experience difficulty controlling their emotions, we may need to intervene. Anger management programs that teach cognitive restructuring to help patients reframe unhealthy thoughts in more positive ways are very useful in this regard.

For the Win: The statement, "Everyone on the same page," is overused to the point of cliché, yet it is nonetheless true. Assure that everyone in your enterprise understands the goal and means to victory.

You Lose: Blindly assuming that everyone understands, agrees, and knows how to proceed without validating means that at a critical moment you will discover a breach in your plan caused by misunderstanding or mutiny.

18. Sun Tzu wrote:

"When the general is weak and without authority, when his orders are not clear and distinct, when there are no fixed duties assigned to officers and men, and the ranks are formed in a slovenly haphazard manner, the result is utter disorganization."

The structure of any organization determines how effectively it can operate. It allows the assignment of responsibilities into entities such as branches, departments, and workgroups. We assign a hierarchy to these teams to facilitate clear command, control, and communication with an assurance that with strong leadership our orders will be carried out. Conversely, we must strip any leader of their authority whose forces fall into disarray and replace them with someone more competent lest we breed uncontainable mayhem throughout our organization.

We may experiment with structure and authority, yet if results prove ineffectual, we must promptly change course, replacing weak leaders who lose their authority before it poisons the ranks and undermines morale. Steven Pinker (1954 –) is a Canadian-American cognitive psychologist, linguist, and author. He wrote, "My politics were pretty anarchistic until 1969 when the Montreal police went on strike. Within hours, mayhem and rioting broke out and the Mounties had to be called in to restore order. It instilled in me that one's convictions can be subjected to empirical test." Likewise, we must plan, test, and course-correct if results do not turn out as expected.

For the Win: Assign a hierarchy to that facilitates clear command, control, and communication and appoint capable leaders to implement your designs.

You Lose: Surround yourself with sycophants, incompetents, or malcontents and your schemes will come crashing down around you.

19. Sun Tzu wrote:

"When a general, unable to estimate the enemy's strength, allows an inferior force to engage a larger one or hurls a weak detachment against a powerful one and neglects to place picked soldiers in the front rank, the result must be rout."

If we wish to probe an enemy's strength, we must do so with skilled, elite forces, as we may not know the adversary's capabilities ahead of time. Throwing untested or inferior troops against a superior foe courts disaster.

Lacking money and manpower to compete directly with the armies of their neighboring states, the Israeli Defense Force (IDF) uses exceptional strategy, stealth, and technology to defeat numerically superior adversaries. Their elite naval commando unit, Shayetet 13 (which translates into English as "Flotilla 13"), is an example of this. Tasked with advanced reconnaissance, infiltration, and sabotage, this unit was involved in one of the most daring missions of the Second Lebanon War in 2006. A small team of Shayetet commandos flew hundreds of miles behind enemy lines, raided the Hezbollah stronghold city of Tyre, killed 30 Hezbollah commanders, and escaped without capture or casualties.

For the Win: Once you have measured the arena, you may astutely decide whether to go into battle, fix your position, or retreat.

You Lose: To hurl your forces against an unknown, unassessed enemy, is a crapshoot. The problem with gambling in war is that our life is on the line and the "house" almost always wins.

20. Sun Tzu wrote:

"These are six ways of courting defeat, which must be carefully noted by the general who has attained a responsible post."

The greater our responsibility, the better we must prepare for any eventuality. Knowing the ways in which we may potentially be defeated forewarns and forearms us. In this fashion, we are able to plan, strategize, and overcome without succumbing to fatal blunders or costly mistakes.

In any endeavor, there are risks, issues, and opportunities that arise along the way. Risks are vulnerabilities that may undermine our success, while issues are problems that have actually occurred and must be mitigated. By identifying risks ahead of time, we are able to create contingency plans that may immediately be initiated whenever issues crop up. For example, business continuity plans assure that an enterprise can continue operations in the event of a natural disaster such as an earthquake, hurricane, tornado, or pandemic by switching to backup facilities, leveraging alternate suppliers, or taking similar actions. In this fashion, we adroitly respond to any eventuality and stay on track.

For the Win: Know the method and means of your own defeat, because the enemy surely does. Now you can plan responsibly.

You Lose: To ignore your weakness leaves your limitations lacking. Only with honest appraisal can you shore things up.

21. Sun Tzu wrote:

"The natural formation of the country is the soldier's best ally, but a power of estimating the adversary, of controlling the forces of victory, and of shrewdly calculating difficulties, dangers and distances, constitutes the test of a great general."

The land, its topography, and resources are instrumental to the outcome of any skirmish. For the foot soldier the finer points of fighting, say identifying sources of cover or concealment on an open plain, are paramount yet for all their individual skill and accomplishment no trooper can survey the entire battlefield while caught up in a firefight. This is the perspective of the commander, to oversee and control the conflict as a whole.

Projects may be planned top-down or bottom-up. When strategies and goals are pushed down from the top, senior executives assure tight alignment of individual efforts with objectives of the enterprise. It takes less time to work this way, but these top-down strategies may miss important details that only those on the front line have noticed. Bottom-up planning, on the other hand, empowers each individual to play a role in the larger plan. It does not work well for time-sensitive decisions but often results in more holistic appraisals. By deliberate use of both top-down and bottom-up planning, we assure the best outcomes for our enterprise.

For the Win: Keen observation and good council assure solid decision-making.

You Lose: No system is immune to failure. Believe otherwise and you accelerate your loss.

22. Sun Tzu wrote:

> *"He who knows these things and in fighting puts his knowledge into practice will win his battles. He who knows them not nor practices them will surely be defeated."*

We must study the lay of the land, understand it, and then discern ways to use the battlefield to our advantage. This creates opportunities for us as much as it helps us create problems for our adversaries. In war, we must pay attention to our surroundings or risk defeat. In this fashion, we control our destiny.

Marcus Aurelius (121 – 180) was a Roman emperor and Stoic philosopher known for his book Meditations, in which he wrote, "Say to yourself early in the morning, 'I shall meet today with ungrateful, violent, treacherous, envious, uncharitable men. All these things have come upon them through ignorance of real good and ill… I can neither be harmed by any of them, for no man will involve me in wrong, nor can I be angry with my kinsman or hate him; for we have come into the world to work together.'" It is easy to let the opinions of others bring us down, yet knowing that others are envious of our position, success, or good fortune means that we're doing something right. Our self-worth should never be determined by anyone but ourselves. After all, we're both our harshest critic and greatest supporter; we know our journey, it's the destination, our progress, and whether any course-correction is truly desirable.

For the Win: Apply your wisdom. The path forward may be challenging, but there is a reason why you earned your position. Think on that and demonstrate it daily.

You Lose: Forget why you got here, letting the slings and arrows of others whipsaw your emotions and control your day. That is a loss every time.

23. Sun Tzu wrote:

"If fighting is sure to result in victory then you must fight even though the ruler forbids it. If fighting will not result in victory then you must not fight even at the ruler's bidding."

Despite the chain-of-command, we must not abide by foolish orders from those who do not understand the art of war. The rules of fighting are immutable and at times can supersede the order of the sovereign. Just because someone is in charge does not always mean that they have a viable plan.

The term "strike while the iron is hot" comes from blacksmithing. It literally means to strike a piece of hot metal while it is still malleable enough to shape without breaking, and has come to mean seizing an opportunity before it passes us by. Oliver Cromwell (1599 – 1658), Lord Protector of the Commonwealth of England, Scotland, and Ireland expanded on this concept by saying, "Not only strike while the iron is hot but make it hot by striking." We know that there are few pivotal moments that can turn the tide of any contest. The instant that we know with certainty that victory is inevitable, we must strike lest we pass that opportunity to our everlasting regret.

For the Win: Only under extraordinary circumstances may you thwart the chain of command. Know that if you act and you're wrong, you will have thrown away everything for nothing.

You Lose: Act against the wishes of the sovereign and you are likely to lose your position if not your head.

24. Sun Tzu wrote:

"The general who advances without coveting fame and retreats without fearing disgrace, whose only thought is to protect his country and do good service for his sovereign, is the jewel of the kingdom."

Mahatma Gandhi (1869 – 1948) wrote, "The best way to find yourself is to lose yourself in the service of others." The greatest leaders set ego aside, doing what must be done simply because it must be done. If we keep our mission in front of us, adhering to the vital elements of our plan, we will do well.

The term "servant leadership" was coined by Robert Greenleaf (1904 – 1990) in 1970, referring to those who put others' needs first, empowering individuals and teams in ways that further the success of their enterprise. Servant leaders must be empathetic, persuasive, self-aware, and committed to the growth and development of those around them. In this fashion, we find the best in ourselves while bringing out the best in others. Unlike management, which requires hierarchical authority, anyone can be a leader. True leadership simply means setting an example that others wish to follow.

For the Win: Set your ego aside and do what must be done simply because it is imperative.

You Lose: Act for your own glory or grandeur over the good of the endeavor and you will obtain neither.

25. Sun Tzu wrote:

"Regard your soldiers as your children and they will follow you into the deepest valleys, look upon them as your own beloved sons and they will stand by you even unto death."

War is not a game like chess; people's lives are at stake. We must never throw "pieces" away haphazardly. If we treat our forces as we would our family, we do what must be done, yet in doing so build unbreakable affiliations. When we truly care about our people they will know; we soon discover that they will run through walls of fire for us. As Theodore Roosevelt (1858 – 1919), the 26th President of the United States of America, once wrote, "People don't care how much you know until they know how much you care."

One of the best ways to demonstrate to others that we care is to listen attentively to them. Active listening is a skill widely taught to business leaders, educators, military, and law enforcement officers because it is so effective. It helps with everything from getting along with our significant other to dealing with violent criminals. There is no downside to this skill, yet most people do not use it, in part because they spend more time thinking about how they will respond than they do paying attention to what the other person in a dialogue is actually saying. In most conversations, person A says something and halfway through the sentence person B has decided what is about to be said, has formulated a reply, and is mentally rehearsing his or her lines. From that point on, person B is not listening. Real communication has already stopped. To be leaders we must listen, truly listen.

For the Win: When you value your forces as if they are your own blood, they will act as such during battle.

You Lose: Treat your men like game pieces and you use and abuse haphazardly, and you throw away not only their lives but also your victory.

26. Sun Tzu wrote:

"If, however, you are indulgent but unable to make your authority felt, kindhearted but unable to enforce your commands, and incapable moreover of quelling disorder then your soldiers must be likened to spoilt children. They are useless for any practical purpose."

No matter how much we care about those around us, we must remain firm when it comes to matters of discipline. If we spoil our men and women it is because we are weak, and in this weakness, we make our forces less effective too. As parents must from time-to-time discipline their children to help them mature and grow, so too must leaders discipline their men and women for the best interests of their team.

A strong work ethic is important. Beyond the inherent appeal of making a contribution, we tend to value things we earn far more than anything we get for free. Look no farther than the difference between how most folks treat rental cars versus vehicles they own to know that this is true. Our work ethic begins early; if children learn the value of hard work, they build habits that stick with them for a lifetime. Hard work and discipline are the fundamental building blocks that breed success.

For the Win: Strong forces, individuals who exhibit both fortitude and proficiency, can only be forged in challenging environments. Embrace adversity to build yourself and your team up.

You Lose: Lavish praise and reward without holding your team accountable and thereby create a weaker team.

27. Sun Tzu wrote:

"If we know that our own men are in a condition to attack but are unaware that the enemy is not open to attack, we have gone only halfway towards victory."

We must have knowledge of not only our own condition but also the enemy's situation as well. Without solid information, we risk grave miscalculation. The more we know, the better prepared we will become.

Randeep Hooda (1976 –) is an Indian actor who wrote, "Knowledge is power. You can't begin a career, for that matter even a relationship, unless you know everything there is to know about it." This is the value of continuous study and self-improvement for both ourselves and our team. It arms us with the power to make informed decisions.

For the Win: Know your disposition and the enemy's nature. Armed with this knowledge you will find the path to victory.

You Lose: Failing to understand both sides of the equation, yours and your enemy's, is like jumping from a plane with half a parachute.

28. Sun Tzu wrote:

"If we know that the enemy is open to attack but are unaware that our own men are not in a condition to attack, we have gone only halfway towards victory."

We cannot seize an opening if we are not prepared to act. We may know the adversary's position and find weakness therein, but must also be certain that our men and women are capable of carrying out our plan before ordering a strike.

The Battle of Argonne Forest in 1918 was part of what became known as the Meuse-Argonne Offensive. While many of the US troops dispatched to Verdun France for the battle had no prior experience in war, General Joseph "Black Jack" Pershing (1860 – 1948) led over a million fresh troops into the fight which began on September 26th with a massive artillery bombardment, after which the Americans slowly but surely forced the German forces back. During the battle, which lasted until the Armistice on November 11, 1918, which marked the end of WWI, American forces advanced about 10 miles, clearing the forest of enemy troops at a cost of 26,277 lives and 90,723 wounded. The French suffered approximately 70,000 casualties, while the Germans lost 126,000 men.

For the Win: Be certain that your troops are capable of carrying out your plan before ordering them to attack.

You Lose: Treating your team like automatons, under the false assumption that they are ever ready for battle without the need for respite.

29. Sun Tzu wrote:

"If we know that the enemy is open to attack and also know that our men are in a condition to attack but are unaware that the nature of the ground makes fighting impracticable, we have still gone only halfway towards victory."

Terrain plays no small role in the battle. Even if our forces are prepared to strike, the enemy open to attack, we must know the lay of the land before we act. Watchfulness and observation are the cornerstones of any successful campaign.

Holly Hunter (1958 –) is an American actress and producer, who said, "Sometimes you have to marinate instead of making a quick decision. I appreciate my instincts, but my instincts can be dead wrong. Circumspection can give you time." This is excellent advice. No matter how honed our instincts, no matter how broad our experience, we cannot make sound decisions without any facts or data. Our intuition helps us know with certainty how much information is required, of course, but it is folly to forge ahead without knowing with some degree of certainty what we face.

For the Win: Conduct a complete pre-battle analysis, it is the first movement of your victory.

You Lose: You cannot make sound decisions without facts and data. Sloppy analysis leads to bad conclusions, uninformed choices, and suboptimal results.

30. Sun Tzu wrote:

"Hence the experienced soldier once in motion is never bewildered, once he has broken camp he is never at a loss."

In this fashion, we cement our victory before we even begin the battle. We have taken a thorough measure of our own forces, our adversary, and the terrain upon which we will fight, thus with sound strategy and adroit tactics we can make no mistakes. Confidence, borne of wisdom and experience, is our fiercest weapon.

In the Battle of Marathon, in 490 BC, King Darius the Great (550 – 486 BC) of Persia invaded Greece with 20,000 men. Despite being heavily outnumbered, the Athenians led by Miltiades, the Younger (550 – 489 BC) waited until the Persian cavalry was out on patrol to launch a fierce counterattack on Darius's infantry encampment. Miltiades tricked the Persians best men into striking at the center of his line, whereupon they were quickly surrounded by the inward-wheeling wings of his formation. After being enveloped, 6,400 Persians were slaughtered and the rest fled back to their ships, all at a loss of only 192 Greek soldiers. According to legend, an Athenian messenger was dispatched from Marathon to Athens, a distance of about 25 miles, where he announced the Persian defeat before dying of exhaustion, the basis for the modern marathon race.

For the Win: Confidence, borne of wisdom and experience, is your fiercest weapon. Use it well.

You Lose: Undermine your experience with slovenly analysis and wisdom dances tantalizingly out of your reach.

31. Sun Tzu wrote:

"Hence the saying, 'If you know the enemy and know yourself your victory will not stand in doubt, if you know heaven and know earth you may make your victory complete.'"

With a keen knowledge of the affairs of men, the seasons of Heaven, and the natural advantages of Earth, an astute student of the art of war cannot fail in achieving victory. American advice columnist Esther Pauline Lederer (1918 – 2002), better known as Ann Landers, wrote, "Know yourself. Don't accept your dog's admiration as conclusive evidence that you are wonderful."

With astute appraisal of our strengths and weaknesses, we may be ready for any challenge. Finding a job is one of them. If asked about our shortcomings during an interview, we must be honest while keeping the job description in mind when providing our answer. The interviewer really wants assurances that we have the requisite skills, experience, and attitude necessary to succeed on the job, and this is one way of probing for that information. To avoid disqualifying answers, we should focus on what we have done to overcome one of our legitimate weaknesses, using examples that demonstrate both self-awareness and personal growth.

For the Win: "If you know the enemy and know yourself your victory will not stand in doubt!" This is the most quoted verse in Art of War; it succinctly encapsulates all of Master Tzu's maxims.

You Lose: Nod knowingly and walk past this declaration without unpacking it. This is the act of a fool.

Chapter 11: The Nine Situations

In this chapter, we delve deeply into nine varieties of ground, dispersive, facile, contentious, open, intersecting, serious, difficult, hemmed-in, and desperate ground, identifying how we may gain advantage offensively and defensively in each. We emulate swiftness and ferocity of the shuai-jan snake; if an adversary strikes at our head we attack with the tail, if attacked at the tail, we counter with the head, and if struck at our middle we attack with both head and tail together. Thus, we maneuver our warriors and affiliations, jealously safeguarding our designs such that the enemy has no forewarning, no safe harbor, and no possibility of victory.

1. Sun Tzu wrote:

"The art of war recognizes nine varieties of ground: (1) dispersive ground, (2) facile ground, (3) contentious ground, (4) open ground, (5) ground of intersecting highways, (6) serious ground, (7) difficult ground, (8) hemmed-in ground, and (9) desperate ground."

There are nine different types of ground that students of the art of war must study, dispersive, facile, contentious, open, intersecting, serious, difficult, hemmed-in, and desperate ground. In this fashion we are prepared for any eventuality, marshaling our forces in the best manner to achieve victory.

The Siege of Orleans, which lasted from October 12, 1428, until May 8, 1429, was a turning point in the Hundred Years' War between France and England. After being surrounded and cut off for four months, a French attempt to break their blockaders' supply line failed at the Battle of the Herrings and the city's leaders were ready to surrender when Joan of Arc (1412 – 1431), the famous "Maid of Orleans," persuaded King Charles VII (1403 – 1461) to make another attempt to relieve the besieged city. French forces took diversionary action against a nearby fort to draw English forces away and deliver needed supplies. Shortly afterward Joan, following Divine inspiration, rallied the citizenry and helped the French retake the banks of the Loire River and defeat their invaders. This unexpected victory bolstered dispirited French morale, likely saving the country from centuries of English rule. Captured, tried for witchcraft and heresy, and burned at the stake in 1431, Joan of Arc's fame far outlived her death. She was eventually canonized by Pope Benedict XV in 1920.

For the Win: Diligently studying the nine types of ground allows you to marshal your forces in the best manner to achieve victory.

You Lose: It is madness to assume that the ground you face will purely be comprised of only one element, hence disregarding the others and proceeding with incomplete plans.

2. Sun Tzu wrote:

"When a chieftain is fighting in his own territory it is dispersive ground."

Fighting in our home territory places our friends and families in danger. While this may harden our hearts to prevail, many men and women may also seize the opportunity under cover of battle to disperse, escorting their loved ones to safety. Familiarity with the terrain affords an advantage for those who wish to move unseen, yet makes it easier for an army to disperse under pressure.

When the stakes are highest, so is the leadership challenge. For example, Admiral Yamamoto (1884 – 1943), commander of the Imperial Japanese Navy during WWII, once said, "You cannot invade mainland United States. There would be a rifle behind each blade of grass." Obviously, such a battle never took place, but we can imagine for a moment that it had, the advantage of a heavily armed population defending their home turf would likely have been insurmountable.

For the Win: When facing dispersed forces, you must control the hubs of communication and commerce, and thereby suppress their activities.

You Lose: If you allow native forces to disperse into their own land, your fight will be long and arduous.

3. Sun Tzu wrote:

"When he has penetrated into hostile territory but to no great distance it is facile ground."

Facile ground is named for its facility toward retreat. When an army first enters enemy territory and encounters resistance their thoughts may turn toward home, yet once they have battled deeper, this buttresses their collective will such that victory can be the only option. In this fashion the benefits of our longer range plan may supersede the shorter term view. It's a disciplined approach, akin to how professionals address opportunities in the stock market.

Day trading is the act of buying and selling financial instruments such as stocks or bonds within the same day, or even multiple times over the course of a day. In this fashion astute traders may take advantage of small price fluctuations to generate substantial income, but only if they diligently adhere to a well-thought-out strategy. Those who follow their whims, make emotional decisions, or become desperate to offset losses are not really trading, they're gambling, and in the long run, those who gamble in the stock market will always lose money.

For the Win: Early contact with enemy is perilous. Create contingency plans within your long term strategy that account for this factor.

You Lose: There will come a time when you must decide whether to pause or proceed. Failing to plan ahead for the eventuality is a weakness that can be exploited in the heat of battle.

4. Sun Tzu wrote:

"Ground the possession of which imports great advantage to either side is contentious ground."

The contentious ground is territory that either side may contend for. With a sound strategy and sufficient will we may overcome, but must wrest this ground away from our adversaries. As it furthers our overall aim, we devise plans to conquer contentious ground.

The Battle of Tours, which took place on October 10, 732, pitted an invading Islamic army, led by Moorish General Abd al-Rahman (731 – 788) against the Frankish forces of Charles Martel (686 – 741). After heavy fighting, the Franks killed al-Rahman, defeated the Moors, and thereby halted their advance into Western Europe. This victory at Tours had immense historical significance, assuring the ruling dynasty of Martel's family, the Carolingians. His son Pepin the Short (714 – 768) became the first Carolingian king of the Franks, and his grandson Charlemagne (742 – 814) was crowned emperor of what became the Holy Roman Empire. Many scholars also believe that if Abd al-Rahman had prevailed, Islam would have become the dominant religion in Europe. This is the import of contentious ground.

For the Win: If it furthers your overall strategy, devise plans to conquer contentious ground. If the cost appears too high, find another way around.

You Lose: Rushing into contentions ground without proper evaluation.

5. Sun Tzu wrote:

"Ground on which each side has liberty of movement is open ground."

Open ground facilitates easy communication, allowing for rapid movement of troops and equipment. Oftentimes this implies an existing network of roads. Both we and our adversaries may freely take advantage of this territory to further our aims.

The ancient Romans built 50,000 miles of hard-surfaced highway to facilitate conquest and administration of subjugated territories, creating a transportation network that extended throughout Italy, Spain, Britain, France, and northern Africa. The first of these roads was called the Appian Way, built by Appius Claudius Caecus (340 – 280 BC) in the year 312 BC using concrete made from volcanic ash and lime. While fashioned from a variety of local materials, these long straight highways were all notable for their solid foundations and chambered surfaces that assured drainage. A testament to their engineering prowess, fragments of that ancient road system still survives today.

For the Win: Open movement without impediment is an opportunity you should never squander. Open ground is a resource not to be enjoyed with leisure, but rather to be used with haste in the furtherance of your plan.

You Lose: Dally in open ground and forget your ultimate goal.

6. Sun Tzu wrote:

"Ground which forms the key to three contiguous states, so that he who occupies it first has most of the empire at his command, is a ground of intersecting highways."

If we create a dominant position at the crossroads of intersecting highways, we may often compel weaker states to become allies in our endeavors. Control of infrastructure creates a dominant position over the surrounding area.

The Mongol invasions of Goryeo (what is now modern-day Korea), between 1231 and 1270, included some 7 major campaigns that ultimately resulted in Korea becoming a vassal state of the Yuan dynasty for about 80 years. After the bloodshed was over, a series of marriages cemented this relationship. For instance, during the reign of Kublai Khan (1215 – 1294), the Korean King Chungnyeol (1236 – 1308) married one of the Khan's daughters to cement an alliance, and a Goryeon princess name Gi (1315 – 1370) married Ukhaantu Khan (1333 – 1368), taking the title of empress. Her son Biligtü Khan (1340 – 1378) grew up to became emperor of the Northern Yuan dynasty in Mongolia.

For the Win: Control commerce and you can compel alliances and avert rebellion. When people see their livelihood at risk they hesitate.

You Lose: Let the flow of commence continue unimpeded and squander control.

7. Sun Tzu wrote:

"When an army has penetrated into the heart of a hostile country leaving a number of fortified cities in its rear it is serious ground."

A deep invasion is a significant endeavor. Whenever an occupying force builds in foreign territory with the intent is to stay, it demonstrates is a serious commitment. Much like purchasing a home, the initial investment is steep and there are ongoing expenses necessary to stay, all the more so if an adversary is trying to push us back out.

Renting is transitory, yet purchasing a home is a significant commitment, typically the largest purchase any individual or couple will make in their lifetime. Before taking the plunge and shopping for a loan, it is vital to realize that in most instances the decision to buy is more of a lifestyle choice than an investment. Home prices may go up, but could just as easily go down, multi-tenant properties are a better investment than single family units, and real estate is an illiquid investment. As owners, we are responsible for utilities, repairs, taxes, insurance, and a host of other costs that renters do not directly experience. If a home is right for us however, we must be picky about which one to buy. Detailed home inspections can help uncover costly issues such as termites, mold, asbestos, leakage, or wiring problems that will make us regret our purchase later on.

For the Win: Build a strong, enduring supply line and robust infrastructure and your intention of occupying conquered lands remains clear.

You Lose: Failing to create lasting outposts and supply lines through conquered territory allows the populace to entertain dreams of revolt.

8. Sun Tzu wrote:

"Mountain forests, rugged steeps, marshes and fens, all country that is hard to traverse, this is difficult ground."

Any terrain that slows our movement becomes the difficult ground. This can span everything from a minor inconvenience to a serious impediment to an outright trap, and merits consideration before moving our forces into such areas. The difficult ground is, by definition, demanding.

The path to success in almost any endeavor is arduous. It takes creativity, enthusiasm, and hard work, yet with a support network, we can lighten the burden. Even world-class professional athletes turn to coaches to tune up their game, likewise, we can find mentors, advisors, and teachers who are willing to share their expertise and help. There's always someone who knows more about our enterprise than we do. Wise leaders know when to ask for help.

For the Win: Difficult ground must be respected, find experts to guide you through.

You Lose: Be too stubborn or prideful to ask for help.

9. Sun Tzu wrote:

> *"Ground which is reached through narrow gorges and from which we can only retire by tortuous paths so that a small number of the enemy would suffice to crush a large body of our men, this is hemmed-in ground."*

Without the ability to move and act freely, our options are markedly reduced. Hemmed-in ground is a quagmire, one that should never be approached willingly, save that we are certain it is unoccupied by our adversaries. Caught in this trap, we must understand that it will take our wits and will to survive. In fact, our willpower is instrumental for a great many things in life.

Rollo Reece May (1909 – 1994) was an American psychologist and author who wrote, "Freedom always deals with 'the possible;' this gives freedom its great flexibility, its fascination, and its dangers." In 1940, May contracted tuberculosis and his doctors gave him a 50% chance of surviving. At that moment he discovered that recovery was as much a mental challenge as it was a physical one. Recognizing that his will to survive would do more than medical care to determine whether or not he lived solidified his existentialist views and also set an example for others to follow. In May's view, it is our awareness of our own mortality is what makes vitality and passion possible.

For the Win: Any situation that restricts your mobility shortens your list of tactical options. This is a risk best avoided.

You Lose: Willingly restricting your own mobility creates an unnecessary burden.

10. Sun Tzu wrote:

"Ground on which we can only be saved from destruction by fighting without delay is desperate ground."

Desperate ground is much like hemmed-in ground, save that escape is no longer possible. Like hiding in a burning building, the environment itself forces our choices as much as any action performed by the enemy. We are forced to fight our way free.

There is an inverse relationship between stress and decision-making. The more stressful the situation, the poorer our decision will likely be. British psychologist William Edmund Hick (1912 – 1974) conducted reaction-time research to develop a model he called Hick's Law, which states that response times increase in proportion to the logarithm of the number of potential stimulus-response alternatives. That is a fancy way of saying that the more choices we have to make, the longer it takes to make a decision. This means that to avoid freezing in a fight, we must limit our choices. Under stress, in battle, we must choose our favorite technique and keep on using it until it stops working, then move to our plan B.

For the Win: Fighters only know how to fight. Warriors, however, not only know how to fight, but also when. Be a warrior not a fighter.

You Lose: If you find yourself in a situation where your only option is to fight, you have made your enemy's assessment all too easy.

11. Sun Tzu wrote:

"On dispersive ground, therefore, fight not. On facile ground, halt not. On contentious ground, attack not."

A wise student of the art of war will use his or her energies to occupying advantageous positions rather than aspiring for some way to counter an adversary's lead. No sense in fighting on dispersive ground, halting on the facile ground, or attacking on contentious ground. The terrain we face determines how and when we fight.

Warren Buffett (1930 –), CEO of Berkshire Hathaway, is one of the most successful investors in recent memory. Nicknamed the "Oracle of Omaha" by the media, Buffet once told reporters, "Risk comes from not knowing what you're doing." Following his own advice, he eschewed the tech bubble (which lasted from ~ 1994 to 2000), passing on short-term gains while assuring longer term accomplishment, and it paid off handsomely. One share of Berkshire stock purchased in January of 1994 at $16,350 was worth $339,155 in January of 2020, a whopping 2,074% increase. Compare this to the Dow Jones Industrial Average (which tracks the 30 largest publicly-traded companies) growth of 553% during that same period of time. Any investment that returns nearly four times the Dow's returns is impressive. When we know what we're doing, as Buffet certainly does, the risk of our endeavor is all but eliminated.

For the Win: Let the terrain you face determine how and when to fight.

You Lose: Seek to counter your enemy's lead rather than forcing the enemy to bring the fight to you.

12. Sun Tzu wrote:

"On open ground do not try to block the enemy's way. On the ground of intersecting highways join hands with your allies."

It is costly and impulsive to attempt to block an enemy's forces on open ground, a waste of men and resources. When the environment allows free, unlimited movement, we cannot easily impede an opponent, though we may draw our forces closer together to assure that the adversary is unable to encircle and cut off some portion of our troop. On the ground of intersecting highways, however, we may be able to join forces with allies to entrap our adversaries.

During the Second Punic War, at the Battle of Ilipa in Spain, Publius Cornelius Scipio Africanus (236 – 183 BC) locked horns with the Carthaginians under command of Hannibal Barca's brother Mago Barca (243 – 203 BC). Although Mago's forces outnumbered Africanus's by some 10,000 men, both armies were comprised of both their own professional forces as well as hired mercenary contingents, and both initially formed their line of battle with the indigenous forces in the middle and mercenaries holding their flanks. This resulted in a stalemate until Africanus switched things around, moving his mercenaries to the middle of his line while the rest of the Roman forces harassed and eventually broke through the opposing mercenaries on the Carthaginian flanks, rolling up and defeating their army. This victory marked an important turning point in Rome's war with Carthage.

For the Win: Call on your friends, build alliances, and work together to entrap and defeat your enemies.

You Lose: Waste resources attempting to impede an enemy on open ground.

13. Sun Tzu wrote:

> *"On serious ground gather in plunder. In difficult ground keep steadily on the march."*

If we intend to stay deep in enemy territory, we must use every available resource to secure our lines of supply. This may include appropriating food and provisions, but care must be taken to not take unjust actions that will disaffect the local population and spark insurgency. When operating in unforgiving, difficult locations we are best off passing quickly and moving on to better locales.

The Townshend Acts, passed by the British Parliament in 1767, imposed duties on colonial imports to the Americas. These unjust fees were met with so much protest that they were repealed three years later, all except for the duty on tea which helped prop up the East India Company. Decrying "Taxation without Representation," a group of 60 American patriots disguised as Mohawk Indians dumped 342 chests of tea into Boston Harbor in protest, an incident that became known as the "Boston Tea Party" on December 16, 1773. In retaliation, the British Parliament passed the series of punitive measures known in the Americas as the "Intolerable Acts," closing the port of Boston to trade pending repayment for the destroyed tea. This punishment backfired, uniting the 13 colonies against British rule, which eventually led to the American Revolutionary War. This insurgency lasted from 1775 to 1783 when the American colonies gained their independence from Great Britain.

For the Win: Appropriate what you need, but do so in a fair and just manner.

You Lose: Take unreasonable actions that spark revolution.

14. Sun Tzu wrote:

"On hemmed-in ground resort to stratagem. On desperate ground fight."

When cornered we have two options, move or fight. Should we find ourselves on the hemmed-in ground, we must trick our adversaries in order to escape. When boxed in we must use all our knowledge, skill, and craftiness to discern a way out. If ultimately, we cannot escape, we must fight so fiercely that the enemy is relieved to let us go.

When faced with danger, our sympathetic nervous system releases an adrenaline-laced hormone cocktail that kicks us into the fight, flight, or freeze mode. If our subconscious believes we have some chance to win, it will prime us for battle. Conversely, if we believe that our adversaries are too powerful to overcome, our natural impulse is to escape. If, in the first few milliseconds of an encounter our subconscious believes that we can neither defeat nor escape the danger we face, we freeze. This reaction may have been evolutionarily useful since predatory animals are often attracted to movement, yet when stymied by fear we're in no position to defend ourselves from danger. Many psychologists postulate that the foremost predictor of those developing PTSD after a traumatic experience is dissociation caused by freezing inappropriately. Thankfully, we can learn to break this freeze through realistic and comprehensive combat training.

For the Win: War is always a dance of deception, but when pinned down your ploys become increasingly desperate. Aim to fight so fiercely that the enemy will be relieved to let you escape to safety.

You Lose: Freeze when cornered rather than moving or fighting.

15. Sun Tzu wrote:

"Those who were called skillful leaders of old knew how to drive a wedge between the enemy's front and rear, to prevent cooperation between his large and small divisions, to hinder the good troops from rescuing the bad, the officers from rallying their men."

When we are able to stymie an adversary's communications, we undermine his or her ability to act. Enemy commanders, being unable to contact their men, are confounded, while those who are used to following orders upon hearing nothing do not know what to do. In this fashion, we may have our way with our enemy.

British actress Emma Thompson (1959 –) once said, "Any problem, big or small, within a family, always seems to start with bad communication. Someone isn't listening." This is true not just for families, but for any human interaction. Every enterprise must effectively transmit strategy and direction up and down its ranks, keeping everyone on the same page in order to succeed. Strong communication is based on active listening.

For the Win: Wedges driven into the enemy's forces can be physical or psychological, both must be used before, during, and after the battle. In this fashion you will prevail.

You Lose: When you fail to heed the simple yet profound statement, "Divide and conquer."

16, 17. Sun Tzu wrote:

"When the enemy's men were united, they managed to keep them in disorder. When it was to their advantage, they made a forward move, when otherwise they stopped still."

Respect from our adversary is the highest praise. When they acknowledge how we dislocated their forces, pushed forward strategically, and stood strong when there was no advantage to gain by attacking, they learn to fear what we are capable of doing. This fear breeds caution, consternation, and undue consideration. In this fashion, our battle is already won before we strike the first blow. Reflecting on the American Civil War, President Ulysses S. Grant (1869 – 1877) wrote, "The art of war is simple enough. Find out where your enemy is. Get at him as soon as you can. Strike at him as hard as you can and as often as you can, and keep moving on."

Faced with an overwhelming disadvantage in manpower, industrial capabilities, and military leadership during the Civil War, the Confederacy also knew that their legitimacy was not recognized by foreign diplomats. This was, no doubt, disconcerting. After a series of key losses at Vicksburg, Gettysburg, Chickamauga, Chattanooga, and Atlanta, more and more Southerners lost faith in their cause. As Northern generals like Grant, Farragut, and Sherman earned rent-free space in the Confederate leader's heads with their battlefield prowess, the war was for all intents and purposes over. And, with Abraham Lincoln's (1809 – 1865) reelection, the Confederacy's defeat was assured.

For the Win: When your enemy respects and fears your prowess you can win without fighting.

You Lose: When your enemy holds you in contempt you lose on multiple levels.

18. Sun Tzu wrote:

> *"If asked how to cope with a great host of the enemy in orderly array and on the point of marching to the attack I should say, 'Begin by seizing something which your opponent holds dear then he will be amenable to your will.'"*

It is challenging to defeat a large, well-organized foe. These adversaries wish to capture our favorable positions and ravage our cultivated lands, all while safeguarding their own communications. We must disrupt their designs by taking something they value greatly. In seizing this initiative, we place our enemy on the defensive, thwarting his or her plans.

The one thing any parent holds most dear is their child. In 1981, 6-year-old Adam Walsh (1974 – 1981) was kidnapped from a Sears store in Hollywood, Florida. Sadly, the perpetrator wasn't after a ransom and the boy's decapitated body was found 2 weeks later. Nevertheless, the case received massive publicity including a made-for-TV movie in 1983, and Adam's father John Walsh (1945 –) was able to leverage this exposure to help other victims of violent crimes, creating the television show America's Most Wanted. Although the prime suspect, convicted serial-killer Ottis Toole (1947 – 1996), was never tried for this particular crime, Walsh's show led to the capture of over 1,200 criminals. In this fashion, something good came from the kidnapping.

For the Win: By quickly taking whatever is most valued by your enemy, you create dismay and despondency in his forces.

You Lose: When you allow the enemy to retain hope for victory.

19. Sun Tzu wrote:

"Rapidity is the essence of war. Take advantage of the enemy's unreadiness, make your way by unexpected routes, and attack unguarded spots."

As the adage states, "Speed kills." Whoever marshals their forces, identifies weakness, and strikes before his or her enemy is prepared will prevail. We may either deploy faster or more silently than the enemy or, having discovered a chink in the adversary's armor, deliver our fatal blow. The Six-Day War between Israel and its Arab neighbors in 1967 is a good example of this principle.

In May of 1967, Egyptian President Nasser (1918 – 1970) mobilized his forces in the Sinai, closed the Gulf of Aqaba to Israeli shipping, and signed a mutual defense pact with Jordan. Shortly afterward, Syria also joined this alliance. Fearing a looming confrontation with hostile neighbors that surrounded them, Israeli Prime Minister Menachem Begin (1913 – 1992) launched a preemptive air assault on June 5th. Catching Egypt's air force completely by surprise, the Israelis destroyed 90% of their enemy's planes while they were still parked on the tarmac. A similar strike incapacitated the Syrian air force. With the only operational air force in the theatre, it took Israel only three days to crush Egypt's ground forces, capture the Gaza Strip, and take over the Sinai Peninsula all the way up to the east bank of the Suez Canal. By June 7th, they had also driven Jordanian forces out of East Jerusalem and most of the West Bank. During the six days of fighting Egypt suffered over 11,000 casualties, Jordan 6,000, and Syria 1,000, with 700 losses on the Israeli side.

For the Win: As the fictional Cobra Kai motto states, "Strike first! Strike hard! No mercy!" Attack your enemy with surprise, aiming for a weak point, and thereby devastate his or her defense.

You Lose: Moving ponderously brings unwelcome transparency to your plan, which gives your enemy both time and perspicacity to prepare. That rarely ends well.

20. Sun Tzu wrote:

"The following are the principles to be observed by an invading force: The further you penetrate into a country the greater will be the solidarity of your troops and thus the defenders will not prevail against you."

The deeper we penetrate into enemy territory, the greater the danger that surrounds us. With no safe avenue of retreat, our men and women will bolster their spirit, draw together in unanimity, and perform their assigned duties without fail. Advancing in camaraderie, with esprit de corps, we become an unbeatable force.

When we dive down deep into the concept of esprit de corps, it is much like looking at an atom. If all the parts are in place—say one hydrogen atom and two oxygen atoms (H2O)—then we get the desired output, which in this example is water. Change the equation to one hydrogen atom and one oxygen atom and the molecule becomes unbalanced. It will seek stability by acquiring another oxygen atom. Similarly, people who lack one of the three essential elements of esprit de corps, will, deference, or self-discipline, are unstable. It is difficult to find balance when one of the three legs on this metaphorical stool is missing. While self-directed people will find this missing element on their own, others need to have it shown to them. The ability to identify the gap, explain the need, and show others the way can make us a great leader.

For the Win: The farther you venture into the unknown, the more your team will bond and bind themselves together.

You Lose: If you fail to recognize and reinforce this cohesiveness.

21. Sun Tzu wrote:

"Make forays in fertile country in order to supply your army with food."

Napoleon Bonaparte (1769 – 1821) wrote, "An army marches on its stomach." Without adequate food and supplies, any war effort must grind to a halt. Consequently, whenever we find ourselves deep in enemy territory stretched beyond our supply lines, we must send foragers to acquire provisions.

The amount of food authorized by an army to feed one soldier for one day is called a "ration." The quality and quantity of these rations affect both troop capabilities and morale. During the American Civil War (1861 – 1865), for example, the Union Army had two types of rations, marching rations and camp rations. Marching rations were relatively lightweight, consisting of 16 ounces of hard bread (known as "hardtack"), 12 ounces of salt pork (or 20 ounces of fresh meat when available), sugar, coffee, and salt. When stores ran low, soldiers resorted to hunting, raiding, and foraging for replenishments. When encamped, officers often received an allowance to purchase supplies and hire cooks rather than receiving camp rations, which were distributed to the rest of the men. Camp rations substituted soft bread, flour, or cornmeal for the hardtack, and included extras such as dried beans or peas, rice, vinegar, molasses, soap, and candles.

For the Win: When you discover a need for resources tangential to your strategic path, make this diversion nothing more than a raid. Grab what you need, and get back on track toward your ultimate goal.

You Lose: When you impulsively follow resources like a child offered candy by a stranger.

22. Sun Tzu wrote:

"Carefully study the well-being of your men and do not overtax them. Concentrate your energy and hoard your strength. Keep your army continually on the move and devise unfathomable plans."

To preserve their fighting spirit, we must see to the needs of our men and women. When well-fed, clothed, bathed and trained, our troops may perform at their best. When forced to arduous marches in field conditions, on the other hand, exhaustion sets in and morale will soon suffer. The capabilities and reputation of our forces play an important role in any war as demonstrated by the Battle of Maling in 342 BC. During the Chinese "Warring States" Period, the independent nation of Qi was invaded by the neighboring Wei army. Wei general P'ang Chuan (? – 342 BC) had little regard for his Qi foe, as their forces had developed a reputation for being poorly trained, ineffective, and insubordinate.

Qi general Sun Pin (? – 316BC), on the other hand, had a trick up his sleeve… In order to make it appear that his forces were beset by desertions, he ordered his men to reduce the number of campfires they lit at night during their advance, cutting them in half the first night, and then in half again on the second. This ploy, which became known as the "Tactic of the Missing Stoves," proved genius. Unknowingly facing a full army of some 100,000 men rather than the 25,000 or so expected, the Qi forces were overwhelmed and defeated at Maling, leading Chuan to commit suicide rather than the face the shame of his defeat.

For the Win: Treat your forces well and they will fight well. It's that simple.

You Lose: Showing little consideration for the needs of your men.

23. Sun Tzu wrote:

"Throw your soldiers into positions whence there is no escape and they will prefer death to flight. If they will face death there is nothing they may not achieve. Officers and men alike will put forth their uttermost strength."

In Sun Tzu's time, the bulk of most armies were conscripts rather than professional soldiers. When faced with near certain death, many of these men who otherwise may have deserted preferred to perish with honor rather than flee in disgrace. In this condition, without the burden of self-preservation, we become capable of virtually anything. This is when men and women, focused on their mission, united in their fellowship, can pass beyond any preconceived limits perform amazing feats of heroism and gallantry.

The Hagakure, written by Tsunetomo Yamamoto (1659 – 1719) in the early 1700s, was about the author's meditations on living and dying with honor at a time when samurai faced the dilemma of maintaining a warrior class during the absence of war. In it, we read, "The way of the samurai is found in death…This is the substance of the way of the samurai. If by setting one's heart right every morning and evening, one is able to live as though his body were already dead, he gains freedom in the way. His whole life will be without blame and he will succeed in his calling."

For the Win: If the only way out is forward, your men will move forward. Spur them in that direction.

You Lose: By giving options, allowing too many choices, you create second-guessing and poor commitment to your cause.

24. Sun Tzu wrote:

"Soldiers when in desperate straits lose their sense of fear. If there is no place of refuge, they will stand firm. If they are in hostile country, they will show a stubborn front. If there is no help for it, they will fight hard."

Placed in a no-win situation, men and women lose their sense of fear, fighting valiantly rather than meekly surrendering to the inevitable. Sometimes this valor can overcome any opposition, sometimes not, yet we never strive harder than when we believe we are making our last stand. One of the most famous last stands in American history was the Battle of the Little Big Horn, which took place on June 25, 1876. The US Army's 7th Cavalry under the command of General George Armstrong Custer's (1839 – 1876) was poorly trained and equipped, armed with single-shot carbines and side arms. They found themselves outmatched and ultimately defeated by the Native Sioux and Cheyenne horde that was armed with over a hundred Winchester, Henry, and Spencer repeating rifles as well as with pistols, bows, and arrows.

Many of the dead soldiers found in archeological excavations were not even in military uniform, jiving with Native accounts their enemy's dread and disorganization during the battle. As it became clear he was about to lose, Custer ordered his men to kill their horses and create a defensive breastwork some 30-feet in diameter, in which his last 40 men succumbed at the end of the fighting. After Custer fell, his remaining soldiers panicked, some attempting to flee toward a nearby cottonwood stand while others turned their guns upon themselves. Afterward, the Natives, believing that the souls of disfigured bodies were doomed to walk the earth forever, scalped and dismembered their enemy's corpses.

For the Win: The perspective of "nothing to lose" is one of a total commitment. Respect this on both sides of the battle line.

You Lose: Suffer unnecessary losses when you battle an enemy with nothing to lose.

25. Sun Tzu wrote:

"Thus, without waiting to be marshaled the soldiers will be constantly on the qui vive *(alert, ready for a duel), without waiting to be asked they will do your will, without restrictions they will be faithful, without giving orders they can be trusted."*

On desperate ground, our men and women are constantly under threat, ready for action, and eager to strike in order to improve their position. Thus fortified, we need not fear delay nor disobedience, but rather can count on our plan being implemented instantaneously and without fail. An example of this principle was the Battle of Rorke's Drift took place on January 22, 1879.

A British mission station at Rorke's Drift in Natal Province, South Africa, was besieged by an army of 4,500 Zulu warriors led by Prince kaMapande (1839 – 1886). The 139 British infantry defenders were led by Lieutenants John Chard (1847 – 1897) and Gonville Bromhead (1845 – 1891). As the battle progressed, the Zulu came ever closer to overrunning the garrison, with wave after wave assaulting the British forces throughout the night. As the soldier's ammunition was exhausted, the defensive perimeter shrank with each attack, eventually devolving into fierce hand-to-hand fighting. Suddenly, at 2:00 AM, the forays stopped. The Zulu, believing they could not prevail, had had enough. By daylight, the Zulu army had vanished, leaving behind their dead. Inexplicably, only 17 British soldiers died during the fighting compared to 350 deaths suffered by the Zulu.

For the Win: Build clarity of vision and unity of purpose, which allows your men to act correctly without detailed direction. In this fashion your team is empowered to prevail.

You Lose: When your forces have no clarity of purpose they will scatter their efforts under stress, requiring moment-by-moment direction to remain on track. This wasteful condition cannot last.

26. Sun Tzu wrote:

"Prohibit the taking of omens and do away with superstitious doubts. Then, until death itself comes, no calamity need be feared."

Strategy, not superstition, builds our battle plans. We must never let our men or women reconnoiter their fortunes with false divinations. Such superstitions create counterfeit trust and timorousness. Our men and women must trust instead in our leadership, for when all doubts and delusions are discarded our forces will never falter in their resolution.

On the roof of the Basilique Notre-Dame de Brebieres in the town of Albert during WWI there was a golden statue of the Madonna holding her child up to the sky. Visible from the front lines in Somme a few miles away, it became an enemy artillery target. Knocked askew by a shell in 1915, superstition grew amongst the French ranks that they would be defeated and Germany would win the war if the statue fell. In 1918, when the Germans recaptured Albert during their spring offensive, the British discovered that the tower was being used as an observation point and bombed it, knocking the statue to the ground. Nonetheless, the incident did not coincide with a German win. In fact, Albert was retaken four months later by the British, with the armistice that ended the war negotiated three months after that. Despite French superstition, the Madonna statue had nothing whatsoever to do with the outcome of the war.

For the Win: Root out superstitions and misconceptions early, addressing talisman thinking before it can take root and undermine morale.

You Lose: Failing to address doubts and delusions.

27. Sun Tzu wrote:

"If our soldiers are not overburdened with money it is not because they have a distaste for riches, if their lives are not unduly long it is not because they are disinclined to longevity."

Everybody desires long life, abundant health, and plentiful riches. We would never discard our valuables, undermine our health, or throw away our lives by choice, but rather only in situations where we perceive no other option. Soldiers being but human, temptations to shirk responsibility in search of wealth or safety should not be sent their way. A soldier's first duty is preparation for war, yet embraced as a higher calling, becoming a warrior is a truly noble profession. There are unique bonds of camaraderie that only combat veterans share. And, most would agree that they would much rather put themselves in danger than leave that duty for others. Pat Tillman was an excellent example of this perspective.

Pat Tillman (1976 – 2004) was an American football player who left a lucrative National Football League career with the Arizona Cardinals to enlist in the Army after the terrorist attacks of September 11, 2001. He trained to become an Army Ranger, where he was assigned to the 2nd battalion of the 75th Ranger Regiment and deployed to Iraq in 2003. In 2004 his unit was sent to Afghanistan to conduct operations against the Taliban and al-Qaeda. Caught in an ambush near the village of Manah, in the Khost province, he was inadvertently killed by friendly-fire due to a communication breakdown amongst segments of his platoon. Awarded a Purple Heart and Silver Star by the military, Tillman's numbers at Arizona State University and with the Arizona Cardinals were both retired in his honor. He was also inducted into the College Football Hall of Fame in 2010. That same year the NFL and the Pat Tillman Foundation joined forces to create an NFL-Tillman Scholarship which honors individuals who "exemplify Pat Tillman's enduring legacy of service."

For the Win: Balance your men's desires with their duty.

You Lose: Ignoring your men's needs is a path to failure. Disregarding their desires dulls your team's commitment.

28. Sun Tzu wrote:

"On the day they are ordered out to battle your soldiers may weep, those sitting up bedewing their garments and those lying down letting the tears run down their cheeks. But let them once be brought to bay and they will display the courage of a Chu or a Kuei (famous Chinese heroes)."

Though soldiers may weep, it is not because they are afraid, but rather because they know that they have been tasked to give up their lives in service to their general and for their country. Once resolved to this fate, however, they may embrace their destiny with courage and fortitude much like the American revolutionaries who in declaring independence from Britain pledged "their lives, their fortunes, and their sacred honor" to their cause.

While little is known of these men today, the fearlessness of Chu and Kuei were legendary in Sun Tzu's day. In 515 BC, Chuan Chu was reportedly hired to assassinate King Wang Liao. Knowing that it was likely a suicide mission he nonetheless set to his task. Using a dagger secreted in the belly of a fish that was served at a state dinner, he succeeded in murdering the monarch but was immediately hacked to pieces by the king's bodyguards afterward. Ts'ao Kuei, on the losing side of a war, was about to conclude a peace treaty in 681 BC when he suddenly seized his adversary, Duke Huan Kung, held a dagger against his throat, and demanded a better deal. Kung, fearing for his life, consented whereupon Kuei flung away his blade and resumed his place amid the assemblage. With this bold stroke, Kuei regained what his side had lost in three protracted battles.

For the Win: Know that your forces are human. They understand what is at risk in your endeavor. True leaders understand and address their men's concerns and anxieties.

You Lose: When you treat your men as if they are cogs in a machine, each resource easily replaceable with another. People are individuals with hopes, dreams, and aspirations, not nameless, faceless headcount.

29. Sun Tzu wrote:

"The skillful tactician may be likened to the shuai-jan. *Now the* shuai-jan *is a snake that is found in the Ch'Ung Mountains. Strike at its head and you will be attacked by its tail, strike at its tail and you will be attacked by its head, strike at its middle and you will be attacked by head and tail both."*

Shuai-jan aptly translates into English as "suddenly" or "rapidly," indicative of swift military maneuvers we use to keep our enemies off their guard and on the defensive. When an adversary probes at our weakness and it becomes our strength. He seeks to circumvent our will only to find himself upset by our plan. In this fashion, our knowledge of the art of war makes us unassailable.

Much like the shuai-jan, the Mongol hordes under Genghis Khan (1162 – 1227) were famous for their agility. As a nomadic people from the Steppes, they were born and bred to horseback, each soldier owning multiple swift, surefooted ponies. The Mongol's mobility helped them prevail over the larger, less nimble foe. Opening engagements often began with a storm of arrows from the Mongol light cavalry, during which they were able to gauge their enemy's maneuvers, before striking a final blow with heavy cavalry. A staple of the Mongol tactics was called the "mangudai," where a select group of warriors would harass the enemy lines, baiting the other side to break ranks and charge after them. The Mongols would pretend to flee, all while continuing to fire arrows by turning backward in their saddles, until pursuing forces became strung out and disorganized. At this moment the entire horde would surround and slaughter their foe.

For the Win: Stay flexible and as a good boxer, being able to strike from any position.

You Lose: Strength should never be confused with rigidity. When you are inflexible you become weak.

30. Sun Tzu wrote:

"Asked if an army can be made to imitate the shuai-jan *I should answer, 'Yes.' For the men of Wu and the men of Yueh are enemies, yet if they are crossing a river in the same boat and are caught by a storm, they will come to each other's assistance just as the left hand helps the right."*

If two enemies may become inclined to join forces during a time of common peril, how much closer may two portions of the same army become? In a well-organized, disciplined military, all aspects of the troop fight with the unity of spirit, working in close cooperation such that they become one body with the general as its head. In this fashion, we are as swift and decisive as the dreaded shuai-jan.

Masters of communicating swiftly across great distances, the Mongol hordes under Genghis Khan (1162 – 1227) used many-pronged invasions to engage their adversaries, moving independently in small groups for stealth and speed, yet uniting into larger formations in battle. Often passing enemy strongholds, they would raid smaller villages and townships, meticulously conquering their adversaries' territory bit by bit. A good example was the Khwarizm campaign, in 1220, when the Mongols took the surrounding smaller cities and fortresses before capturing the principal city of Samarqand, in modern Uzbekistan. This tactic not only cut off the principal city from seeking aid from its neighbors but also sent a steady flow of refugees fleeing to Samarqand, straining the resources and damaging the morale of that final stronghold. By the time the horde attacked Samarqand, it easily fell before their might.

For the Win: Leverage the full breadth and depth of your team, irrespective of role or troop configuration, to solve problems and further your cause.

You Lose: Create a rigid hierarchy and organizational structure that restricts your team's ability to share unique and creative solutions with each other. In this fashion synergy passes you by.

31, 32. Sun Tzu wrote:

> *"Hence it is not enough to put one's trust in the tethering of horses and the burying of chariot wheels in the ground. The principle on which to manage an army is to set up one standard of courage which all must reach."*

The ideal army is far stronger than the sum of its parts, operating as one organic whole. When we set a high standard to which everyone aspires, we bolster each and every individual on the team. No one will consider failing their brother or sister, such that even the lesser troops are buoyed in courage and endurance. In this fashion heroism becomes contagious. Consider Audie Murphy (1924 – 1971) by way of example. In 1942, 17-year-old Murphy forged his birth certificate and tried to enlist in the military at the outset of WWII. He was turned down by both the United States Marines and Paratroopers for being too small, underweight, and slightly built. When the Army finally accepted him, they tried to make him serve as a cook… until he reached the battlefield.

Beginning his service as Private, Murphy's bravery and valor helped him quickly rise to the enlisted rank of Staff Sergeant before being given a battlefield commission as a 2nd Lieutenant. In two years of service at the European front, Murphy killed 240 German soldiers in documented firefights. He fought in 9 major campaigns across the European Theater and survived the war, earning the Medal of Honor, the Distinguished Service Cross, the Legion of Merit, the Silver Star (twice), and the Bronze Medal (twice). He was also awarded the Purple Heart three times for combat injuries plus a variety of other honors totaling some thirty-two medals. This made him the most decorated combat veteran of WWII. Not bad for a little skinny guy, huh?

For the Win: The strong and the brave must be put in positions where they can demonstrate with their exploits what lesser men must emulate.

You Lose: When you fail to address any weakness of spirit in your team. It is not enough to assume it will pass.

33. Sun Tzu wrote:

> *"How to make the best of both strong and weak; that is a question involving the proper use of ground."*

Our goal as leaders is to eliminate the differences between strong and weak individuals in our command, assuring that everyone is given a role in which they can best succeed. By knowing our men and women, and leveraging their strengths, we develop an unassailable force.

The Myers-Briggs Type Indicator (or MBTI®) is a widely used personality assessment that has proven valuable for understanding the role of individual differences in personality type and the implications thereof for learning, team building, and effective communication. In this fashion, we can better understand the strengths of those on our team. Developed by the mother and daughter combination of Isabel Myers and Katherine Briggs, it operationalized Jungian psychology. Used successfully during WWII for placing civilians in jobs required by the war effort, it has since been revised several times. Constantly being tested for validity and reliability, it has proven invaluable for virtually any enterprise.

For the Win: Associations amongst forces can be contagious; place weak with weak and collectively they will become weaker. Pair the weak with the strong to give them a chance to rise.

You Lose: If you write off or sacrifice your lesser forces, you will never know what capability has been lost.

34. Sun Tzu wrote:

"Thus the skillful general conducts his army just as though he were leading a single man, willingly by the hand."

Clearly, there are differences amongst individuals, yet the superior leaders are able to forge their team into a single body with all the strengths and none of the weaknesses of the men and women under their command. Through clear communication backed by judicious use of discipline and reward, leading a large team is no more difficult than leading a single individual.

Leadership can stem from an authority, expertise, or example. With the exception of hierarchical authority, being placed in charge, any example that others want to follow is leadership. While styles vary greatly, traits of good leadership consistently apply to everyone. Leveraging natural charisma is valuable, of course, but it is far less important than behaviors that demonstrate character. Without good character, people will not follow any leader over the long run. The essential attributes of leadership include being consistent, visionary, fair, honest, courageous, inspirational, and productive. We must embrace these attributes, modeling principled behaviors that others may follow, while identifying and rewarding men and women in our organization who exhibit these same characteristics.

For the Win: If the spirit is willing the body follows. The reverse is also true. Know your men's disposition, leverage their strength, and build cohesion through judicious discipline and reward.

You Lose: Overlook your team's shortcomings, letting results and relationships trump principle.

35. Sun Tzu wrote:

"It is the business of a general to be quiet and thus ensure secrecy, upright and just, and thus maintain order."

Secrecy is vital to successful warfare, so as generals we may not disclose our full plans, yet it remains imperative that our men and women willingly follow our commands. To this end we must be seen as forthright and fair, setting clear expectations and holding everyone high and low alike accountable. In this way, our troops come to trust us when we withhold information that spies could take advantage of.

Nancy Wake (1912 – 2011) was one the best spies of WWII. Trained in espionage, sabotage, and able to drink most of her male counterparts under the table, she was instrumental to the success of the French Resistance. An expert in hand-to-hand combat, she killed more than one German with her bare hands, yet she earned her nickname, "The White Mouse," by talking and flirting her way out of trouble. "A little powder (makeup) and a little drink on the way, and I'd pass their (German) posts and wink and say, 'Do you want to search me?'" she once told reporters. "God, what a flirtatious little bastard I was." By 1942, she wound up at the top of the Gestapo's most-wanted list, with a five-million-franc award on her head, which forced her to leave France and take up residence in Britain. There she joined the Special Operatives Executives, quickly became an officer, and found herself in charge of 7,500 men.

For the Win: You needn't reveal every aspect of your plans or intentions so long as your team is aligned and everyone knows what they must do. Create a clear vision, delegate effectively, and thereby assure that the parts and pieces of your design move forward in concert.

You Lose: Reveal your plan in its entirety to those who do not need to know.

36. Sun Tzu wrote:

"He must be able to mystify his officers and men by false reports and appearances and thus keep them in total ignorance."

Spies are everywhere. To guard against espionage, we cannot bring our troops into our plans at the beginning. Even our officers may only know their own role, and perhaps those they must work most closely with, safeguarding the entirety of our design. With confidence in our leadership and track record, the troops will faithfully carry out our commands, celebrating the outcome when they discover afterward what we collectively have done.

Yoshiko Kawashima (1907 – 1948) was a Chinese princess of Manchu descent who was born in Japan and went on to become a secret agent for the Imperial Japanese forces during the Sino-Japanese War. Known as the "Eastern Mata Hari," she served as a spy for General Kenji Doihara (1883 – 1948), who led the Japanese invasion of Manchuria, on whose orders she pursued numerous undercover missions, often disguised as a man. As a figurehead for the territory of Manchukuo, she made radio appearances, cut records, and released stories of her exploits to reporters to further Japanese propaganda. She was captured and arrested in 1945 by Chinese counter-intelligence officers, held in prison in Beijing, and executed by firing squad on March 25, 1948. Afterward, her body was put on public display, a shameful end for a famous spy.

For the Win: Spies are everyplace. If you know they are spies, they are not effective spies, which means that the superior ones appear to be friends. Consequently, safeguards must be put in place to keep information vital to your endeavor close. A company's Critical Technical Information (CTI), for example, is often not patented (as patents are publicly disclosed) so that its secrets can be held close.

You Lose: When you overly reveal your designs, enemies may cross you at any time.

37. Sun Tzu wrote:

"By altering his arrangements and changing his plans he keeps the enemy without definite knowledge. By shifting his camp and taking circuitous routes he prevents the enemy from anticipating his purpose."

War is based on deception. At times we must deceive not only the enemy but also our own soldiers. Nevertheless, we must inspire our men and women to follow us unquestionably, without letting them know why we do what we do. Spurred by our men and women's belief in our leadership, we safeguard the success and inevitability of our plan.

In 1965 Harvard psychologist Robert Rosenthal (1933 –) and elementary school principal Lenore Jacobson (1963 –) conducted a "Pygmalion in the Classroom" experiment, telling teachers that certain children were "growth spurters," based on results of a fictitious Harvard Test of Inflected Acquisition. While chosen completely at random, teachers set higher expectations of their first-and second-grade students whom they believed would be high achievers, which in turn influenced how well the kids scored on IQ tests later on. This study demonstrates deception used in a positive way, based on the self-fulfilling prophecy principle that when folks believe they can succeed they often will.

For the Win: At times you must not only deceive the enemy but also our own men. Build rapport and trust such that this action does not come back to bite you.

You Lose: If you don't have a track record and reputation for success, the prudent act of withholding information will be met with dissention amongst your team.

38. Sun Tzu wrote:

> *"At the critical moment, the leader of an army acts like one who has climbed up a height and then kicks away the ladder behind him. He carries his men deep into hostile territory before he shows his hand."*

A decisive action which makes it impossible for our forces to turn back unless victorious will spur them to battle. This advice may at first blush appear ill-considered, but unlike modern volunteer forces, armies were largely comprised of conscripts during the "Warring States" period in ancient China. The very real probability of desertion materially influenced Sun Tzu's perspective on how generals should treat their men and women.

Eddie Slovik (1920 – 1945) was the only US soldier shot for desertion during WWII. Slovik had a rough upbringing, spending time in reformatory school and prison before being drafted into the army infantry in 1944. In northern France he came under artillery fire in August before even reaching his unit, fleeing to the safety of a Canadian Military Police (MP) troop before finding and joining his regiment two months later in October. Officers were willing to accept his return without asking too many questions or pressing charges, yet when assigned to a rifle platoon by Captain Ralph Grotte (1920 – 1945) of Company G, he turned around and walked away from the front stating that he would desert if sent to combat again. This landed him in the stockade, where he was tried a month later, convicted, and shot dead by a dozen men from his regiment. In keeping with tradition, one rifle carried a blank so that no one would know for certain who killed the prisoner. All the other eleven shots hit their target.

For the Win: When given only one way out, your forces will fight furiously.

You Lose: Allow too many options, or weak leadership, such that the chain-of-command is not respected and your men become reluctant to follow your orders.

39. Sun Tzu wrote:

"He burns his boats and breaks his cooking-pots, like a shepherd driving a flock of sheep he drives his men this way and that and nothing knows whither he is going."

The men and women under our command are fully aware of orders to hold or move, attack or retreat, yet remain unaware of the strategic reasons behind these instructions. We steer them to suit our purpose much like a shepherd herds his or her sheep. There is no cruelty inherent in this treatment, but rather an abiding appreciation for the value of guile and secrecy in winning any war. The troops know their role, but not the larger objective.

Isabelle Boyd (1844 – 1900) was a spy for the Confederacy during the American Civil War (1861 – 1865). She was in Martinsburg, Virginia fundraising for the Southern war effort in 1861 when that town was occupied by Union forces. Quartered in the same residence as General James Shields (1806 – 1879), she overheard the Union officer's plans to withdraw and blow up the town's bridges to cover their retreat, undertook a hazardous journey across the battle lines to inform General Stonewall Jackson (1824 – 1863) about what she'd heard, and thereby thwarted the plan. In 1864 she was sailing on a blockade runner to England with letters from Confederate President Jefferson Davis (1808 – 1889) when her ship was intercepted. She flirtatiously distracted the ship's prize master Samuel Wylde Hardinge (1836 – 1866), facilitating the Confederate captain's escape. While Hardinge was court-martialed and discharged from the navy for this failure, he later moved to England and married Boyd in 1864.

For the Win: When your forces trust you, they will fight willingly, even without knowing all the details.

You Lose: Engaging in any risky endeavor without the full faith and focus of your team.

40. Sun Tzu wrote:

"To muster his host and bring it into danger, this may be termed the business of the general."

After mobilizing our forces and solidifying our plans there should be no delay in carrying them out. As with any good leader, the laudable general is decisive, courageous, and swift. We must not waste time with words when action is called for. British Prime Minister Neville Chamberlain (1869 – 1940) could be considered the poster boy for this admonishment.

Chamberlain is infamous for his policy of appeasement toward Adolf Hitler (1889 – 1945) and the German expansionist policies before the outbreak of WWII. With the Munich Agreement, which was signed on September 30, 1938, Chamberlain and Edouard Daladier (1884 – 1970), the Premier of France, granted almost all of Hitler's demands, including that Czechoslovakia cede the Sudetenland to Germany. He returned to England blathering about of "peace with honor" and "peace for our time," but quickly had to swallow his words when the Nazis seized the rest of Czechoslovakia, eventually resigning in disgrace on May 10, 1940 when Germany invaded Belgium, the Netherlands, and Luxembourg.

For the Win: Be decisive, courageous, and swift. Once prepared, and you know the time is right, you must strike.

You Lose: When you hesitate needlessly, resorting to words when actions are necessary.

41. Sun Tzu wrote:

"The different measures suited to the nine varieties of ground, the expediency of aggressive or defensive tactics, and the fundamental laws of human nature. These are things that must most certainly be studied."

Our strategy is informed by a deep understanding of the terrain, tactics, and mankind. In this fashion, we know with certainty beforehand what we face, how our adversaries are likely to act, and how we may best bring our forces to bear in order to prevail. What's true in warfare, often works much the same in the business world where corporations can create empires by swallowing-up smaller companies.

In 2006, the Walt Disney Company took a major step in conquering the entertainment industry by acquiring Pixar for $7.4 billion. Pixar began in 1979 as Graphics Group, a part of Lucasfilm's computer division, before being spun-off as a standalone corporation in 1986 with funding from Apple co-founder Steve Jobs (1955 – 2011) who became a billionaire as their majority shareholder. By the time Disney took an interest, Pixar had an impressive portfolio including the first two Toy Story movies, Finding Nemo, and The Incredibles. By 2019 they had produced 21 hit movies generating billions in the box office, streaming, and merchandising revenue. Toy Story 3, Finding Dory, Incredibles 2, and Toy Story 4 are all among the 50 highest-grossing films of all time. Disney already owned ABC/Capital City (1995) and Fox (2001) before the Pixar deal, and further acquired Marvel Entertainment for $3.96 billion in 2009 and Lucasfilm in 2012 for $4.05 billion, cementing their entertainment empire.

For the Win: Comprehensive understanding of the lay of the land, the abilities of the enemy, and the human experience are keys to winning the day. Leverage your mastery of the art of war to succeed in any worthy endeavor.

You Lose: Taking action without sufficient knowledge and understanding.

42. Sun Tzu wrote:

> *"When invading hostile territory, the general principle is that penetrating deeply brings cohesion, penetrating but a short way means dispersion."*

In war we must be confident; halfhearted attempts never prevail. Like the thrust of a sword to our enemy's vitals, we must penetrate deeply for the best effect. While a terrible, bold strike emboldens our men and disheartens the adversary, a timid invasion is easily dispersed and destroyed. This is exactly what happened at The Bay of Pigs.

The Bay of Pigs was an abortive invasion attempted on April 17, 1961, when 1,500 Cuban exiles landed at a beach on the south-central coast of Cuba to conduct a guerrilla war against Fidel Castro (1926 – 2016) and his Communist regime. Plans for US CIA-backed invasion were initiated during Eisenhower's presidency and implemented during the Kennedy Administration, but Castro was warned by three half-hearted bombing runs on his airbases two days earlier, hence was prepared. It took just two days for better-armed Cuban forces to capture or kill 1,100 of the insurgents. In the aftermath of this failure, critics charged the CIA with supplying faulty information to the new president, noting that in spite of Kennedy's orders supporters of Cuban dictator Batista (1901 – 1973) were included in the invasion force, whereas members of the more capable anti-Castro group, the non-Communist People's Revolutionary Movement, were not. Regardless of any politics behind the debacle, from a pure military perspective this fainthearted incursion was doomed from the start.

For the Win: If you are going to fight, go all in for the win.

You Lose: Much like you cannot be a "little bit pregnant," you cannot go to war just a little. Halfhearted attempts end badly.

43. Sun Tzu wrote:

"When you leave your own country behind and take your army across neighboring territory you find yourself on critical ground. When there are means of communication on all four sides the ground is one of intersecting highways."

In this passage, Sun Tzu refers to ground separated from our home by an adjacent state whose territory we have had to cross. This puts us in a position that is not far enough advanced to truly be called facile, yet not near enough to home to be dispersive. While this was a rare occurrence in his time, hence not included in the nine situations, it is a circumstance that he believed must be addressed nonetheless. In this position, we must settle our business quickly and move on or risk becoming entrapped.

When Napoleon Bonaparte (1769 – 1821) placed an embargo on the British in 1806, Russian Czar Alexander I (1777 – 1825) initially went along with the prohibition but stopped complying 4 years later due to its deleterious effect on his economy. Additionally, Alexander rebuffed Napoleon's request to marry one of his sisters and further imposed import duties on French luxury products, enraging the emperor. Bonaparte naturally retaliated, raising a "grand army" of some 650,000 men. The smaller Russian army, numbering about 200,000, avoided most major battles, letting weather, disease, and desertion whittle away at the French forces. Napoleon did manage to invade Moscow on September 14th, 1812, but took so long getting there that he found the city abandoned. Faced with sub-zero temperatures, Napoleon was forced to retreat back to France a month later, arriving with only 20,000 soldiers still in fighting condition. One could say that Alexander defeated Napoleon, but in reality, it was the Russian winter that did him in.

For the Win: Move quickly from critical ground lest you become entrapped.

You Lose: Allowing your forces to move into a situation where they must defend 360 degrees is a failure of both leadership and opportunity.

44. Sun Tzu wrote:

"When you penetrate deeply into a country it is serious ground. When you penetrate but a little way it is facile ground."

This point is so important that it bears repeating. The beginning of any incursion into enemy territory is fraught with danger, not only based on actions from the adversaries but also from any lack of unity, discipline, or resolve within our troops. As we move deeper and deeper, we not only demonstrate the merits of our strategy but also create cohesion amongst our team as the troops understand that there is no course available but toward victory.

The US Army defines "morale" in its Field Manual on Leadership as, "The mental, emotional, and spiritual state of the individual. It is how he feels—happy, hopeful, confident, appreciated, worthless, sad, unrecognized, or depressed." Evaluations by the US Military of casualty rates during WWII definitively concluded that it is not strength in numbers of troops that bring victory in war, but rather, "Whichever army goes into battle stronger in soul, their enemies generally cannot withstand them." In other words, those units with better pre-deployment morale performed better in achieving their objectives and suffered fewer casualties (by as much as 38%) than units with lower esprit de corps. This is the power of morale.

For the Win: Start with a strong, cohesive team and let your small successes and early victories build toward total triumph.

You Lose: If your actions as a leader are not serious, or not perceived as such, your forces will behave indiscriminately despite the consequences. Low morale will undermine your endeavor.

45. Sun Tzu wrote:

> *"When you have the enemy's strongholds on your rear and narrow passes in front, it is hemmed-in ground. When there is no place of refuge at all it is desperate ground."*

Sometimes we run out of options, stuck between the proverbial rock and hard place, with nowhere to turn. When there is no safe harbor, we must fight our way out. During the Korean War, the Battle of the Chosin Reservoir, which took place between November 27th and December 13th of 1950, was a good example. When United Nations Command troops advanced up the western side of the Korean peninsula and began pushing the North Vietnamese back toward Pyongyang, the battle pretty much went according to plan until China entered the fray.

In a surprise attack, more than 100,000 Chinese troops trapped a contingent of US Marines in a remote mountainous area during the heart of winter. With temperatures falling under 25-degrees below zero, it was too cold to dig foxholes without explosives or bulldozers, so combatants resorted to piling up frozen bodies in lieu of sandbags. The American troops managed to escape, embarking on a harrowing 70-mile trek where they fought their way down a narrow road through several mountain passes, bridged a chasm, and finally reached the safety of transport ships on the coast. The Americans fighting spirit thwarted disaster despite a monumental setback. By the end of the battle, the Chinese had suffered around 50,000 casualties, while the Americans lost 17,843 men.

For the Win: On desperate ground let your fighting spirit prevail.

You Lose: Giving your enemy ample choices creates a hazardous crossroads you will be unable to defend.

46. Sun Tzu wrote:

"Therefore, on dispersive ground I would inspire my men with unity of purpose. On facile ground I would see that there is close connection between all parts of my army."

With the unity of purpose and close cooperation amongst our troops, we guard against both the possibility of a surprise attack by our adversaries as well as the prospect of desertion by our own men and women. On the march our forces coordinate routes and missions, staying in constant contact, whereas once positioned we drive continuity across our encampments such that all our independent companies act as one united team.

Creating alignment is essential to building and maintaining any healthy organization, be it a small business, large corporation, elite military unit, or sports team. Inconsistencies can confuse stakeholders, driving conflict, undermining productivity, and disheartening the team. There are six critical questions that need to be answered to assure that everyone is on the same page: (1) why does our organization exist, (2) how do we behave, (3) what do we do, (4) how will we succeed, (5) what is important right now, and (6) who must do what to assure our success? Candidly discussing these questions and coming to consensus on the answers helps assure team cohesion.

For the Win: Assure unity of purpose and close cooperation amongst your entire team.

You Lose: Tolerate poorly expressed intention, unclear plans, or estranged forces and you hand victory to your enemy before the battle begins.

47. Sun Tzu wrote:

"On contentious ground, I would hurry up my rear."

On contentious ground, speed is of the essence, yet we must neither arrive in disarray nor too exhausted to fight. When a favorable position on the contested ground is identified, we should detach a small group to swiftly capture it, baiting the enemy to bring a fight with his full numbers and then unexpectedly fall upon his flanks with our main body of soldiers. In this fashion, our victory will be assured.

Six months after the attack on Pearl Harbor on June 3rd, 1942, Japanese Fleet Admiral Isoroku Yamamoto (1884 – 1943) attempted to draw American aircraft carriers that had not been sunk in the earlier attack into an ambush by invading Midway Atoll, a US-island near Hawaii. What he didn't know was that US Navy cryptanalysts had broken the Japanese communication codes and knew weeks ahead of time what Isoroku was up to, setting up a counter-ambush. In the resulting battle, Japan lost 3,000 men, including more than 200 of their most experienced pilots, 300 aircraft, a heavy cruiser, and 4 aircraft carriers whereas the Americans only lost 2 ships, 145 aircraft, and approximately 360 men. This outcome emboldened the Allies, materially changing the balance of power in the Pacific Theater during WWII.

For the Win: Tightly align your forces and move as swiftly as possible.

You Lose: Allow your forces to straggle and disperse when threatened, leaving you vulnerable to attack.

48. Sun Tzu wrote:

"On open ground I would keep a vigilant eye on my defenses. On ground of intersecting highways, I would consolidate my alliances."

While we may like to go it alone, at times even the strongest enterprises must seek outside help. The idea of creating strategic alliances applies as much to business as it does to geopolitics or warfare, and can be beneficial in almost every arena. Combining forces with other leaders who have complementary capabilities can create an alliance more powerful than any of its individual partners had they chosen to go forward alone. That means creativity can create a win in circumstances where victory was far from assured. Sometimes the best alliances appear dubious at first blush. Consider Luxottica and Google by way of example.

Luxottica, who owned Lens Crafters, Sunglass Hut, Ray-Ban, and Oakley, was a high-end eyewear manufacturer whose products had been increasingly undercut on price by big-box retailers like Costco. Google was… well, everybody knows Google, but the original Google glass headset was a failure in part because their eyewear appealed to technology, not fashion. Luxottica's brands spoke to fashion, not tech, hence the opportunity for a joint venture. In their press release, Google wrote, "Luxottica will bring design and manufacturing expertise to the mix and, together, we will bring even more Glass style choices to our Explorers. In addition, Luxottica's retail and wholesale distribution channels will serve us well when we make Glass more widely available down the road."

For the Win: When exposed, reach out to allies.

You Lose: Ignoring weaknesses (and opportunities) by needlessly going it alone.

49. Sun Tzu wrote:

"On serious ground I would try to ensure a continuous stream of supplies. On difficult ground I would keep pushing on along the road."

Our supply lines are vital for the conduct of war. After all, without provisions and ammunition, we cannot accomplish our mission. While safeguarding our baggage trains and communication networks is imperative, speed and agility may dictate the need for forage and plunder as well. We must balance momentum with security as the ground dictates.

The British-Zulu War began when British troops under the command of Lieutenant General Frederic Augustus (1827 – 1905) invaded Zululand from the southern African republic of Natal in 1879. Less than two weeks into the war, a British contingent set upon what they believed to be the main Zulu camp at Isandlwana, only to discover that it was nearly empty. While searching the area they were surprised by an army of 20,000 warriors who quickly surrounded them. Overwhelmed by the sheer number and ferocity of their foes, three quarters of the 1,800-man force was wiped out, their baggage and supplies destroyed. The remaining British were forced to flee. The Zulu took 1,000 casualties driving the invaders off of their turf, though the British tried again much more successfully about 7 months later.

For the Win: Balance momentum with security as the ground dictates.

You Lose: Lose provisions such that you cannot accomplish your mission.

50, 51. Sun Tzu wrote:

"On hemmed-in ground I would block any way of retreat. On desperate ground I would proclaim to my soldiers the hopelessness of saving their lives. For it is the soldier's disposition to offer an obstinate resistance when surrounded, to fight hard when he cannot help himself, and to obey promptly when he has fallen into danger."

There are few things more terrifying than a warrior who is willing to fight to the death for his or her cause. Sometimes this is done out of devotion to the team, a sense of patriotism, or religious fervor, and sometimes it is simply because there is no choice but to prevail or perish, yet whatever their underpinning motivation when someone sets aside their instinct for survival in pursuit of their objectives, they become virtually unstoppable. During WWII, Japanese Tokubetsu Kogekitai (Special Attack Units), or kamikaze, were a famous example of this principle.

The Japanese word kamikaze translates into English as, "divine wind," a reference to a typhoon that unexpectedly dispersed a Mongol invasion in 1281, and refers to both planes and pilots who made suicide attacks by crashing into enemy ships. The practice was most prevalent from the Battle of Leyte Gulf, which took place during October of 1944, until the end of the war as things got more and more desperate for the Japanese Imperial forces. Most kamikaze planes were nothing more than ordinary fighters or light bombers that carried both bombs and extra gasoline tanks. Kamikaze attacks sank 34 ships and damaged hundreds of others during the war. At Okinawa they inflicted the greatest losses ever suffered by the US Navy in a single battle, killing just under 5,000 men.

For the Win: A force with no way out will fight to the end. If you have no escape, leverage your predicament as motivation.

You Lose: Stand in the way of someone who has set aside his instinct for survival in pursuit of his objectives at your peril.

52. Sun Tzu wrote:

"We cannot enter into alliance with neighboring princes until we are acquainted with their designs. We are not fit to lead an army on the march unless we are familiar with the face of the country—its mountains and forests, its pitfalls and precipices, its marshes and swamps. We shall be unable to turn natural advantages to account unless we make use of local guides."

Whenever we align with foreign powers, we risk misfortune from both misunderstanding and betrayal. Consequently, we must diligently evaluate their motivation and purpose to be certain if the proposed partnership may prove beneficial. If so, we must learn to know our neighbors as ourselves, so we can influence their terrain in battle as well as we use our own.

To evaluate any potential partnership in business, we must understand what synergies may be obtained by the union. If it appears mutually beneficial, that there's "profit in it" so to speak, then we must go deeper, asking ourselves whether or not our values and priorities are in alignment. These are the fundamentals, without which there is no good match, because cultural misalignment has sunk more mergers than any other root case. From there we can delve into the level of "fit," ascertaining the other party's level of commitment, analyzing the opportunities and risks, and deciding if we wish to move forward to negotiate a deal.

For the Win: Be discerning in your choice of allies.

You Lose: Fail to understand your allies' motivations and your call for help will go unanswered. Or worse, it will be answered by someone who purposefully or by accident torpedoes your endeavor.

53. Sun Tzu wrote:

"To be ignored of any one of the following four or five principles does not befit a warlike prince."

If in attacking a powerful state we can divide their forces then we overcome despite bringing smaller numbers to the field of battle. Conversely, if we are inherently stronger, we may use our might to dominate our adversaries. Anytime we overawe one opponent, their neighbors become frightened and in so doing will refrain from joining that enemy against us. In this fashion our fierce reputation both advances and safeguards our plans. Few leaders held a more fearsome reputation than Vlad the Impaler (1431 – 1476).

Vlad III, better known as Vlad the Impaler, was likely the real-life inspiration for Bram Stoker's (1847 – 1912) character Dracula. A prince (military governor) of Walachia, he was considered a national hero who fought tirelessly against the Ottoman Empire, but his fondness for impaling both foreign and domestic enemies on stakes and leaving them to die slow, horrible deaths also made him one of the most feared men in history. His cavalry used hit-and-run tactics against numerically larger enemies, striking and then quickly retreating. As he fled one battle in 1462, he left a field filled with thousands of impaled victims as a deterrent to pursuing Turkish forces. Legend states that he placed a solid gold cup in the Targoviste town square (a city in modern-day Romania) declaring that anybody could drink out of it, but that it must never leave the marketplace. Some 60,000 people lived in the town at the time, many of them quite poor, yet Vlad was so feared that during his entire reign (1456 – 1462) the cup was never stolen.

For the Win: As Niccolò Machiavelli (1469 – 1527) wrote, "It is better to be feared than loved, if you cannot be both." Heed his words, building a fierce reputation that both advances and safeguards your plans.

You Lose: Rule through fear alone and lose respect, ultimately undermining your plans. You cannot be both a leader and a tyrant.

54. Sun Tzu wrote:

"When a warlike prince attacks a powerful state, his generalship shows itself in preventing the concentration of the enemy's forces. He overawes his opponents and their allies are prevented from joining against him."

If a powerful state can be defeated before summoning allies, then the lesser states will fear our prowess and refrain from massing their forces against us. In this fashion victory begets victory. This principle of inter-state conflict is much like fighting multiple attackers in interpersonal self-defense scenarios. If we are forced to fight a group, we can realistically engage only one adversary at a time. Once the first threat has been defeated, we may have a chance to escape to safety or we may have to move on to defeat the next attacker and then get away.

The challenge is that despite what is often portrayed in the movies, the other guys won't line up and wait for us to attack each one in turn. Defense against a group must be handled by strategically engaging one person at a time in a manner that confounds the other's ability to reach us. Our response is a form of triage, striking for the greatest impact or taking on the most dangerous threat first. If we can instantaneously and dramatically disable someone, leaving him huddled in a pool of his own blood, the psychological advantage over the rest of the group will be enormous.

For the Win: Keep your enemy dispersed, forcing them to communicate over great distances, and then make that difficult as well.

You Lose: Allowing acts of the enemy, or the lay of the land, to isolate your forces from one another.

55. Sun Tzu wrote:

"Hence he does not strive to ally himself with all and sundry nor does he foster the power of other states. He carries out his own secret designs, keeping his antagonists in awe. Thus, he is able to capture their cities and overthrow their kingdoms."

Secure against any combination of enemies, we can afford to reject entangling alliances in favor of pursuing our designs for conquest. This is the power of prestige; it enables famed generals to pick and choose amongst partnerships that may be forced upon (or be beyond the reach of) lesser leaders.

According to the Harvard Business Review, business alliances account for nearly a third of many companies' revenue and value yet paradoxically the failure rate for partnerships runs around 60% to 70%. A few principles can break past this conundrum and help us assure success. First, focus cultural alignment, determining how compatible our organizations truly are. If this foundation is strong, our next focus must be on the relationship itself, letting the way in which the companies can best work together determine viability and structure of the alliance. Next, we must implement governance that measures and manages not only the business goals but also the partnership objectives so that benefits are not lost in the confusion of emerging imperatives and daily work. Finally, rather than trying to eliminate the differences between organizations we must influence them to create value.

For the Win: An alliance must be beneficial—it must answer a need that is wanting, a necessary resource gained.

You Lose: Forming an alliance simply to make an alliance. An alliance built without purpose is a lot like playing a sport without any method for keeping score. Energy is spent, yet nothing meaningful is accomplished.

56. Sun Tzu wrote:

"Bestow rewards without regard to rule, issue orders without regard to previous arrangements, and you will be able to handle a whole army as though you had to do with but a single man."

Underlings adapt to their overseer's preferences, yet it takes time to get used to a different style, even if it's better than what came before. Consequently, new leadership is often pressured to do things in the same way as the previous administration despite any needed change in direction or known shortcomings in what was done previously. Just because a person, program, or process historically held favor does not mean that it advances our current cause. We must re-baseline, building measures that reward behaviors that move our enterprise forward while punishing those who stubbornly cling to dysfunctional methods of the past.

Change can be harder for some to swallow than others. Sometimes histrionics are necessary for people to get things off their chest, progress past the emotion, and move on to more productive things. Other times we need to snap them out of it. In those instances, it is prudent to wait for the other person to wind down and then ask the question, "Why are you not taking action on this now?" Sometimes the act of having to own their own words points out to people how extreme a position they have taken in a non-threatening manner.

For the Win: Wipe away old rules, tools, and methods if they're holding you back.

You Lose: Blindly retain the shortcomings of those who came before you and prove yourself a follower not a leader.

57. Sun Tzu wrote:

"Confront your soldiers with the deed itself; never let them know your design. When the outlook is bright bring it before their eyes; but tell them nothing when the situation is gloomy."

As leaders we issue orders, but oftentimes must not explain to the troops the reasons behind our instructions lest they intuit our overall plan. When things are going well, we should hold up our progress to spur our men and women onward, yet must be cautions to not undermine morale when the inevitable setback is encountered. This may seem disingenuous, yet most men and women are prone toward negative thinking on their own. As leaders we cannot engage in nor reinforce flawed reasoning.

Whatever our endeavor, whatever our goal, we will never achieve it if we limit ourselves or our imagination with negative thinking. To optimize our chances for success, it is paramount to identify our objectives in writing, documenting what we wish to accomplish as well as the exact reasons why that is important to us. Keeping that objective in mind, we can visualize success and thereby help eliminate obstacles in our path. We can maintain our motivation by creating a set of stretch goals against which we can monitor our performance and see progress over time. In this fashion we remain positive and realistic at the same time.

For the Win: Not everybody needs to know everything about everything. Communicating necessary information, however, motivates the rank and file without overloading them.

You Lose: Open up the strategy for all to see and comment upon. The old idiom, "Too many cooks spoil the broth," is as true today as it ever was.

58, 59. Sun Tzu wrote:

"Place your army in deadly peril and it will survive; plunge it into desperate straits and it will come off in safety. For it is precisely when a force has fallen into harm's way that is capable of striking a blow for victory."

In Sun Tzu's time armies were largely comprised of conscripts, so the strategy of placing them in harm's way in order to bring out their best effort was commonplace. Only on the front lines in close quarters with the enemy could they make a difference in the outcome of the war. Battle-hardened veterans who survived a number of these skirmishes continuously honed their skills enriched their spirits, and thereby fought with ever-increasing ferocity. In other words, success begat bravery, which in turn produced a triumph.

This principle is not so different from growing a startup business. Even with experienced mentors, new companies must go through a process of trial-and-error to get things up and running effectively. The more deeply entrepreneurs come to understand their enterprise and marketplace the more adroit their decision-making becomes. Building on the success and learning from failures they earn "battle scars" to become more and more accomplished over time.

For the Win: Winning fixes a lot of problems. Triumph over a weak opponent will fix many difficulties. Even more is mended with victory over a strong opponent.

You Lose: Go a long time without a win, no matter how small, and the spirit for fighting evaporates like morning mist in the heat of the sun.

60. Sun Tzu wrote:

"Success in warfare is gained by carefully accommodating ourselves to the enemy's purpose."

We know that all warfare is based on deception. Oftentimes this means feigning foolishness to draw our foe into making a mistake. If, for example, our enemy shows an inclination to advance, we can lure him in. If he is anxious to retreat, we might simulate delay so that he may carry out his intention. Once our adversary is convinced by our foolhardiness and lowers his guard, we may finish him with ease. This strategy is commonly used by hackers to gain access to sensitive information by tricking people into letting them in.

For example, in 2016 the US Department of Justice (DOJ) fell for a social engineering attack that compromised the personal information of approximately 20,000 FBI agents and about 9,000 Department of Homeland Security (DHS) employees. The subterfuge began with a hacker calling the department's help desk number, claiming to be a new employee, and asking for assistance in accessing their systems. Using email credentials stolen from a DOJ employee, he obtained full access to their network, stealing information from a variety of sensitive systems including employee contact information, military emails, and credit card data. All of this was accomplished without any sophisticated technology, specialized software, or advanced computer skills.

For the Win: What is your adversary's endgame? What does he consider victory? Know this and you will discern your enemy's methods.

You Lose: Fail to understand the ultimate objective of your enemy. Without this discernment, you are like a rudderless ship, tossed from wave to wave.

61, 62. Sun Tzu wrote:

"By persistently hanging on the enemy's flank, we shall succeed in the long run in killing their commander-in-chief. This is called ability to accomplish a thing by sheer cunning."

When we are able to continuously shadow and harass our enemy's forces, we eat away at their capabilities until they are no longer able to wage war successfully. In this fashion, we outright kill our adversary or see him deposed by his sovereign or by the men and women who paid the price in blood and treasure for his folly. Either way, victory is ours. Consider the battle of Issus by way of example. In 333 BC, Darius III (380 – 330 BC), led his Persian hoard into battle against Alexander the Great (336 BC – 323 BC), who commanded a significantly smaller Macedonian force.

These adversaries met at Issus, a plain on the coast of the Gulf of Iskenderun (Southern Turkey in present-day), with the Persian army drawn up on one side of the Pinarus River and the Macedonian forces arranged on the other side. Darius, who had proclaimed himself King of Kings, made the critical mistake of choosing a battlefield which was too small to allow him the full advantage of numbers yet well-suited for Alexander's smaller, more mobile forces. The Macedonian cavalry crushed the Persian's left flank and then joined with Alexander's infantry phalanx to roll up and overcome the enemy's forces. It was the first time in history that a Persian King had been personally defeated in battle. While Darius managed to escape, his family was captured and the army he left behind was slaughtered by the Macedonians.

For the Win: By adhering to the enemy you may act as a parasite, slowly weakening his ability to campaign against you.

You Lose: Seek consistent head-to-head battles and you will quickly discover that these fights are detrimental to both your resources and your spirit.

63. Sun Tzu wrote:

"On the day that you take up your command, block the frontier passes, destroy the official tallies, and stop the passage of all emissaries."

Once placed in charge we must assure that our forces immediately recognize our authority. One method for doing this is to repeal the previous leader's orders, issuing new commands that demonstrate our superiority. To exert complete control, we may additionally arrest-free passage, destroy official tallies that might challenge our position, and temporarily retain foreign emissaries who could prematurely inform our adversaries of the situation. Secure in our station, we will have free reign to solidify our position and begin to implement our plans.

While this principle may seem a bit excessive in peacetime, it is really not so different from what often happens when new leaders take over an organization in government, academia, or the corporate world. Prior organizational structures and operating principles are often thrown away as we reorganize to best suit our strategy and objectives. Clearly, we must get to know the team and learn its history and culture before creating new agreements for working together, yet abandoning the old to institutionalize the new is a time-honored method of establishing fresh leadership.

For the Win: Your forces must see immediate and tangible change when new leadership takes power. Even the smallest act that reinforces this change can prove valuable.

You Lose: When "Why did we change?" becomes the chorus of your men and women, you do not remain their leader for long.

64. Sun Tzu wrote:

"Be stern in the council-chamber, so that you may control the situation."

Senior leaders in the sovereign's council often have their own agenda, working at cross-purposes to undermine each other while earning the king's favor. Politics aside, one cannot be appointed to the high station without being intelligent, accomplished, and outspoken. Nevertheless, we cannot allow our expertise in the art of war to be overruled or countervailed by lessor accomplished yet highly opinionated men or women lest the kingdom suffer. Consequently, it is important to control the agenda, showing no weakness, protecting the security of our deliberations, and insisting that the sovereign endorse our battle plans. In this fashion, we best serve the interests of both the state and ourselves.

Politics are activities associated with the governance of a country or organization, especially the debate or conflict amongst individuals or parties having or hoping to achieve power. Despite this definition, they are not inherently good or evil; like any tool, it's how we use them that matters. Activities undertaken to influence stakeholders to get the right things done for the good of the enterprise are "good" politics. Actions used for self-aggrandizement, personal recognition, or gratuitous reward as well as those used to undermine others without cause (or purely for personal advancement) are "bad" politics. We do not need to be altruistic, yet we must be moral in our use of political weapons just as we are with weapons of war.

For the Win: The idiom of "the tail wagging the dog" refers to actions conducted in the incorrect order. Stay clear in thought when assessing order and action. Do not allow the tail to wag the dog that is your enterprise.

You Lose: Strong personalities tend to be successful. They are a necessary part of your team yet must remain a part of the enterprise. Let strong personalities become a force unto themselves with their own separate agenda and you have lost the team.

65. Sun Tzu wrote:

"If the enemy leaves a door open, you must rush in."

Warfare is often arduous and plodding yet sometimes we find opportunities that are simply too good to refuse. When we face an enemy who is reckless, foolish, or simply unlucky, one who leaves the proverbial door open for conquest, we must take advantage of it. Consider the siege of Tenochtitlan by way of example. At the beginning of the 16th century, the Aztecs controlled a vast empire in South America subjugating nearly 500 vassal states. Their capital, Tenochtitlan, was the most densely populated city to ever exist in Mesoamerica with some 140,000 inhabitants. The center of their power was safely concealed on an artificial island in the middle of Lake Texcoco where it seemed impenetrable.

The Aztec empire's delusion of unassailability abruptly ended in 1521 when they encountered Don Hernan Cortes (1485 – 1547) and his cohort of about 800 Spanish conquistadores. In May, Cortes laid siege to Tenochtitlan by portaging his ships overland in segments and reassembling his armada of 13 ships at the lakeside. Armed with modern weapons and cannon, Cortes was able to cut off the Aztec's food and water supply. Aided by tens of thousands of indigenous allies and a fortuitously-timed smallpox outbreak that ravaged the city, the Spaniards wore down the Aztec defenders and toppled a 900-year-old empire in a mere 93 days.

For the Win: When you discover that the enemy has failed to guard a path, seize it quickly before they recognize their error and don't let go until you have triumphed.

You Lose: Fail to act and squander opportunity. Or, act in haste, without forethought, and find yourself caught in the enemy's trap.

66. Sun Tzu wrote:

"Forestall your opponent by seizing what he holds dear and subtly contrive to time his arrival on the ground."

If we identify a favorable position for battle yet our enemy does not meet us there, the advantage we wished to achieve is nullified. Consequently, we must entice the enemy to come to us at the time and place of our choosing. The battle of Adwa provides an example. In 1895 Italy invaded Ethiopia in an attempt to build an empire in Africa. Ethiopian Emperor Menelik II (1844 – 1913) had an army of some 100,000 men, all trained and armed with modern weaponry, yet shrewdly downplayed his strength spreading rumors of discord amongst his forces.

Emboldened by Menelik's tales of disgruntlement and discontent, Italian General Oreste Baratieri (1841 – 1901) led 14,500 men against the Ethiopians, making contact on March 1, 1896, at Adwa, a city in North-Central Ethiopia. Without reliable maps, the Italians arrived disorganized and were quickly routed by the larger force, with 70% of their men captured or killed in battle. It was the first defeat of a European power by African forces during the colonial era and led to the Treaty of Addis Ababa, signed in October of 1896, which dissolved the Italian protectorate and gave Ethiopia its freedom.

For the Win: What is the most important thing to the enemy? Know it, take it, and then tempt them with it.

You Lose: Emotionally responding to an enemy's action gives them rent-free space in your head. While you're embroiled with angst, worrying over what he might or might not do, the adversary remains free to act unfettered and take you down.

67. Sun Tzu wrote:

"Walk in the path defined by rule and accommodate yourself to the enemy until you can fight a decisive battle."

By strictly following the art of war we know the principles that lead to victory, though oftentimes must delay action until the ideal moment arises for us to strike. For example, during the War of 1812, American forces tried numerous times to push past English and Canadian defenses to attack Montreal. On March 30, 1814, Major General James Wilkinson (1757 – 1825) led 4,000 men and 11 artillery pieces across the Lacolle River to attack a garrison manned by Major Richard Handcock (1791 – 1861) with a force of 180 British soldiers and 160 Canadian troops.

Since Wilkinson was positioned where he could only fire three of his artillery pieces at the enemy, his initial bombardment caused only superficial damage to the stone building they were hiding in. Nevertheless, the British and Canadian defenders quickly ran low on ammunition during their counterattack. In desperation, Handcock ordered a charge to try to capture the American artillery. Outnumbered nearly 12 to 1, his initial charge failed, but he led a second charge later in the day, briefly capturing the enemy's guns before being forced to retreat again that evening. During the fighting, the Americans suffered 254 losses compared to 61 on the British side. In this fashion, a mere 340 men blocked the American invasion of Canada. Unable to secure his objective, Wilkinson returned home in disgrace where he was relieved of duty on April 11, court-martialed, and later acquitted.

For the Win: Keep your discipline. If given a choice, only fight when it is clear that you have an advantage.

You Lose: When you lose sight of your discipline, training, or stratagem. Lose these fundamentals and you will lose everything.

68. Sun Tzu wrote:

"At first, then, exhibit the coyness of a maiden until the enemy gives you an opening; afterwards emulate the rapidity of a running hare and it will be too late for the enemy to oppose you."

We must feign timidity, patiently awaiting the right opportunity, and the strike swiftly when that time arrives so that the enemy cannot respond. Consider the Battle of Gate Pa by way of example. In 1864 the British began confiscating Maori lands in New Zealand because the natives refused to accept their colonial authority. On April 27, 1864, they attacked Gate Pa, a Maori fortress defended by 235 warriors. Leading the assault was British commander Duncan Cameron (1808 – 1888) who brought along 1,700 soldiers and 17 artillery pieces. Numerically speaking this should have been a slaughter. It wasn't.

The Maori, under the command of Rawiri Puhirake (? – 1864), weathered two days of intense bombardment. After a couple dozen of their men were killed, the stopped shooting back in retaliation and hid in bunkers, trenches, and under the fortress's floorboards, hoping to make the British believe that they had been annihilated by their artillery. Falling for this trick, the British captured the fortress, began to relax after the battle, and then suddenly found themselves under fire when the natives popped out of their hiding places and counterattacked. About 120 British soldiers were killed in the first few minutes and the Maori were able to slip away during the mayhem, capturing many of the British field weapons as they fled.

For the Win: Disguise your true ability prior to battle.

You Lose: If you mistake the enemy's presentation of weakness for truth.

Chapter 12: The Attack by Fire

In this chapter, we discover that fire was the medieval weapon of mass destruction, denigrated for causing inglorious death, yet invaluable if used correctly nonetheless. In attacking with fire, we must be prepared for five possible outcomes, formulating a strategy for each one. We must know that there is a proper season and special days when the winds are favorable for conflagration, which can throw the enemy into disarray, yet understand that the use of fire remains an intense and irrevocable decision, one that may be used against us if we do not remain on guard.

1. Sun Tzu wrote:

"There are five ways of attacking with fire. The first is to burn soldiers in their camp; the second is to burn stores; the third is to burn baggage trains; the fourth is to burn arsenals and magazines; the fifth is to hurl dropping fire amongst the enemy."

In Shakespeare's play, The Life and Death of King John, the bard wrote, "Be stirring as the time; be fire with fire; threaten the threatener and outface the brow of bragging horror." Thus, when we "fight fire with fire," as the adage states, we employ more extreme measures than may normally be warranted. Fire is a horrifying weapon. It is difficult to control, burns indiscriminately, and destroys everything in its path, including enemy weapons or supplies which we might want to appropriate. Nevertheless, at times it is the only tool that will do the job.

Operation Meetinghouse, the bombing of Tokyo, which took place between March 9th and 10th 1945, is often cited as one of the most destructive acts in the history of warfare. An armada of 334 American B-29 bombers under the command of Major General Curtis LeMay (1906 – 1990) dropped 1,665 tons of incendiaries, including a half-million cylinders of napalm and white phosphorus, on Japan's capital city, where dry, windy conditions quickly spread the conflagration. The resulting firestorm, later known as the "Night of the Black Snow," utterly destroying 16 square miles of the densely populated city, causing more devastation than the bombings of Dresden, Hiroshima, or Nagasaki, the latter two of which were destroyed with nuclear weapons! Although the precise death toll is unknown, conservative estimates suggest that somewhere between 80,000 and 100,000 Tokyo residents perished in a single night, leaving over a million people homeless afterward.

For the Win: The act of literally or metaphorically burning of an enemy leaves nothing in its wake. Know this and act prudently.

You Lose: Assuming that restoration of burned territory is easy or cheap. It is neither.

2. Sun Tzu wrote:

"In order to carry out an attack, we must have means available. The material for raising fire should always be kept in readiness."

While we must avail ourselves of favorable winds and dry weather to assure success, the materials necessary for attacking with fire should be readied, hence available whenever we need them. Unlike unsheathing a sword, raising spear, or unleashing an arrow, it takes time and preparation to execute an attack by fire. To assure success, a well-honed plan must be in place ahead of time and considerable coordination must be performed during the operation.

One of the largest, best coordinated, and most impactful military maneuvers in history, Operation Overlord (the D-Day invasion of Normandy), took place on June 6, 1944, when 156,000 American, British, and Canadian forces made a coordinated landing on five beaches along the coast of France. It was the largest amphibious assault in history, the culmination of years of thought and over seven months of detailed planning. Logistics for this attack were staggeringly complex, including moving over 9 million tons of equipment across the Atlantic Ocean to supply the endeavor while at the same time launching deception campaigns to draw German strength away from the landing zones. Due to all this diligent preparation and careful execution, Operation Overlord was a success. By late-August all of northern France was liberated and by the following spring, Allied forces had completely defeated Nazi Germany.

For the Win: When you have the ability to bring fire to the battle, keep that fire within reach.

You Lose: When you are not prepared, with resources and mindset, to bring fire to the battlefield key opportunities to change the outcome of battle are lost.

3. Sun Tzu wrote:

"There is a proper season for making attacks with fire, and special days for starting a conflagration."

As with any delicate procedure, there is a time and location when attacks with fire are most likely to succeed. Students of history identify repeating cycles that may predict future events with a high degree of precision. When it comes to weather, critical when weaponizing fire, farmers are adroit at recognizing seasonal variations in temperature, rainfall, and prevailing winds that may affect their crops. We can learn from this analysis and apply it to our enterprise.

Seasonal changes in surface winds, for example, are impacted by variations in land and sea temperatures. While land has a greater influence in the tropical Atlantic than in the Pacific Ocean where there is more balance of both land and sea, these cycles can be observed and used to anticipate what conditions we may face at various times throughout the year. Observed globally, these patterns show predictable cycles, such as annual typhoons that are generated from the China Sea and affect Southeast Asia, hurricanes that begin in the Caribbean and affect the southeastern United States and Central America, and tornadoes that travel through the American Midwest. The ability to predict direction, duration and velocity of winds is obviously critical to attacking with fire.

For the Win: Consider the lay of the land, both literally and metaphorically. Your plans must thoughtfully account for everything that will be burned as winds carry the fire you have set.

You Lose: Lighting a fire for the sake of using fire. This is mayhem; it has no order and no purpose… and, it will surely spin out of control.

4. Sun Tzu wrote:

"The proper season is when the weather is very dry; the special days are those when the moon is in the constellations of the Sieve, the Wall, the Wing, or the Crossbar, for these four are all days of rising wind."

These days are, respectively, the 7th, 14th, 27th, and 28th of the 28 stellar mansions which reflect the movement of the moon during each lunar month, corresponding to the constellations of Sagittarius, Pegasus, Crater, and Corvus. During Sun Tzu's time, the odds of favorably dry weather and predictable winds occurring on these days was high. Since we know that these times are beneficial for attacking with fire, so too must our adversaries, hence even as we make plans for assault, we must diligently guard others taking the same tact.

While fire has been a psychologically terrifying aspect of warfare since the time of the ancient Greeks, the flamethrower came into common use during WWII, with both motorized and man-portable units deployed across the battlefield. Effective at clearing trenches, bunkers, and buildings, it was pioneered by the Germans and adopted by virtually all combatants by the end of the war. Portable units typically used two tanks, one holding non-flammable nitrogen gas and the other filled with compressed air, which when mixed together and ignited created an intense stream of fire. Using an attached hose containing an ignition and trigger system, the operator could kill targets out to a distance of approximately 80 feet.

For the Win: There are natural times to use fire that are better than others. Know these times and act accordingly, making the most out of your most fearsome weapons while simultaneously guarding against the likelihood of your adversary doing the same.

You Lose: Arsonists set fires when it is easy to start fires. They don't fight the season or environment. Attempt to countermand this natural understanding and you will fail.

5. Sun Tzu wrote:

"In attacking with fire, one should be prepared to meet five possible developments:"

The use of fire in battle has predictable outcomes. Knowing ahead of time what may happen, and how it will impact our adversaries and ourselves, we can pragmatically use this insight in formulating our plans. This is similar to planning for any battle, of course, but given the seriousness of attacking with fire, our preparation for its use merits additional diligence and consideration.

Every violent act has consequences. When we fight, even a simple skirmish has the potential to escalate into something with life-altering consequences. We must think about that, asking ourselves ahead of time what is really worth fighting for. Clearly, a whacked-out drug-a-holic lunging at us with a knife in his hands and murder in his eyes warrants a dynamic defense. But, is it worth fighting over a hurtful comment? Probably not. What about a carjacker who's trying to steal our fully insured vehicle? Is it better to take the risk and fight, or to hand over your keys and call 911 or whatever the local emergency number is? Thoughtfully anticipating scenarios and outcomes ahead of time affords us the opportunity to forearm ourselves, making skillful decisions under pressure.

For the Win: It is difficult, but all possible ramifications of your intended actions must be considered and prepared for before you act.

You Lose: Act like an adolescent in full tantrum, failing to think past your initial action.

6. Sun Tzu wrote:

"(1) when fire breaks out inside to enemy's camp, respond at once with an attack from without."

Saboteurs, spies, and turncoats are often used to attack with fire from inside an enemy's camp. Consequently, our timing of battle must coincide with our collaborators' activity, both to assure effective engagement as well as to cover their escape. Oftentimes the outbreak of fire itself is the signal for attack since it requires no additional communication. Prepared and positioned ahead of time, the moment our troops see the flames they should fall upon the enemy without mercy. In this fashion our adversary is forced to fight both the flames and our forces.

Unfortunately outbreaks of fire in an enemy camp aren't always a component of combat. During WWII, American prisoners of war on Palawan Island in the Philippines were tasked to build an airfield for their Japanese captors, hauling and crushing coral gravel by hand and pouring concrete, seven days a week. Treatment was inhumane, with prisoners suffering starvation, torture, and various forms of brutality. As the war turned against the Japanese, the treatment continuously got worse. On December 14, 1944, the surviving prisoners were herded into air raid shelters, doused with buckets of gasoline, and burned alive. Those few who outlasted the flames and explosions were bayonetted or shot to death with machineguns. Of 150 men held at Palawan, only 11 survived the massacre. They later testified against their Japanese captors, 16 of which were convicted and sentenced to death in August of 1948, but all were later released during a general amnesty.

For the Win: When a fire breaks out in the enemy camp, be it in real or metaphorical terms, they will turn inward to face it. Take advantage of this.

You Lose: When internal strife embroils the enemy, they suddenly have two fronts to battle. Failure to create a third one, to seize this moment, is a squandered opportunity which constitutes a triple-loss.

7. Sun Tzu wrote:

"(2) if there is an outbreak of fire but the enemy's soldiers remain quiet, bide your time and do not attack."

If there is an outbreak of fire and the enemy does not respond, that either means that they have not yet noticed or that it is a part of their plan. Consequently, we must survey the situation and ascertain whether or not it is appropriate to attack. In this fashion, we assure that our eagerness to attack does not lead us into a trap.

The word "booby," as used in the term booby trap not the anatomical reference of the same name, comes from the term "bobo," which is Spanish for "stupid," "naive," or "foolish." This, in turn, originated with the Latin word, "balbus," meaning "to stammer," as stammering was considered a symbol of stupidity during Roman times. Thus, "booby traps" refer to traps that idiots, or boobs, fall victim to. Some are innocuous pranks like whoopee cushions, yet in warfare, these are deadly pitfalls like tiger traps, punji sticks, snake pits, flag bombs, cartridge traps, tripwires, and improvised explosive devices. We cannot afford to be foolish when faced with these deadly threats.

For the Win: Tricks and deception are part and parcel to the trade of combat. Scrutinize your enemy's actions to see past his duplicities and discern the truth.

ou Lose: When you confuse recklessness with aggressiveness.

8. Sun Tzu wrote:

> *"(3) when the force of the flames has reached its height follow it up with an attack if that is practicable, if not stay where you are."*

In the right conditions, once a fire starts it can spread quickly. Whipped by winds or inertia, an initial spark will quickly consume nearby combustible materials, spread, and grow, before building into an inferno. Prepositioned and prepared, our forces can monitor the progress of the blaze, and, knowing its likely behavior, attack with the assurance that they will not be caught up in the flames along with the enemy.

Once a fire begins, fuel sources, weather, and topography determine its growth and trajectory. With wildfire, for example, when the wood is heated to its flashpoint (572 degrees Fahrenheit) it releases hydrocarbon gases that mix with oxygen in the air and combust. In this fashion, a forest fire can spread at a rate of up to 14.29 mph, consuming everything in its path. As it spreads the fire often takes on a life of its own, throwing embers which may ignite brush or trees miles away. As long as there is something to burn it becomes self-sustaining because heat and smoke cause potential fuel's moisture to evaporate, making it easier to ignite when the fire reaches it. When it gets large enough, a forest fire can even create its own weather patterns, such as fire whirls, vortices that act like miniature tornadoes.

For the Win: Any natural factor that aids your cause should be embraced. Act in concert with natural forces to lighten your use of resources.

You Lose: Failing to working together with natural events that moving in your direction is a failure of both resources and leadership.

9. Sun Tzu wrote:

"(4) if it is possible to make an assault with fire from without do not wait for it to break out within but deliver your attack at a favorable moment."

While awaiting progress from saboteurs within our enemy's camp, we may discover an opportune moment to attack with fire from without. In such instances, we are best served by launching our assault right away since we cannot know for certain whether our agents have been captured, thwarted, or even turned against us. In this fashion, we accomplish our goal no matter any tactical circumstances beyond our control. The best plans are multifaceted, guarding against any single point of failure.

Without intentional fault-tolerance, plans are easily thwarted. For example, Roman emperor Antonius Caracalla (188 – 217) was warned by the officer he left in charge of his urban cohorts while out on a campaign of an assassination plot hatched by rival Marcus Opellius Severus Macrinus (165 – 218). The message was sealed and given with other letters to a courier of the imperial post who completed his journey without haste, not realizing what he was carrying. Caracalla received the note, but instead of reading it himself he turned all of the daily dispatches over to Macrinus, who promptly disposed of the incriminating letter. Because he was afraid that Caracalla's servant might try to warn the emperor again, Macrinus moved up his plot, assassinating and shortly thereafter succeeding Caracalla as emperor.

For the Win: Even if your plans are moving forward well, should a better opportunity arise you must seize it.

You Lose: Rigidity of planning and execution is the mark of a failed campaign.

10. Sun Tzu wrote:

"(5) when you start a fire, be to windward of it. Do not attack from the leeward."

When we attack with fire, we can expect the enemy to retreat away from the flames. If we oppose his retreat, he will fight desperately which will not be conducive to our success. Furthermore, positioning ourselves leeward of the fire exposes our forces to the same smoke and heat that assaults our enemy. While we might hope to suffer adversity and drive our adversaries back into the fire, our best chance of success is to attack from the windward side. The formations we use in battle reflect the ground we fight on, oftentimes not just the battlefield itself but also the environmental conditions and technology employed by our forces as well. Consider the Macedonian pike phalanx, an infantry formation developed by Philip II (382 BC – 336 BC) and used by his son Alexander the Great (356 BC – 323 BC) to conquer one of the largest empires in the ancient world.

The phalanx formation closely resembles an American Revolutionary War-era volley line, even though at first blush spears and muskets appear to have little in common. Massed fire against charging cavalry, especially with early firearms that lacked rifling and aerodynamic bullets, was much more effective than carefully aimed potshots, making volley lines extremely useful in battle. Further, as soldiers ran out of ammunition or when the enemy pressed close enough that there was no time to reload their single-shot weapons, the men could attach bayonets to their long-rifles creating an actual phalanx. It wasn't as invulnerable as its ancient counterpart, but that formation still got the job done.

For the Win: When you launch a firestorm, place your forces in a position where they will not inadvertently be caught up in it. This, of course, applies not just for literal fires, but also to metaphorical firestorms such as those that erupt in social media, legal, and regulatory arenas as well.

You Lose: When you lob attacks by fire with no consideration for prevailing winds, weather, or the lay of the land.

11. Sun Tzu wrote:

"A wind that rises in the daytime lasts long, but a night breeze soon falls."

As a general rule, a day breeze dies down by nightfall whereas a night breeze winds down long before daybreak. While this phenomenon is commonly observed, it is by no means guaranteed. Nevertheless, the better we know the prevailing weather trends in areas where we operate, the better we can factor that knowledge into our plans. Weather impacts all kinds of battle plans, not just those involving fire.

For example, during the US Civil War, Atlantic storms delayed and eventually disrupted the Union navy's attempt to capture a vital Confederate stronghold at Wilmington, North Carolina in late 1864. The planned mid-December amphibious landings against Fort Fisher, the South's final remaining ocean port, had to be postponed twice due to foul weather. When the Union finally began landing troops near the Confederate positions between December 23rd and 27th, another storm swept through the area scattering the landing boats. With some forces dispersed along the beach and others swept out to sea, the entire operation had to be called off and restaged again later on in 1865.

For the Win: To best use the winds to aide your attack you must act when the winds are strong. This is the same for people, oftentimes they are strongest during the day and weaker at night.

You Lose: Attempting to set your fire when the winds, physical or metaphorical, are unfavorable. As media consultants say, "That story doesn't have legs."

12. Sun Tzu wrote:

"In every army the five developments connected with fire must be known, the movements of the stars calculated, and a watch kept for the proper days."

We must not only know how and when to attack our enemies with fire but also be on guard against these same tactics being used against us. Our adversaries also study the art of war, hence may come to the same conclusions we do on where, when, and how to strike. Just as we are preparing to use fire to attack, so too may the enemy. And, knowing that the time is ripe, they may sow the seeds of our undoing by baiting a trap for us to walk into.

To avoid our adversary's trap, we must get to know him, studying his strategy and tactics. Armed with this knowledge we can train for both what we reliably expect to face based on his predilections as well as for flexibility in combat so that we can quickly react to any unexpected tactics we may have overlooked. In this fashion, and with the disciplined execution of our strategy, we may reliably counter whatever we face.

For the Win: Once set, fire burns with a mind of its own. Wise leaders account for this challenge before starting a blaze.

You Lose: Reckless use of uncontrollable weapons is the equivalent of trying to place a bet on which horse will win when you are watching a baseball game.

13. Sun Tzu wrote:

"Hence those who use fire as an aid to the attack show intelligence, those who use water as an aid to the attack gain an accession of strength."

Attacking with fire causes terror and destruction. Under the right conditions, it is relatively easy to get started and swings the outcome of a fight, but in doing so it also damages or destroys everything in its path. While this may bolster a fearsome reputation, this action does little to strengthen or resupply our forces. If we wish to capture and usurp supplies from our enemy, we must choose another path, in this case, water. Harnessed properly the power of a flood can turn the tide of battle, yet in the aftermath, much of what isn't swept away remains reusable. Similarly, cutting off or contaminating an adversary's water supply swiftly speeds his demise leaving his possessions untouched.

While burning or drowning our foes are certainly viable options for victory, there are a variety of psychological methods that have been used throughout time to crush an enemy's spirit. Since few battles end with total annihilation, psychological warfare is a viable way to speed an adversary's surrender. Historical examples include the Aztec death whistles, designed to sound like people howling in agony, Ramses II's (1303 – 1213 BC) war chariots, with which he slaughtered foot soldiers with ease, Tamerlane's (1336 – 1405) pyramids of skulls, and Vlad II's (1431 – 1476) impaling spikes. Using psychological and physical warfare in concert, we gain the upper hand against our foe.

For the Win: We like to point to a single act, a single moment in which we prevail, but it is always a combination of moments and actions that sets the table for a victory. Let each and every action further your end game.

You Lose: When you only look for the "one shot kill," the one magical thing that once unleashed will win the day with a single stroke.

14. Sun Tzu wrote:

"By means of water an enemy may be intercepted but not robbed of all his belongings."

Water does not have the same kind of destructive potential as fire, though it can also be channeled and used as a weapon. For instance, flooding a valley encampment or marshy field, though the act diverting streams and watercourses is arduous and rarely done with complete surprise. Cutting off or contaminating an enemy's water supply is often easier, and can break a siege, cause famine, or provoke disease.

Fire and water are useful weapons in war, but few know that insects can be weaponized as well. They can be used to destroy an enemy's crops, spread disease, or even incapacitate a foe. For example, during the Third Mithridatic War, Mithridates (135 BC – 63 BC) ordered grayanotoxin-laden honey, created by rhododendron-foraging bees, to be left along roads where Roman invaders would find it. Legionnaires who ate the honey became sick, suffering hallucinations, which earned it the nickname "mad honey." Thus incapacitated, Romans became easy prey for Mithridates' army.

For the Win: The nature of a water attack is it is not the water itself but what it carries. The debris in the tsunami does more damage than the water. Leverage both direct and indirect means to accomplish your goals.

You Lose: When you fail to see a weapon beyond its initial use. Failing to consider the collateral benefit and impact of every weapon is short-sighted, leading to unintended consequences that can undermine your endeavor.

15. Sun Tzu wrote:

"Unhappy is the fate of one who tries to win his battles and succeed in his attacks without cultivating the spirit of enterprise, for the result is waste of time and general stagnation."

To succeed in battle, we must seize favorable moments as they arise and not shrink on occasion from extreme measures such as resorting to attacks with fire, water, insects, and similar means. What we must not do, however, is sit back and hold onto the advantages we currently have without using our resources to further our cause. Failure to act is a dereliction of duty.

From primitive tribes using poison dart frogs to coat their arrowheads with a toxin to nerve gas, chlorine, and phosgene deployed on the battlefield during WWII, chemical and biological warfare is nearly as old as mankind. In fact, the Greek word for a poisoned arrow is toxicon, which is derived from toxon (meaning bow or arrow). The Romans modified it to toxicum (meaning any kind of poison), from which we get the English words "toxic" and "toxin." Although the Geneva Protocol of 1925, which the US didn't sign until 1975, seemingly outlawed the use of biological weapons, countries can still own and study them today. It's by no means a stretch of the imagination to predict that chemical and biological weapons will raise their ugly heads again on some battlefield of the future. Consequently, militaries around the world prepare and train for that eventuality.

For the Win: Expend whatever resources are necessary to assure the progress of your endeavor.

You Lose: Hoarding resources is different than prudently using them. Hoarding is useless and burdensome.

16. Sun Tzu wrote:

"Hence the saying: The enlightened ruler lays his plans well ahead; the good general cultivates his resources."

As generals, we direct our troops by the power of the authority invested in us by our sovereign. Nevertheless, command authority is not enough. We must hold the army together with good faith, using rewards and punishments to make them strong and keep them serviceable. If we allow the men and women in our command's faith in their leadership to decay, there will be disruption to our plans. If rewards are deficient or punishments excessive, our commands will not be respected.

According to exit interviews, one of the primary reasons that people leave organizations is a lack of recognition for their contributions. Some individuals may be more motivated by a challenging assignment than they ever would be from any certificate or cash award, so it's important to know your team and act accordingly. Acknowledgment reinforcing meritorious behaviors can be anything from a kind word to a letter to framed artwork to stock options; it's not the recognition so much as how and when we do it that matters. The best rewards are sincere, meaningful to the person being honored, relevant to their achievement, and timely. In this fashion, we not only motivate our best people but also inspire others to follow their example.

For the Win: The good leader is multidimensional—sometimes you are a coach, other times a taskmaster. Sometimes you're a mentor, teacher, or confidant. Occasionally you're even a confessor. All this must be understood and played appropriately to further your endeavor.

You Lose: Being skilled in only one area is narrow, finite, and not transferable to the majority of your forces. This is a path of failure.

17. Sun Tzu wrote:

"Move not unless you see an advantage, use not your troops unless there is something to be gained, fight not unless the position is critical."

Win or lose, any action in battle uses valuable resources, weakening our capabilities if we do not replace what was expended. Consequently, we must assure that the return for our actions is worth the cost. Sometimes this means taking risks for small gain whereas other times that means waiting for the optimal conditions to carry out a significant operation in furtherance of our plan. The Battle of the Bulge during WWII is a good example of waiting for the right time to execute one's plan (though thankfully it didn't exactly work out as planned).

After suffering five months of losses along the Western Front, the Nazi's planned a counteroffensive in December of 1944. Clear skies and sunshine, however, kept them from launching their Ardennes Offensive into Belgium. With newly-trained reserves from the Volkssturm (home guard) in position, dwindling fuel and ammunition stockpiled, the Germans waited two weeks for the weather to worsen so that a thick blanket of clouds could cover their assault. Although the initial onslaught of what became known as the "Battle of the Bulge" on December 16th created a "bulge" in their enemy's lines, the Allies quickly regained the initiative. Germany lost over 120,000 men and critical stores of ammunition and supplies they could not afford to replace during the battle. With this defeat, they were well on their way to losing WWII a few months later. Germany surrendered to the Western Allies on May 8th and to the Russians on May 9th on what became known as V-E (Victory in Europe) Day.

For the Win: Move when you better your position.

You Lose: When you move for movement's sake out of anxiety or frustration.

18. Sun Tzu wrote:

"No ruler should put troops into the field merely to gratify his own spleen, no general should fight a battle simply out of pique."

The maxim, "Don't cut off your nose to spite your face," means that we should never do something out of spite that will end up causing more harm to ourselves than to our enemy, needlessly throwing our men and women's lives away out of spite, selfishness, or intemperance. This adage was reportedly inspired by Viking raiders during the 9th Century.

The Scandinavian term Viking referred to a profession rather than a specific ethnic group, derived from the Old Norse phrase "fara i viking" meaning "to go on expedition (by raiding other people's lands)." In the year 870, while Danish, Norwegian, and Swedish Vikings were raping, pillaging, and plundering their way across the British Isles, a group of raiders laid siege to the Coldingham Priory. Saint Aebee the Younger (? – 870) exhorted the nuns who lived there to avoid being raped by voluntarily disfiguring themselves, setting an example by cutting off her own nose and upper lip. When the Vikings broke into the convent and saw the self-mutilated nuns, their lust naturally turned to disgust. Unfortunately, this act of defiance didn't entirely work out as planned... The Vikings locked everyone inside, set fire to the place, and left.

For the Win: It is immoral to fight for fighting's sake. Never go to war, literal or metaphorical, simply to satisfy a personal shortcoming.

You Lose: Be guided by your emotions to justify battle and soon those emotions will guide you to your grave.

19. Sun Tzu wrote:

"If it is to your advantage make a forward move, if not stay where you are."

There is a cost both to action as well as to inaction. If we are ensconced in a secure position and it furthers our aims to send out raiding parties or even advance our entire force into enemy territory, we should take action. If, however, there is little to be gained there is no point in wasting valuable resources pursuing targets of low merit. Such decisions must be made thoughtfully lest our inaction invites attack from the enemy. Consider the Raid on Medway by way of example.

The Anglo-Dutch War began in 1665. Two years in, King Charles II (1630 – 1685) found himself running low on resources to continue the fight and attempted to call off the hostilities, yet was unable to reach a reasonable peace with his Dutch counterpart Johann de Witt (1625 – 1672). During the negotiations, the English blocked their navigable channel with a massive chain that stretched from shore to shore. Thinking themselves secure behind this barricade, they bided their time sending emissaries back and forth. Dutch engineers, however, were able to use the lull in the fighting to break past the chain on June 12, 1667, and sail 60 ships up the Thames River into the heart of England. During the fight they captured two ships, including the British flagship, and burned the rest of the English armada in the harbor, losing only their sacrificial "fire ships" in the process.

For the Win: Movement should only be done when an advantage is seen and within your grasp.

You Lose: Let nervousness and apprehension drive your choice to move. The last word of losers is frequently, "Well, we have to do something."

20. Sun Tzu wrote:

"Anger may in time change to gladness, vexation may be succeeded by content."

Great leaders are never ruled by emotion. We know that most frustrations are short-lived. It's easy to become angered, but hard to stay that way overlong. Consequently, we must never make decisions in a fit of rage that we may come to regret later on. Sadly, many leaders throughout history had to learn this lesson the hard way.

When Iraqi Dictator Saddam Hussein (1937 – 2006) held a grudge, he often took things to extremes. After Iraq's defeat during the First Gulf War in 1991, he developed a deep, personal, and abiding hatred for US President George H. W. Bush (1924 – 2018) whose coalition beat him, expressing this rage with a huge mosaic of Bush's face on the floor of the al-Rashid hotel in Baghdad. Upon entering the hotel, visitors would walk across the US President's face, a grave insult in a culture where striking someone with the sole of your shoe is a sign of disrespect. Ironically when US forces overthrew Saddam's regime during the Second Gulf War in 2003, soldiers dug out the mosaic of the former US President and replaced it with a portrait of Saddam himself.

For the Win: Know that the phrase, "This time it's personal," is a movie cliché designed to manipulate the emotions of the audience.

You Lose: Adopt a Hollywood cliché as a justification for your action. Not only do you look foolish, but you're on a path to be both foolish and dead.

21. Sun Tzu wrote:

"But a kingdom that has once been destroyed can never come again into being, nor can the dead ever be brought back to life."

What we lose in battle is destroyed forever. No one knows this better than a seasoned general. We understand that the consequences of failure or folly are severe; there will be no way to undo any damage that we cause to our country, our troops, or our reputation. We must, therefore, always keep the art of war at the forefront of our mind, prudently using its principles to prevail in all our endeavors. Consider how their defeat in WWII affected the leadership of Japan.

Losing the war did not sit well with the Japanese High Command. War minister Anami Korechika (1887 – 1945) committed seppuku (ritual suicide) following an argument with Emperor Hirohito (1901 – 1989) in which he advocated for continuing the fight despite the emperor's support for surrender in August of 1945. Following his suicide, a number of junior officers who also favored continuing the war attempted a coup against the emperor, something unthinkable in pre-war Japanese society where the emperor was called Tennō, literally "heavenly sovereign," the embodiment of supreme power in the country after the Meiji Restoration of 1867. Commander of the Eastern District Army, General Tanaka Shizuichi (1887 – 1945), helped thwart that rebellion, yet also committed suicide by shooting himself ten days later.

For the Win: Know that going to battle changes everything. All elements engaged in the fight are forever and permanently impacted. Win or lose, nothing remains the same.

You Lose: Assuming you know what the long-term results of your actions in battle will be.

22. Sun Tzu wrote:

"Hence the enlightened ruler is heedful, and the good general full of caution. This is the way to keep a country at peace and an army intact."

Empires can expand through conquest, but it does not always have to be that way. More often than not, periods of peace bring greater prosperity for the populace. As a commander in peacetime, we must always be ready for war, maintaining the readiness of our troops, yet we should never needlessly seek out conflict. Consider the Pax Romana, or "Roman Peace," by way of example.

Pax Romana was a state of unprecedented peace, stability, and prosperity throughout the ancient world that lasted from the reign of Augustus Caesar (27 BC – 14 AD) until the reign of Marcus Aurelius (161 – 180). Augustus laid the foundation by creating a beneficial condition where individual provinces paid taxes and accepted Roman military protection yet were able to make and administer their own local laws. During that 200-year period, the empire grew to span from England in the north to Morocco in the south to Iraq in the east, with roughly 70 million people under its rule. The "peace dividend" of Pax Romana included significant advances in literature, poetry, philosophy, and engineering, including the discovery of the formula for concrete, which facilitated the construction of the extensive Roman aqueducts and highways, some of which still exist today.

For the Win: Consider thoughtfully before acting. War is expensive, its outcomes long-lasting, and results are by no means guaranteed, even for those who study the art of war.

You Lose: When you act rashly, leaping into battle without forethought. Your impetuousness demonstrates your immaturity and lack of vision.

Chapter 13: The Use of Spies

In this chapter, we learn the full cost in blood and treasure that comes with war. Unless we are constantly informed of the enemy's condition, such that we remain ready to strike him at the opportune moment, conflict may drag on for years. The only way to obtain intelligence critical for the success of our conquest is through building a network of spies, of whom we may place in five classifications. Adroitly using these agents, we learn the names and predilections of those who oppose us, and in this fashion gain the information necessary to achieve great results from our conduct of the art of war.

1. Sun Tzu wrote:

"Raising a host of a hundred thousand men and marching them great distances entails heavy loss on the people and a drain on the resources of the State. The daily expenditure will amount to a thousand ounces of silver. There will be commotion at home and abroad and men will drop down exhausted on the highways. As many as seven hundred thousand families will be impeded in their labor."

The total cost to train, equip, and deploy one US infantry soldier for one year today runs somewhere in the $400,000 +/- range, depending on that warrior's role. This includes his or her education, training, salary, benefits, equipment, weapons, ammunition, transportation, etc. By comparison, it costs approximately $10,900,000 to qualify a pilot to fly the Lockheed-Martin F-22 Raptor air superiority fighter. The jet itself runs about $334,000,000 apiece, with an additional flight cost per hour of roughly $60,000 (excluding any munitions expended during the mission). Imagine that kind of burden placed upon an agrarian state where peasants rarely made actual cash money but rather paid a tithe to the government based on the value of their crops or trade goods and we begin to understand Sun Tzu's message here. A standing army is expensive, a deployed one more so.

While an arms race can create technological spin-offs, job creation, infrastructure improvements, and the like, military expenditures displace other, often more-productive forms of investment. Even when weapons and supplies are exported, excessive military spending creates adverse economic consequences. For example, the former Soviet Union's (1922 – 1991) economic troubles were exacerbated by the high proportion of their gross domestic product (GDP) devoted to their Cold War arms race with the United States. The more productive US economy outpaced the Soviet economy by a GDP ratio of 5:1, which is a large part of why the Soviets lost the Cold War and subsequently dissolved into component states.

For the Win: Project your losses, and then double your calculations. Project your gains, and cut them in half. This is a sensible equation on which to make your decisions.

You Lose: Engaging in delusional projections, based on emotions without fact.

2. Sun Tzu wrote:

"Hostile armies may face each other for years striving for the victory which is decided in a single day. This being so, to remain in ignorance of the enemy's condition simply because one grudges the outlay of a hundred ounces of silver in honors and emoluments, is the height of inhumanity."

The only way to obtain information about our endeavor is to employ spies. These men and women must be rewarded for the risks they take and the intelligence they provide. This may prove expensive, but the cost of an active or cold war is an incalculably greater sum. Since the burden of funding our armies ultimately falls heavily on the shoulders of the poor, neglecting to use spies is nothing short of a crime against humanity!

In 1943, Gene Grabeel (1920 – 2015), an American mathematician and cryptanalyst in the US Army's Signal Intelligence Service, started Project Venona in order to decipher the USSR's secret encryption system. Soviet spies used numerical codebooks that allowed only the sender and receiver to understand the message. These books were intended to only be used a single time and then destroyed, rendering their codes unbreakable, but the sheer volume of messages meant that some of the codebooks were reused or reprinted, giving Grabeel and her code breakers a chance to figure them out. Project Venona successfully unmasked double agents like atomic spies Klaus Fuchs (1911 – 1988), Julius Rosenberg (1918 – 1953), and Ethel Rosenberg (1915 – 1953). Both Rosenbergs were convicted of espionage and executed by electric chair at Sing-Sing Prison in 1953 for their treachery.

For the Win: Information is everything in preparing for and engaging in any worthy endeavor. Operatives are not only necessary, but cannot be neglected. Use them wisely.

You Lose: Assume you know everything you must to prevail yet fail to gain full information prior to taking action.

3. Sun Tzu wrote:

"One who acts thus is no leader of men, no present help to his sovereign, and no master of victory."

The true purpose of war is to create peace. Through military prowess, we preserve order, assure harmony amongst nations, and create conditions where the populace may thrive. If we cannot commit resources and valor toward our important enterprise, we have no business leading it. War is not a game; it ends with victory or destruction.

Chariot racing was as popular in ancient Constantinople as soccer is today (with roughly 4.2 billion fans worldwide), with devotees often acting like ruffians in much the same way, albeit more barbarically, as modern soccer hooligans. The two biggest gangs in Constantinople were the Blues and the Greens. A riot erupted in January 532, when Emperor Justinian (482 – 565) refused to release two members of these gangs who had been condemned to death for their crimes. In a rare moment of agreement, the two factions banded together and started a massive insurrection. They burned the city prefect's headquarters, killed hundreds of imperial guards, and tried to overthrow the emperor, crowning one of their own number in his stead. Faced with a full-scale revolution over a chariot race, Justinian bribed the Blues to gain their support and then turned his army loose on the remaining hoodlums. By the end of the counterattack, more than 30,000 citizens were killed and the riot vanquished utterly.

For the Win: Avoiding confrontation is not always possible, yet a prudent leader foresees shifts and trends, course correcting as necessary in a good faith effort to avoid conflict.

You Lose: Having a cavalier attitude. This was brilliantly expressed by General "Buck" Turgidson (played by George C. Scott) in the movie Dr. Strange Love. "Mr. President, I'm not saying we wouldn't get our hair mussed. But I do say no more than ten to twenty million killed, tops. Uh, depending on the breaks."

4. Sun Tzu wrote:

"Thus, what enables the wise sovereign and the good general to strike and conquer, and achieve things beyond the reach of ordinary men, is foreknowledge."

Foreknowledge of our adversaries' disposition and likings allows us to craft and implement strategies that overcome their designs. Such is the value of our network of spies, for forewarned is forearmed. We have access to intelligence that ordinary men do not, hence are able to achieve the greatness they can only aspire to.

Throughout history, knowledge has always meant power, but never more than today. Over the last decade or so, data has become one of the most valuable commodities in the world. In fact, it has turned into a new revenue model for many enterprises, with data science used to create value, solve problems, remediate fraud, market effectively, and retain customers. For example, data-driven predictive maintenance creates a competitive advantage for manufacturers whose products become more reliable and cheaper to operate than their competitors' offerings that lack this vital information. Data not only creates new products and services but also makes existing ones more valuable.

For the Win: Understand that communication and information are the lifeblood of proper planning for battle and acquire the data necessary to support your plans.

You Lose: Failing to ask again, enquire again, and ponder once more before taking action, thereby creating failure before you take your first step.

5. Sun Tzu wrote:

"Now this foreknowledge cannot be elicited from spirits, it cannot be obtained inductively from experience nor by any deductive calculation."

Knowledge of our enemy can neither be intuited with guesswork nor determined through calculation. We cannot magically conjure knowledge nor consult with arcane spirits to better understand our foe. Without close, personal observation and evaluation we cannot know precisely what we face. This principle is as unquestionable as the setting of the sun or rising of the tide.

It was extremely challenging for Western forces to gain accurate intelligence from inside xenophobic Japan during WWII, yet that's exactly what Richard Sorge (1895 – 1944) managed to accomplish. He was a German reporter who led a successful Soviet espionage ring in Tokyo at the beginning of the war. After service in the German army during WWI, Sorge joined the Communist Party in 1919 while earning his doctorate at the University of Hamburg, later moving to Moscow in 1924. Working in China, Germany, and later Japan, he proved himself an accomplished spy. In August of 1941, Sorge reported that the Japanese Army was planning to advance southward against Pacific targets rather than northward against the USSR. His information freed Soviet troops along the Manchurian border for service against enemies in the west. On October 18, 1941, Sorge's activities were discovered, he was arrested by the Japanese, jailed throughout most of the war, and eventually executed on November 7, 1944. Twenty years later Sorge was posthumously declared a Hero of the Soviet Union for his service.

For the Win: Prognosis is not built from a single element, but many. Analyze the environment like a scientist studying lab results and thereby move forward with confidence.

You Lose: By forgetting that nature always wins. Choosing to ignore facts that countermand or fail to support your narrative is a dead general's playground.

6. Sun Tzu wrote:

"Knowledge of the enemy's dispositions can only be obtained from other men."

We may comprehend the natural world through science and experimentation. It may be possible to understand the spirit world through prayer or divination. Immutable laws of the universe can be verified through calculation. The only way to take an accurate measure of our adversaries, however, is through direct, personal observation and appraisal. This can only come from other men or women.

Nathan Hale (1755 – 1776) attended Yale University and became a schoolteacher, first in East Haddam and then later in New London. As rumblings of the American Revolutionary War became evident, he joined a Connecticut army regiment in 1775, served in the siege of Boston, and was commissioned a captain in 1776. He went to New York that September with forces under the command of William Heath (1737 – 1814), capturing a British ship filled with provisions from under the guns of a Man-of-War, but was captured while attempting to return to the unit. Accused of spying, Hale was hanged without trial the next day on September 22, 1776. Just before his execution he famously said, "I only regret that I have but one life to lose for my country," solidifying his places as a hero and martyr of the American Revolution.

For the Win: Prostitution is said to be the world's oldest profession. Spying may very well be the second oldest. These vocations are still around because they work. Advance your strategy by evaluating your adversary through direct observation and appraisal.

You Lose: Decide that you can replace the eyes and ears of human spies with technology and you have lowered your ability to truly understand, hence overcome your enemy.

7. Sun Tzu wrote:

"Hence the use of spies, of whom there are five classes: (1) local spies, (2) inward spies, (3) converted spies, (4) doomed spies, and (5) surviving spies."

Knowing that direct, personal observation and appraisal can only come from spies, we understand that we must employ them. In doing so, however, we must also appreciate that there is more than one type of spy that we may hire, coopt, or cajole into our service. By classifying agents into five different categories we are able to make the best use of their skills and information.

During the American Civil War, the Confederate Signal Corps ran an effective intelligence operation known as the Secret Service Bureau. Headed by William Norris (1820 – 1896), a Baltimore lawyer, they operated a semaphore system and courier network to communicate amongst troops in the field. Norris's agents also passed coded messages from the heart of their operations in Richmond to Confederate agents operating in throughout the North and Canada, some even reaching allies across the ocean in Europe.

For the Win: Spies are assets with prodigious value. Treat them in a manner reflecting their distinct character and significance for your cause.

You Lose: Fail to know what role your spies must play, neglect to use them properly, or fail to act prudently on their information and you doom both your plans and your agents.

8. Sun Tzu wrote:

> *"When these five kinds of spy are all at work, none can discover the secret system. This is called 'divine manipulation of the threads.' It is the sovereign's most precious faculty."*

Manipulating a network of all five types of spies enables an irreproachable arrangement, one that cannot be destabilized or thwarted. We combine data from multiple sources, checking one and balancing it against the others, for holistic appraisal. In this fashion, our ability to deduce the truth is near godlike in its exactitude.

Allan Pinkerton (1819 – 1884) founded a detective agency in Chicago and later worked for General George B. McClellan (1826 – 1885) during the American Civil War, setting up the Union's first espionage operations. Though he called this operation the US Secret Service, military intelligence was decentralized at that time, so Pinkerton worked directly for McClellan rather than reporting to President Abraham Lincoln (1809 – 1865) or other generals in the Army of the Potomac. Using the alias E. J. Allen, Pinkerton built a counterintelligence network in Washington, sending undercover agents to Richmond to spy on the Confederacy.

For the Win: Spies may coordinate, but this interaction puts them at risk. Divide up your network to test the veracity of your information.

You Lose: Let your agent's information and relationships cross-pollinate. Hybrid information and agendas cloud true information.

9. Sun Tzu wrote:

"Having local spies means employing the services of the inhabitants of a district."

In enemy territory, we must find scouts who intimately know and can guide us through the terrain. To fill this need, it is better to win over locals with kind treatment or payment rather than by conscripting their services. Because these agents are intimately familiar with the district they live in, their information often proves invaluable, especially for stealthy infiltration and exfiltration.

Harriet Tubman (1820 — 1913) escaped slavery and became a leading abolitionist before the American Civil War. She led over 300 of her fellow Southern slaves to freedom in the North using a secret network of safe houses stretching from Maryland to Canada that came to be known as "The Underground Railroad." During the war, she also helped spy on the Confederates, bringing information about troop movements, warehouses, munition dumps, and the like to the Union army. Sadly, she was paid so little for her wartime service that she had to support herself by baking and selling homemade bread and pastries.

For the Win: Great spies blend in. Leverage those born and raised within the village you wish them to spy upon.

You Lose: Inject your spies into situations where they lack intimate knowledge of the terrain, hence stand out suspiciously.

10. Sun Tzu wrote:

"Having inward spies, making use of officials of the enemy."

Inward spies come from amongst the enemy's officials, those who know him best. This may include aggrieved officers who been demoted or overstepped, retainers who may carry a grudge, fickle turncoats looking to hedge their bets or men and women who worship gold beyond honor. Additionally, we must not overlook the recruitment of body servants, concubines, or courtesans who may overhear affairs of state during the course of their duties or become privy to vital secrets with pillow talk.

Henry Thomas Harrison (1832 – 1923) was a Confederate soldier who spied for General James Longstreet (1821 – 1904) during the American Civil War. He was paid in gold for the information he gathered, much of which proved instrumental to the outcome of the war. On June 28, 1863 he reported that General George Meade (1815 – 1872) had replaced General Joseph Hooker (1814 – 1879) as commander of the Army of the Potomac and that Union forces were advancing northward out of Frederick, Maryland. This report, when read by General Robert E. Lee (1807 – 1870), convinced him to move his forces out of central Pennsylvania where they were spread out indefensibly and concentrate them at Gettysburg. The three-day battle that followed was a pivotal moment in the Civil War, with roughly 51,000 casualties overall, 23,000 for the Union and 28,000 for the Confederacy.

For the Win: Turning an enemy's official into your spy is difficult. The stakes are high, expenditures higher, yet the value is incalculable.

You Lose: Fail to grasp opportunities to turn an enemy's representatives to your cause and miss learning secrets vital for your cause.

11. Sun Tzu wrote:

"Having converted spies, getting hold of the enemy's spies and using them for our own purposes."

Converting an enemy's agents is the process of counterintelligence. We may succeed either by planting false information upon his agents without their participation through guile, by luring these individuals fully into our service, or through some combination of bribes and threats. These double-agents, when faithful, often prove our most valuable assets.

Oleg Penkovsky (1919 – 1963) was the Cold War-era spy who personally prevented nuclear Armageddon. Codenamed "Hero," Penkovsky was a colonel in the Soviet Military Intelligence who informed the United States that his country was preparing to install an intercontinental ballistic missile system in Cuba, sparking the Cuban Missile Crisis in October of 1962. More importantly, however, he also provided evidence that the CIA had materially overestimated Russian nuclear capabilities, helping prevent a shooting war. Reportedly abducted while driving near Moscow, charged with treason, and executed, many theorize that he was actually planted by the Soviets specifically to prevent nuclear war. Rather than actually being killed, he supposedly took on a new identity and disappeared.

For the Win: Enlist double-agents with inside information, longstanding relationships, and high official capacity to subvert the enemy's cause and support your own.

You Lose: Failing to recruit spies from within the enemy's camp.

12. Sun Tzu wrote:

"Having doomed spies, doing certain things openly for purposes of deception and allowing our spies to know of them and report them to the enemy."

At times we may doubt the loyalty or competency of our spies, and choose to deceive them by leading them to believe that we have inadvertently disclosed information we secretly wish the enemy to know. We may let them overhear conversations, obtain documents, or even appear to turn members of our household or staff to gain this disinformation. When these individuals report one tactic yet we pursue another their duplicity will be discovered, often leading to their execution. Their usefulness having run its course, if the enemy has not already put them to death we certainly will, hence the term "doomed" spies.

Dr. Humam Khalil Abu-Mulal al-Balawi (1977 – 2009) was a triple agent who led one of the deadliest attacks against the CIA in Afghanistan. While studying medicine in Istanbul, Turkey, intelligence officers discovered his radical leanings, recruited him as a double-agent, and sent him to Afghanistan to infiltrate Al-Qaida and report on their activities. While he provided just enough intelligence to win over the CIA's confidence, he was secretly a jihadist all along. Claiming to have time-critical information about Al-Qaida leader Ayman al-Zawahiri (1951 –) he went to the CIA command office at Camp Chapman near Khost, Afghanistan on December 30, 2009, where instead of providing intelligence at the meeting he blew himself up using a bomb sewn into his vest. His suicide killed seven American CIA officers, a Jordanian Intelligence officer, and an Afghan working for the CIA. His widow, Defne Bayrak (1979 –) celebrated his martyrdom, telling reporters afterward, "My husband was anti-American; so am I."

For the Win: Misinformation is like a weaponized virus, it kills the host into which it is injected, yet once propagated your enemy can be inoculated against its contamination. Use it sparingly

You Lose: Using misinformation while failing to guard against enemies who would take the same tactics against you.

13. Sun Tzu wrote:

"Surviving spies, finally, are those who bring back news from the enemy's camp."

Surviving spies are those who capture valuable intelligence from within the enemy's camp and bring it back us intact. These individuals merit significant rewards. Few individuals have the wit, courage, and perseverance to succeed in spy craft once let alone repeatedly. These men and women must be counted among our most valuable assets.

Arthur Owens (1899 – 1957) was a Welshman who built boat batteries for a living. Before WWII he worked for both the British Royal Navy and the German Navy as a contractor. After the war started, he moved to Germany and joined the Abwehr. After spying for the Germans, he also contacted MI5, soon becoming the first known double-agent of WWII. While Owens identified 120 German spies working in the UK and helped MI5 and MI6 feed false information to the Nazi's, it became evident in 1941 that he was working both sides. MI5 arrested Owens and had him imprisoned in a hospital until the end of the war, yet afterward he threatened to publish his memoirs if the British government failed to adequately pay him for his services, a demand with which they complied. His daughter Patricia Owens moved to Hollywood where she became an actress, best known for her role in the 1958 movie The Fly.

For the Win: Surviving spies are the best spies, for obvious reasons. Safeguard their services.

You Lose: When your spies are scooped up by the enemy all your intelligence is placed at risk. You can no longer know who and what information to trust.

14. Sun Tzu wrote:

"Hence it is that which none in the whole army are more intimate relations to be maintained than with spies. None should be more liberally rewarded. In no other business should greater secrecy be preserved."

Interactions with our spies must be privileged, kept in strict secrecy for both their safety and ours. The identities of these agents should never be revealed to our troops or to each other, the better to safeguard both our spies and their vital information. Their value is proven, these men and women must be richly rewarded for their service.

Shi Pei Pu (1938 – 2009) was a male Chinese opera singer and secret agent who met French embassy clerk Bernard Boursicot (1944 –) in 1964 at a time when Boursicot taught English to diplomats' families in Beijing. Reportedly convincing the Frenchman that he was a woman dressed as a man, Shi seduced Boursicot, sparking a love affair that lasted over 20 years, all the while tricking Boursicot into handing over 150 French embassy documents to his Chinese spymasters. At one point in their relationship, Shi pretended to have born Boursicot's lovechild, producing a baby boy that he purchased from corrupt officials at a local hospital. In the early 1980s, Boursicot brought Shi and his son to France, where the deception was revealed. Both Shi and Boursicot were arrested, charged with espionage, and sentenced to six years in prison, though they were released after only 11 months on incarceration. Shi's bizarre, real-life story of clandestine sex and espionage reportedly inspired the play (and film) M. Butterfly by David Henry Hwang (1957 –).

For the Win: Treat your spies well. Effective agents are rare and important, and must be handled accordingly.

You Lose: Fail to treat your agents well and you'll you lose them… likely into the service of your enemy.

15. Sun Tzu wrote:

"Spies cannot be usefully employed without a certain intuitive sagacity."

Skilled spies are highly effective at blending in, deeply understanding the culture they wish to infiltrate to the point where they are able to wear the right clothes, speak with the right dialect, imitate the right habits, and tell the right tales necessary to perform their clandestine tasks without stirring suspicion from anyone around them. They are keen observers with strong interpersonal skills, excellent memories, and powerful intuition, hence able to handle the unexpected without breaking their cover. And, they can think quickly, lie effortlessly, make snap decisions, and keep their composure in the toughest situations. Clearly such individuals are rare.

Jonathan Pollard (1954 –) was a US civilian intelligence analyst caught spying for Israel. After failing to earn a job with the CIA in the late 1970s, Pollard was hired by the Navy Field Operational Intelligence Office in Maryland. In 1984, he was assigned to the US Navy's Anti-Terrorist Alert Center where he obtained access to a wide range of classified materials. After contacting officials at the Israeli embassy, he began supplying them with information from the Departments of State, Defense, and Justice, as well as from the CIA and the National Security Agency. On October 25, 1985, he was spotted carrying a suspicious bundle of documents from his office which he placed in his wife's car. After nearly a month of covert surveillance, the US government had all the evidence they needed. Pollard was arrested outside the Israeli embassy in Washington on November 21st where he was likely seeking asylum. He pled guilty to espionage and cooperated with investigators but was, nevertheless, sentenced to life in prison in 1987. After 28 years of incarceration, Pollard was paroled in 2015. This incident strained the relationship between America and its Middle East ally, leading then Prime Minister Shimon Peres to apologize for Pollard's illicit activities and dissolve the spy agency that worked with him.

For the Win: Anyone can spy, but great spies are born not made. Seek out skillful spies and treat them well.

You Lose: Average spies don't last long. You must be ready to wash your hands of them quickly. Failure to know this and prepare for the eventuality, such as with compartmentalization of information, will undermine your cause.

16. Sun Tzu wrote:

"They cannot be properly managed without benevolence and straightforwardness."

Spies are naturally both astute and apprehensive. Consequently, when working with them we must be both forthright and generous lest we drive them away or turn their allegiance toward our enemies. In other words, while spies may be attracted to our cause with substantial offers, we must treat them with absolute sincerity to uphold our end of the deal.

Virginia Hall (1906 – 1982) was the first woman, as well as the first civilian, to be awarded the Distinguished Service Cross during WWII. After attending both Radcliffe and Barnard Colleges, and completing her education in Europe, she came to speak both French and German fluently. While she wanted to work for the US State Department, she had lost her left leg below the knee in a hunting accident and they refused to hire anyone with a false limb, so she took a job as an ambulance driver with the French Army instead. During the war, Hall joined a British Resistance organization in occupied Southern France, earning the nickname, "The Limping Lady," from the German Gestapo operatives she routinely thwarted. Later in the war, she joined the Office of Strategic Services, the predecessor of the CIA, received training, and went back to France to perform undercover work. After the war, Hall worked at the CIA until forced out by mandatory retirement at age 60.

For the Win: Know your agents needs and desires, treating them with sincerity, generosity, and candor.

You Lose: Cross a spy once and the damage becomes irreparable. Your actions will always be held in a tainted light.

17. Sun Tzu wrote:

"Without subtle ingenuity of mind, one cannot make certain of the truth of their reports."

The manipulative skills necessary to deceive a spy into thinking that he or she is serving an adversary when in fact that agent is damaging our adversary's interests is beyond many leaders. Likewise, the investigative skills necessary to intuit when our agent may have double-crossed us are of the highest order. Consequently, we must always be on our guard against the possibility of spies going over to the service of the enemy, continuously testing and validating the veracity and usefulness of information received and transmitted throughout our spy network.

Supposition, innuendo, and various forms of verbal judo can be utilized to avoid speaking the truth, yet lies can often be detected if we pay close attention to the subconscious clues which become perceptible with changes to other person's normal facial expressions, body language, or speech patterns when they evade the truth. For example, fidgeting, rapid eye blinking, or lip biting may indicate prevarication. Oftentimes this is combined with slight changes in the fraudster's tone and cadence, especially when their sentences become longer or more complex as they begin overthinking while spinning their tall tale. Finally, many liars attempt to psychologically distance themselves from their lies, hence useless self-references (such as I, me, or my) than normal when they speak. The better we know a person, the easier it is to distinguish when they lie.

For the Win: Spies provide data. It's your job to analyze that information, place it in context, validate with other sources, and ultimately turn that information into something that furthers your plan.

You Lose: Assuming a spy's report is all-encompassing and accurate. No single source of data is ever comprehensive or unimpeachable, no person without imperfection. If you are unable to discern truth from fiction your plans will fail.

18. Sun Tzu wrote:

"Be subtle! Be subtle! And use your spies for every kind of business."

Espionage is primarily about gathering information, but secret agents can perform a variety of important tasks such as sabotage, blackmail, misinformation, or assassination as well. Done right, information is compartmentalized such that each spy within our network only knows his or her own mission, hence cannot inadvertently disclose or be tortured into revealing vital information such as the names, locations, or missions of other spies. And, in this fashion, we may also validate the veracity of our agents by comparing and contrasting the information they provide.

Not all spies are human. Carrier pigeons were crucial to communication during WWI. The most honored of the 600 birds owned and flown by the US Army Signal Corps in France was Cher Ami (which means "Dear Friend" in French). He delivered dozens of important messages, but in 1918 his heroics directly saved the lives of 194 Americans trapped behind enemy lines. After Major Charles Whittlesey (1884 – 1921) released the carrier pigeon begging for help for his lost battalion, Cher Ami flew through both enemy and friendly fire to deliver the note. For his bravery, the Black Check cock carrier pigeon was awarded the French Croix de Guerre (Cross of War) with palm. He was returned to the United States and died at Fort Monmouth, New Jersey on June 13, 1919. Cher Ami was later inducted into the Racing Pigeon Hall of Fame in 1931 and received a gold medal from the Organized Bodies of American Pigeon Fanciers in recognition of his service.

For the Win: Use each and every weapon to its full capability in pursuit of your endeavor. Spies can do a lot more than simply gather information. Consider this, adapting to each opportunity as the situation warrants.

You Lose: See your agent as only a spy and thereby lose a dynamic segment of your capability.

19. Sun Tzu wrote:

"If a secret piece of news is divulged by a spy before the time is ripe, he must be put to death together with the man to whom the secret was told."

Even with compartmentalization, whenever a spy divulges information about our plan before it has come to fruition, then both that spy and anyone he or she talked to must be put to death to assure that the breach cannot undermine our plan. Clearly, Sun Tzu's admonishment may seem callous or unjust, yet he was speaking from the worldview of his time period about conquest designed to further interests far greater than any individual. Even today, when the security of the state is on the line, few things are beyond consideration.

Krystyna Skarbek (1908 – 1952) was adept at horsemanship, skiing, shooting, and charming members of the opposite sex. A Polish national working with the British Secret Service, she hatched a bold plan to ski into Nazi-occupied Poland and deliver British propaganda to help to fuel the resistance after their government fled their country. Audacious and daring, she was once stopped by the German border patrol while carrying a map of the area that would have blown her cover but rolled it up into a headscarf, greeted the Nazis with a smile, and strolling on by without capture. Another time she was captured, she raised her hands above her head at the German's command, revealing grenades she'd secreted under both arms. She threatened to pull the pins, causing the guards to flee, and promptly escaped. Despite her adventurousness, she survived the war but was stabbed to death by a jealous lover, Dennis Muldowney (1911 – 1952), on June 15, 1952. Muldowney was hung later that year on September 30th for her murder.

For the Win: Spies who cannot be controlled are dangerous. Keep your agents on a short leash.

You Lose: Allow a spy to dictate the terms of your relationship and find yourself undone.

20. Sun Tzu wrote:

"Whether the object be to crush an army, to storm a city, or to assassinate an individual, it is always necessary to begin by finding out the names of the attendants, the aides-de-camp, and doorkeepers and sentries of the general in command. Our spies must be commissioned to ascertain these."

Our spies must know the names and dispositions of everyone close to our adversaries, those who attend his person as well as those who provide him with vital information, and as such may intelligently advise us on who poses the most threat to our designs, who may be compromised, and who may be co-opted. Without this information, our knowledge of the enemy is incomplete, hence we must task our network of spies to obtain it expeditiously. Only then may we lay our plans for conquest.

Spies have been used throughout history to further military endeavors and affairs of state. For example, ancient Egyptian hieroglyphs reveal the presence of court spies who the Pharos used to expose disloyal subjects, understand their enemy's strengths and weaknesses, and locate weaker populations that could be conquered and enslaved. Their spy networks extended through Greece and Rome, where agents carried out acts of espionage, sabotage, and assassination. In fact, Egyptian spies were the first in known history to develop and use poisons, derived from both flora and fauna, in furthering their nefarious work.

For the Win: To identify an enemy's weakness and understand how best to exploit it you must look to those placed closest to him.

You Lose: Failure to examine the makeup and structure of the enemy's organization and know the disposition of everyone therein means lost opportunity.

21. Sun Tzu wrote:

"The enemy's spies who have come to spy on us must be sought out, tempted with bribes, led away, and comfortably housed. Thus, they will become converted spies and available for our service."

We have two options for dealing with enemy spies: extermination or cooptation. The challenge with attempting to kill our adversary's agents is threefold—whatever useful information they could have imparted will be irrevocably lost, once one spy is eliminated another will soon take his or her place, and we can never know for certain if we have discovered them all. Consequently, it is far more useful to turn these spies to our service, tempting them with bribes, enticements, and kind treatment. Through the conversion of our adversary's spies, we may learn what we need to know about his condition.

In the late 1500s, religious reforms and a schism with the Catholic Church under the rule of Henry VIII (1491 – 1547) prompted him to create a secret police force to locate, infiltrate, and terminate Catholic loyalist cells that he believed threatened the English monarchy. When Henry's daughter, Elizabeth I (1533 – 1603), ascended to the throne at the age of 25, political upheaval threatened her reign so she extended Henry's already impressive network and improved the capabilities of her intelligence services. These agents, renowned for their ruthlessness and effectiveness, were no longer ill-trained military officers or patriots dallying in espionage. They were professional undercover operatives recruited from the ranks of intellectuals, linguists, scholars, engineers, and scientists who were specially trained for their profession. They used telescopes for surveillance, employed mathematical encryption, invisible inks, and dead drops to clandestinely communicate, and utilized small pistols, poisons, and daggers to do their dirty work.

For the Win: Agents may become spies from faith in your cause, a desire to enrich themselves, a lust for power, or a variety of other admirable or dishonorable motivations. Know each person's purpose and discover how to best make them your asset.

You Lose: Assuming potential agents are easily manipulated plays into the enemy's hands.

22. Sun Tzu wrote:

"It is through the information brought by the converted spy that we are able to acquire and employ local and inward spies."

Information is the lifeblood of spies. In the process of tempting an adversary's agent into our service, we may use his or her insight to identify other nobles, courtiers, artisans, or courtesans who may also be interested in joining our cause. These spies already recognize whose greed, avarice, or lust we may leverage to bring additional allies into our endeavor, eliminating some of the risky and time-consuming process of recruiting operatives. We may also discover methods of capturing or corrupting the communication process by which our adversary manages his spy network.

On May 24, 1844, American inventor Samuel Morse (1791 – 1872), sent the first message via telegraph saying, "What hath God wrought!" His Morse code system of dots and dashes that represented letters revolutionized communication; anyone who understood this code could transmit and receive messages in a matter of moments despite being hundreds of miles apart. As soon as this invention caught on, individuals and governments alike began to use telegraphs extensively, with lines stretching across the country. It was the principle means for transmitting information by wire or radio waves for more than a century, which of course sparked a need for spies to learn how to tap the lines and intercept the transmissions. This, in turn, led to the development of complex cryptography to safeguard messages. By the turn of the 20th century, intelligence agencies around the world were tapping both wired and wireless telegraphs.

For the Win: The spy game is one of push and pull, lies, temptations, and manipulations. Deceit takes place at all levels. Like a good chess match, you must only sacrifice your game pieces when the payoff is considerable.

You Lose: Recklessly give up your players and you will experience a rapid, painful loss.

23. Sun Tzu wrote:

> *"It is owing to his information, again, that we can cause the doomed spy to carry false tidings to the enemy."*

While a converted spy knows how the adversary can best be deceived, using him or her in this capacity can be fraught with risk. While the benefits may be high, eventually most double-agent's duplicity will be discovered. The more we use each asset, the better the chances that they will be caught, so we must be strategic in our choices, taking best advantage of each opportunity. And, we must leverage multiple spies such that no single individual becomes the linchpin of our operation. We can never know the full import of an agent's information in the moment. Its value plays out over time, yet even something as insignificant as a pastry shop can start a war.

During a military coup in 1828, large portions of Mexico City were destroyed by rioting mobs. One of the victims was a French pastry chef Monsieur Remontel (whose full name is unknown) whose shop in nearby Tacubaya was ransacked. Once the order was reestablished, Chef Remontel asked the Mexican government for 60,000 pesos as reimbursement for his losses but his pleas fell on deaf ears in part because his shop was valued at less than 1,000 pesos, so he took a longshot and petitioned the French government for compensation. His request finally came to the attention of King Louis-Philippe (1773 – 1850) a decade later. At that time Mexico already owed France millions in unpaid loans, which irritated the king, so he used Remontel's request as an excuse to demand an additional 600,000 pesos to compensate the pastry chef. When Mexican authorities pushed back, Louis-Philippe sent an armada to blockade the city of Veracruz in 1838. While the war never progressed beyond minor skirmishes, Remontel eventually received 600,000 pesos in the brokered peace deal.

For the Win: Know that spies are spies, their nature is deception. Their information must be verified before you put it to use.

You Lose: Trust your spies 100% all the time.

24. Sun Tzu wrote:

> *"Lastly, it is by his information that the surviving spy can be used on appointed occasions."*

Generally speaking, there are four motivations for people to become spies, money (e.g., debt, expensive tastes), ideology (e.g., political, religious, or social causes), compromise (e.g., blackmail, extortion), or ego (e.g., self-importance, sense of intellectual superiority). Regardless of their reasons for becoming involved, once our spies have proven their value, we are able to ascertain when and for what missions they should be utilized. Given the right opportunity, these skilled agents will inflict severe damage upon our adversaries.

Eli Cohen (1924 – 1965) was an Egyptian-born Israeli spy who, posing as a Syrian businessman, infiltrated the highest ranks of the Syrian government. At one point he was reportedly on the shortlist to become Syrian Deputy Minister of Defense in President Amin al-Hafez's (1921 – 2009) administration. Despite a considerable talent for espionage, Cohen played fast and loose with the rules, and this carelessness allowed Syrian counterintelligence officials to catch him in the act of sending a coded radio transmission back to his handlers in Israel in January of 1965. He was arrested, tortured for information, put on trial, convicted, and publicly hanged the following May.

For the Win: Like a good sniper, an effective spy can create havoc amongst the enemy's ranks, pin them down, or preemptively dispatch emerging threats. Use your spies to the full breadth and depth of their capabilities.

You Lose: A captured spy means both compromised intelligence and embarrassment. Failure to be prepared for fallout of a failed mission ahead of time puts you behind the curve.

25. Sun Tzu wrote:

"The end and aim of spying in all its five varieties is knowledge of the enemy, and this knowledge can only be derived in the first instance from the converted spy. Hence it is essential that the converted spy be treated with the utmost liberality."

Converted spies not only provide valuable information themselves but also make it much easier to use the four other kinds of spies to our best advantage. As such, they must be rewarded commensurate with their value. These individuals can literally change the course of history.

Dudley Bradstreet (1711 – 1763) was an Irish-born spy who worked for the Dukes of Newcastle and Cumberland to monitor and report on the activities of Jacobite supporters of Prince Charles Edward Stuart (1720 – 1788), known as Bonnie Prince Charlie. An accomplished con artist, Bradstreet held few scruples, often preying on superstitious fools to enrich himself such as "bottle conjuring" where he ostensibly summoned benevolent spirits from empty bottles for cash. As a spy, Bradstreet played both sides, making up information that both "proved" his worth and filled his pockets. His reports of a make-believe army of some 9,000 soldiers in Northampton ready to fight the Scots persuaded Bonnie Prince Charlie to turn back at a council of war in Derby in 1745, undermining the Jacobite's hopes of seizing London.

For the Win: Treat a converted spy well, but listen carefully to what he or she says. These two acts are necessary to discern the truth and see the lies.

You Lose: Treating a converted spy poorly is tantamount to killing him. Either way he'll be silent.

26. Sun Tzu wrote:

"Of old, the rise of the Yin dynasty was due to I Chih who had served under the Hsia. Likewise, the rise of the Chou dynasty was due to Lu Ya who had served under the Yin."

Sun Tzu's suggestion here is that the Hsia and Yin dynasties were toppled by former ministers who changed sides and thus were able to impart vital information to their enemies. Whenever we can obtain the services of high-ranking officers or confidants, those who know our adversaries best, we will find that their intelligence invaluable. In this fashion, our strategy incorporates intimate knowledge of our foes' predilections, idiosyncrasies, weaknesses, and blind spots.

Colonel Oleg Gordievsky (1938 –) was a senior KGB officer who switched sides, providing invaluable information to the British Secret Intelligence Service for over a decade. His insight was instrumental for the West's understanding of their adversaries who ran the Politburo (The Central Committee of the Communist Party of the Soviet Union). Interestingly, he took action not out of greed but rather out of ideological conviction. His eidetic memory and direct access to classified information made him one of the most influential and successful spies in history, exposing vast Soviet spy networks and providing critical intelligence about misinformation campaigns, media manipulation, forgeries, abductions, and murders. His information is even credited with helping avert nuclear war. Even though the USSR collapsed in 1991, his former KGB handlers had a long memory. He survived an assassination attempt in 2008 when an acquaintance slipped him poisoned sleeping pills that left him unconscious for three days, eventually recovering in the hospital.

For the Win: Turncoats can provide information and insight that external observation of the enemy can never replace. Use their intimate knowledge to inform your strategy.

You Lose: Converted spies are both as helpful and as dangerous as double-edged swords, they can cut both ways. Consider only the sharp front edge and risk impaling yourself on the point or being slashed by the other side of the sword.

27. Sun Tzu wrote:

"Hence it is only the enlightened ruler and the wise general who will use the highest intelligence of the army for purposes of spying and thereby they achieve great results. Spies are a most important element in water, because on them depends an army's ability to move."

An army without spies is blind, unable to move, yet overreliance on spies can bring misfortune too. Just as water can float a boat safely to its destination, so too can that same water overturn or sink the vessel and drown its passengers. Nevertheless, with the shrewd implementation of the art of war, using all five types of spies, we gain an unrecoverable advantage over our adversaries.

In July 1975, the KGB sent Boris Yuzhin (1942 –) to San Francisco to pose as a reporter for the Soviet Tass news agency while collecting intelligence information, but while living in America he came to question his ideology and his country's policies. Three years later he became a double-agent working for the FBI, where he was often tasked to take pictures of sensitive documents using a tiny camera disguised as a cigarette lighter. He did well until another double-agent, CIA officer Aldrich Ames (1941 –), who was clandestinely working for the KGB, ratted him out on February 21, 1994. Rather than being executed, the fate of most Soviet traitors, he was sentenced to six years in prison in Siberia.

For the Win: Know that spies are essential. They will be used by your enemy so you must employ them as well.

You Lose: In assuming you are not being spied upon at this very moment and acting accordingly.

Thank you!

Thank you for your purchase! Publishing is an arduous process and it's folks like you who make our efforts worthwhile. With roughly 4 million new titles created every year, unbiased customer reviews are indispensable in helping readers identify books that are worth buying. To that end, if you found value from this work please let other people know. Publish an Amazon review and send us the link at http://www.stickmanpublications.com/contact/ along with your contact information and you will be entered into a drawing to win autographed versions of our four bestselling titles.

Bibliography

Books:

Abraham, Jay. *Getting Everything You can out of All You've Got: 21 Ways you can Outthink, Outperform, and Out-Earn the Competition.* New York, NY: St. Martins Press, 2000.

Ayoob, Massad. *The Truth About Self-Protection.* New York, NY: Bantam Books (Police Bookshelf), 1983.

Baron-Cohen, Simon. *The Essential Difference: Men, Women and the Extreme Male Brain.* New York, NY: Penguin Publishing, 2007.

Block, Peter. *The Empowered Manager: Positive Political Skills at Work.* San Francisco, CA: Jossey-Bass Publishers, 1987.

Carroll, Pete (with Yogi Roth). *Win Forever: Live, Work, and Play Like a Champion.* New York, NY; Penguin Publishing, 2010.

Charan, Ram. *Action Urgency Excellence: Seizing Leadership in the Digital Economy.* Houston, TX: Electronic Data Systems Corp., 2000.

Christensen, Loren and Dr. Alexis Artwohl. *Deadly Force Encounters: What Cops Need To Know To Mentally And Physically Prepare For And Survive A Gunfight.* Boulder, CO: Paladin Enterprises, Inc., 1997.

Christensen, Loren. *Far Beyond Defensive Tactics: Advanced Concepts, Techniques, Drills, and Tricks for Cops on the Street.* Boulder, CO: Paladin Enterprises, Inc., 1998.

Christensen, Loren. *Warriors: On Living with Courage, Discipline and Honor.* Boulder, CO: Paladin Enterprises, Inc., 2004.

Covey, Stephen M. R. and Rebecca R. Merrill. *The Speed of Trust: The one Thing that Changes Everything.* New York, NY: Simon & Schuster, 2008.

Covey, Stephen R. and David K. Hatch. *Everyday Greatness: Inspiration for a Meaningful Live.* Nashville, TN: Thomas Nelson, 2006.

Covey, Stephen R. *The 7 Habits of Highly Effective People: Powerful Lessons in Personal Change.* New York, NY: Simon & Schuster, 1989.

De Pree, Max. *Leadership is an Art.* East Lansing, MI: Michigan State University Press, 1987.

DeBecker, Gavin. *The Gift of Fear: Survival Signals That Protect Us From Violence.* New York, NY: Dell Publishing, 1998.

Drucker, Peter F. *The Effective Executive.* New York, NY: Harper & Row, 1966.

Dungy, Tony (with Nathan Whitaker). *Quiet Strength: The Principles, Practices, and Priorities of a Winning Life.* Winter Park, FL: Legacy LLC, 2007.

Giles, Dr. Lionel. *The Art of War by Sun Tzu*. Overland Park, KS: Neeland Media, LLC, 2016.

Grant, Adam. *Give and Take: A Revolutionary Approach to Success*. New York, NY: Viking Press, 2013.

Greenleaf, Robert K. *The Servant as Leader*. Westfield, IN: The Greenleaf Center for Servant Leadership, 2008.

Grossman, David A. and Loren Christensen. *On Combat: The Psychology and Physiology of Deadly Conflict in War and Peace*. Belleville, IL: PPCT Research Publications, 2004.

Grossman, David A. *On Killing: The Psychological Cost of Learning to Kill in War and Society*. New York, NY: Little, Brown, and Company, 1995.

Hartley, Gregory and Maryann Karinch. *Get People to Do What You Want: How to Use Body Language and Words for Maximum Effect*. Newburyport, MA: Career Press, 2019

Kane, Lawrence A. and Kris Wilder. *The Little Black Book of Violence: What Every Young Man Needs to Know About Fighting*. Wolfeboro, NH: YMAA, 2009.

Kane, Lawrence A. *Surviving Armed Assaults: A Martial Artists Guide to Weapons, Street Violence, and Countervailing Force*. Boston, MA: YMAA, 2006.

Kane, Lawrence A., and Kris Wilder. *The Little Black Book of Violence: What Every Young Man Needs to Know About Fighting*. Wolfeboro, NH: YMAA, 2009

Kaye, Beverly and Sharon Jordan-Evans. *Love 'Em or Lose 'Em: Getting Good People to Stay*. San Francisco, CA: Berrett-Koehler Publishers, 1999.

Lewis, James P. *Working Together: 12 Principles for Achieving Excellence in Managing Projects, Teams, and Organizations*. New York, NY: McGraw-Hill, 2002.

Lombardi, Vince Jr. *The Lombardi Rules: 26 Lessons from Vince Lombardi—The World's Greatest Coach (Mighty Mangers Series)*. New York, NY: McGraw-Hill, 2003.

Lott, Jr. John R. and William M. Landes. *Multiple Victim Public Shootings, Bombings, and Right-to-Carry Concealed Handgun Laws: Contrasting Private and Public Law Enforcement*. University of Chicago, 1999.

Lovret, Fredrick J. *The Way and the Power: Secrets of Japanese Strategy*. Boulder, CO: Paladin Enterprises, Inc., 1987

MacYoung, Marc. *A Professional's Guide to Ending Violence Quickly*. Boulder, CO: Paladin Enterprises, Inc., 1993.

MacYoung, Marc. *Cheap Shots, Ambushes, and Other Lessons: A Down And Dirty Book On Streetfighting and Survival*. Boulder, CO: Paladin Enterprises, Inc., 1989.

MacYoung, Marc. *Fists, Wits, and a Wicked Right: Surviving On the Wild Side of the Street*. Boulder, CO: Paladin Enterprises, Inc., 1991.

MacYoung, Marc. *Floor Fighting: Stompings, Maimings, and Other Things to Avoid When a Fight Goes to the Ground*. Boulder, CO: Paladin Enterprises, Inc., 1993.

MacYoung, Marc. *Knives, Knife Fighting, And Related Hassles: How to Survive A Real Knife Fight*. Boulder, CO: Paladin Enterprises, Inc., 1990.

MacYoung, Marc. *Pool Cues, Beer Bottles, & Baseball Bats: Animal's Guide to Improvised Weapons for Self-Defense and Survival*. Boulder, CO: Paladin Enterprises, Inc., 1990.

MacYoung, Marc. *Street E & E: Evading, Escaping, and Other Ways to Save Your Ass When Things Get Ugly*. Boulder, CO: Paladin Enterprises, Inc., 1993.

Maxwell, John C. *The 5 Levels of Leadership: Proven Steps to Maximize Your Potential*. New York, NY: Hachette Book Group, 2011.

McKay, Matthew, PhD. Davis, Martha, PhD. Fanning, Patrick. *Thoughts and Feelings: Taking Control of Your Moods and Your Life*. Oakland, CA: New Harbinger Publications, Fourth Edition, 2011.

Miller, Rory A. *Facing Violence: Preparing for the Unexpected*. Wolfeboro, NH: YMAA Publication Center, 2011.

Miller, Rory A. *Force Decisions: A Citizen's Guide to Understanding How Police Determine Appropriate Use of Force*. Wolfeboro, NH: YMAA Publication Center, April 2012.

Miller, Rory A. *Meditations on Violence: A Comparison of Martial Arts Training and Real-World Violence*. Wolfeboro, NH: YMAA Publication Center, 2008.

Miller, Rory and Lawrence A. Kane. *Scaling Force: Dynamic Decision Making Under Threat of Violence*. Wolfeboro, NH: YMAA Publication Center, 2012.

Miller, Rory. *Conflict Communication A New Paradigm in Conscious Communication*. Washougal, WA: Wyrd Goat Press, 2014.

Miller, Rory. *Drills: Training for Sudden Violence (A Chiron Manual)*. Washougal, WA: Wyrd Goat Press, 2011.

Niednagel, Jonathan P. *Your Key to Sports Success*. Laguna Miguel, CA: Laguna Press, 1997.

Panné, Jean-Louis and Andrzej Paczkowski, Karel Bartosek, Jean-Louis Margolin, Nicolas Werth, Stéphane Courtois, Mark Kramer, and Jonathan Murphy. *The Black Book of Communism: Crimes, Terror, Repression*. Cambridge, MA: Harvard University Press, 1999.

Peterson, David B. and Mary Dee Hicks. *Development First: Strategies for Self-Development*. Minneapolis, MN: Personnel Decisions International, 1995.

Peterson, David B. and Mary Dee Hicks. *Leader as Coach: Strategies for Coaching and Developing Others*. Minneapolis, MN: Personnel Decisions International, 1996.

Pink, Daniel H. *Drive: The Surprising Truth about What Motivates Us*. New York, NY; Penguin Publishing, 2009.

Pollard, C. William. *The Soul of the Firm*. New York, NY: Harper Business, 1996.

Quinn, Peyton. *Real Fighting: Adrenaline Stress Conditioning through Scenario-Based Training*. Boulder, CO: Paladin Enterprises, Inc., 1996.

Rath, Tom and Barry Conchie. *Strengths Based Leadership: Great Leaders, Teams, and Why People Follow*. New York, NY: Gallup Press, 2008.

Roberts, Dan. *Unleashing the Power of IT: Bringing People, Business, and Technology Together*. Hoboken, NJ: John Wiley & Sons, 2011.

Rosenthal, Robert and Lenore Jacobson. *Pygmalion in the Classroom: Teacher Expectation and Pupils' Intellectual Development*. Norwalk, CT: Crown House Publishing Company, LLC, 1992

Savage, Charles M. *5th Generation Management: Integrating Enterprises through Human Networking*. San Francisco, CA: Digital Equipment Corporation, 1990.

Scherkenbach, William W. *The Deming Route to Quality and Productivity*. Rockville, MD: Mercury Press, 1986.

Scott, Susan. *Fierce Conversations: Achieving Success at Work and in Life, One Conversation at a Time*. New York, NY: The Berkley Publishing Group, 2002.

Senge, Peter M. *The Fifth Discipline: The Art and Practice of the Learning Organization*. New York, NY: Currency Doubleday, 1990.

Siddle, Bruce K. *Sharpening the Warrior's Edge: The Psychology and Science of Training*. Millstadt, IL: PPCT Research Publications, Inc., 1995.

Sockut, Eugene. *Secrets of Street Survival – Israeli Style: Staying Alive in a Civilian War Zone*. Boulder, CO: Paladin Enterprises, Inc., 1995.

Stouffer SA, Lumsdaine A. A., Lumsdaine M. H., et al. *The American Soldier*. Princeton, NJ: Princeton University Press; 1949.

Suarez, Gabe. *The Combative Perspective: The Thinking Man's Guide to Self-Defense*. Boulder, CO: Paladin Enterprises, Inc., 2003.

Taubert, Robert K. *Rattenkrieg! The Art and Science of Close Quarters Battle Pistol*. North Reading, MA: Saber Press, July 1, 2012.

Thompson, George. *Verbal Judo: The Gentle Art of Persuasion*. New York, NY: HarperCollins, 1993.

Waddington, Tad. *Lasting Contribution: How to Think, Plan, and Act to Accomplish Meaningful Work*. Evanston, IL: Agate Publishing, 2007.

Wilson, William Scott and Tsunetomo Yamamoto. *Hagakure: The Book of the Samurai*. Boston, MA: Shambhala Press, 2002.

Wooden, John and Steve Jamison. *Wooden on Leadership: How to Create A Winning Organization*. New York, NY: McGraw-Hill, 2005.

Websites:

16 Personalities (www.16personalities.com)
AT Kearney Purchasing Chessboard (www.atkearney.com/web/the-purchasing-chessboard)
CNN News (www.cnn.com)
Encyclopedia Britannica (www.britannica.com)
Force Science Institute (www.forcescience.org)
Fox News (www.foxnews.com)
Harvard Business Review (www.hbr.org)
History Net (www.historynet.com)
How Stuff Works (www.howstuffworks.com)
Khan Academy (www.khanacademy.org)
Life Hacker (www.lifehacker.com)
LOTAR Combat (www.lotarcombat.com)

Marc MacYoung (www.nononsenselfdefense.com)
National Do Not Call Registry (at www.donotcall.gov)
National Institute of Mental Health (www.nimh.nih.gov)
Psychology Today (www.psychologytoday.com)
Society for Human Resource Management (www.shrm.org)
Society for Organizational Learning (www.solonline.org)
Stratfor Geopolitical Intelligence Platform (www.stratfor.com)
The Bureau of Justice Statistics (www.bjs.gov)
The Federal Bureau of Investigation (www.fbi.gov)
The History Channel (www.history.com)
The New York Times (www.nytimes.com)
The People History: (www.thepeoplehistory.com)
The Quotations Page (www.quotationspage.com)
The Seattle Times (www.seattletimes.com)
Unified Crime Reports (www.fbi.gov/about-us/cjis/ucr/ucr)
United States Army Combined Arms Center (https://usacac.army.mil)
United States Bureau of Labor Statistics (www.bls.gov)
Warfare History Network (www.warfarehistorynetwork.com)

About the Authors

Lawrence A. Kane, ECOP, CSP, CIAP

Lawrence was inducted into the Sourcing Industry Group (SIG) Sourcing Supernova Hall of Fame in 2018 for pioneering leadership in strategic sourcing, procurement, supplier innovation, and digital transformation. An Executive Certified Outsourcing Professional, Certified Sourcing Professional, and Certified Intelligent Automation Professional, he currently works as a senior leader at a Fortune® 50 corporation where he gets to play with billions of dollars of other people's money and make really important decisions.

A martial artist, judicious use-of-force expert, and the bestselling author of 19 books, he has won numerous awards including the 5th Annual Beverly Hills Book Award and Presidential Prize, the 13th Annual USA Best Book Awards winner, the 11th Annual National Indie Excellence Awards winner, a Next Generation Indie Book Awards winner, 3 ForeWord Magazine Book of the Year Award finalists, 5 USA Book News Best Books Award finalists, 3 Next Generation Indie Book Awards finalists, 2 Beverly Hills Book Awards finalists, and an eLit Book Awards Bronze prize.

Since 1970, Lawrence has studied and taught traditional Asian martial arts, medieval European combat, and modern close-quarter weapon techniques. Working stadium security part-time for 26 years he was involved in hundreds of violent altercations, but got paid to watch football. A founding technical consultant to University of New Mexico's Institute of Traditional Martial Arts, he has also written hundreds of articles on martial arts, self-defense, countervailing force, and related topics.

He has been interviewed numerous times on podcasts (e.g., Art of Procurement, Negotiations Ninja Podcast), nationally syndicated and local radio shows (e.g., Biz Talk Radio, The Jim Bohannon Show), and television programs (e.g., Fox Morning News) as well as by reporters from Computerworld, Le Matin, Practical Taekwondo, Forbes, Traditional Karate, and Police Magazine, among other publications. He was once interviewed in English by a reporter from a Swiss newspaper for an article that was published in French, and found that oddly amusing.

Lawrence lives in Seattle, Washington. You can contact him directly at lakane@ix.netcom.com or connect with him on LinkedIn (www.linkedin.com/in/lawrenceakane).

Kris Wilder, BCC

Kris Wilder is a Board-Certified Coach and internationally renowned martial arts expert who was inducted into the US Martial Arts Hall of Fame in 2018. He runs the West Seattle Karate Academy, a frequent destination for practitioners from around the world which also serves the local community. Sensei Wilder has earned black belt rankings in three styles, karate, judo, and taekwondo, and often travels to conduct seminars across the United States, Canada, and Europe.

A National Representative for the University of New Mexico's Institute of Traditional Martial Arts, Kris has also taught self-defense and lectured at Washington State University and Susquehanna University. He spent about 15 years in the political and public affairs arena, working for campaigns from the local to national level. During this consulting career, he was periodically on staff for elected officials. His work also involved lobbying and corporate affairs. And, he was also a member of The Order of St. Francis (OSF), one of many active Apostolic Christian Orders.

Kris is the bestselling author of 21 books, including a Beverly Hills Book Award and Presidential Prize winner, a USA Best Book Awards winner, a National Indie Excellence Awards winner, and a Next Generation Indie Book Awards winner. He has been interviewed on CNN, FOX, The Huffington Post, Thrillist, Nickelodeon, Howard Stern, and more.

Kris lives in Seattle, Washington. You can contact him directly at Kriswilder@kriswilder.com, follow him on Twitter (@kris_wilder), on Facebook (www.facebook.com/kris.wilder) or Instagram (https://www.instagram.com/thekriswilder/).

Authors' Note

There are hundreds if not thousands of interpretations of Sun Tzu's Art of War you could have purchased. We hope you found this one entertaining, enlightening, and useful. We certainly enjoyed writing it, and learned some fascinating historical insights in the process.

Between us we've now published 40 books with the release of this title, no small accomplishment. If you're an aspiring author and would like some inspiration to follow in our footsteps, here are a couple of free articles you will find valuable:

- Getting that book out of your head and into the marketplace: https://www.linkedin.com/pulse/getting-book-out-your-head-marketplace-lawrence-kane-cop-gov/
- Three keys to writing books that sell: https://www.linkedin.com/pulse/three-keys-writing-books-sell-lawrence-kane-cop-gov/

On a personal note, you may be interested in knowing that the process of grinding out a new book is arduous. Between research, writing, editing, proofreading, photo shoots, layout, and the like, the process takes 9 to 12 months, sometimes longer. To ease the burden, we often listen to music to focus our minds and stay on task while working. The playlist is eclectic, but for the record, there's something ever so right with the universe when Manowar's heavy metal (the song Sons of Odin to be specific) pops up just as you begin explaining how the Swiss Eidgenossen (oath brothers) kicked the sh!t out of the Hapsburgs and Duke Leopold II back in 1315. Just sayin' ☺

Best,

Lawrence   Kris

Other Works by the Authors

Non-Fiction Books:

Musashi's Dokkodo (Kane/Wilder)

"The authors have made classic samurai wisdom accessible to the modern martial artist like never before" – **Goran Powell**, award winning author of *Chojun* and *A Sudden Dawn*

Shortly before he died, Miyamoto Musashi (1584 – 1645) wrote down his final thoughts about life for his favorite student Terao Magonojō to whom *Go Rin No Sho*, his famous *Book of Five Rings*, had also been dedicated. He called this treatise *Dokkodo*, which translates as *"The Way of Walking Alone."* This treatise contains Musashi's original 21 precepts of the *Dokkodo* along with five different interpretations of each passage written from the viewpoints of a monk, a warrior, a teacher, an insurance executive, and a businessman. In this fashion you are not just reading a simple translation of Musashi's writing, you are scrutinizing his final words for deeper meaning. In them are enduring lessons for how to lead a successful and meaningful life.

The Little Black Book of Violence (Kane/Wilder)

"This book will save lives!" – **Alain Burrese**, JD, former US Army 2nd Infantry Division Scout Sniper School instructor

Men commit 80% of all violent crimes and are twice as likely to become the victims of aggressive behavior. This book is primarily written for men ages 15 to 35, and contains more than mere self-defense techniques. You will learn crucial information about street survival that most martial arts instructors don't even know. Discover how to use awareness, avoidance, and de-escalation to help stave off violence, know when it's prudent to fight, and understand how to do so effectively when fighting is unavoidable.

The Big Bloody Book of Violence (Kane/Wilder)

"Implementing even a fraction of this book's suggestions will substantially increase your overall safety." – **Gila Hayes**, Armed Citizens' Legal Defense Network

All throughout history ordinary people have been at risk of violence in one way or another. Abdicating personal responsibility by outsourcing your safety to others might be the easy way out, but it does little to safeguard your welfare. In this book you'll discover what dangers you face and learn proven strategies to thwart them. Self-defense is far more than fighting skills; it's a lifestyle choice, a more enlightened way of looking at and moving through the world. Learn to make sense of "senseless" violence, overcome talisman thinking, escape riots, avert terrorism, circumvent gangs, defend against home invasions, safely interact with law enforcement, and conquer seemingly impossible odds.

Dude, The World's Gonna Punch You in the Face (Wilder/Kane)

"As an emergency room physician, I see a lot of injuries. This book can save you a lot of pain and trauma, not just physical but also emotional and financial as well. Do yourself a favor, read it, and stay out of my Emergency Room." – **Jeff Cooper**, MD

We only get one shot at life. And, it's really easy to screw that up because the world wants to punch us all in the face. Hard! But, what if you knew when to duck? What if you were warned about the dangers—and possibilities—ahead of time? Here is how to man-up and take on whatever the world throws at you. This powerful book arms young men with knowledge about love, wealth, education, faith, government, leadership, work, relationships, life, and violence. It won't prevent all mistakes, nothing will, but it can keep you from making the impactful ones that you'll regret the most. This book is quick knowledge, easy to read, and brutally frank, just the way the world gives it to you, except without the pain. Read on. Learn how to see the bad things coming and avoid them.

Sensei Mentor Teacher Coach (Wilder/Kane)

"Finally, a book that will actually move the needle in closing the leadership skills gap found in all aspects of our society." – **Dan Roberts**, CEO and President, Ouellette & Associates

Many books weave platitudes, promising the keys to success in leadership, secrets that will transform you into the great leader, the one. The fact of the matter is, however, that true leadership really isn't about you. It's about giving back, offering your best to others so that they can find the best in themselves. The methodologies in this book help you become the leader you were meant to be by bringing your goals and other peoples' needs together to create a powerful, combined vision. Learn how to access the deeper aspects of who you are, your unique qualities, and push them forward in actionable ways. Acquire this vital information and advance your leadership journey today.

Dirty Ground (Kane/Wilder)

"Fills a void in martial arts training." – **Loren W. Christensen**, Martial Arts Masters Hall of Fame member

This book addresses a significant gap in most martial arts training, the tricky space that lies between sport and combat applications where you need to control a person without injuring him (or her). Techniques in this region are called "drunkle," named after the drunken uncle disrupting a family gathering. Understanding how to deal with combat, sport, and drunkle situations is vital because appropriate use of force is codified in law and actions that do not accommodate these regulations can have severe repercussions. Martial arts techniques must be adapted to best fit the situation you find yourself in. This book shows you how.

Scaling Force (Kane/Miller)

"If you're serious about learning how the application of physical force works—before, during and after the fact—I cannot recommend this book highly enough." – **Lt. Jon Lupo**, New York State Police

Conflict and violence cover a broad range of behaviors, from intimidation to murder, and require an equally broad range of responses. A kind word will not resolve all situations, nor will wristlocks, punches, or even a gun. This book introduces the full range of options, from skillfully doing nothing to employing deadly force. You will understand the limits of each type of force, when specific levels may be appropriate, the circumstances under which you may have to apply them, and the potential costs, legally and personally, of your decision. If you do not know how to succeed at all six levels covered in this book there are situations in which you will have no appropriate options. More often than not, that will end badly.

Surviving Armed Assaults (Kane)

"This book will be an invaluable resource for anyone walking the warrior's path, and anyone who is interested in this vital topic." – **Lt. Col. Dave Grossman**, Director, Warrior Science Group

A sad fact is that weapon-wielding thugs victimize 1,773,000 citizens every year in the United States alone. Even martial artists are not immune from this deadly threat. Consequently, self-defense training that does not consider the very real possibility of an armed attack is dangerously incomplete. You should be both mentally and physically prepared to deal with an unprovoked armed assault at any time. Preparation must be comprehensive enough to account for the plethora of pointy objects, blunt instruments, explosive devices, and deadly projectiles that someday could be used against you. This extensive book teaches proven survival skills that can keep you safe.

The 87—Fold Path to Being the Best Martial Artist (Kane/Wilder)

"The 87—Fold Path contains unexpected, concise blows to the head and heart... you don't have a chance, but to examine and retool your way of life." – **George Rohrer**, Executive and Purpose Coach, MBA, CPCC, PCC

Despite the fact that raw materials in feudal Japan were mediocre at best, bladesmiths used innovative techniques to forge some of the finest swords imaginable for their samurai overlords. The process of heating and folding the metal removed impurities, while shaping and strengthening the blades to perfection. The end result was strong yet supple, beautiful and deadly. As martial artists we utilize a similar process, forging our bodies through hard work, perseverance, and repetition. Knowing how to fight is important, clearly, yet if you do not find something larger than base violence attached your efforts it becomes unsustainable. *The 87-Fold Path* provides ideas for taking your training beyond the physical that are uniquely tailored for the elite martial artist.

How to Win a Fight (Kane/Wilder)

"It is the ultimate course in self-defense and will help you survive and get through just about any violent situation or attack." – **Jeff Rivera**, bestselling author

More than 3,000,000 Americans are involved in a violent physical encounter every year. Develop the fortitude to walk away when you can and prevail when you must. Defense begins by scanning your environment, recognizing hazards and escape routes, and using verbal de-escalation to defuse tense situations. If a fight is unavoidable, the authors offer clear guidance for being the victor, along with advice on legal implications, including how to handle a police interview after the altercation.

Lessons from the Dojo Floor (Wilder)

"Helps each reader, from white belt to black belt, look at and understand why he or she trains." – **Michael E. Odell**, Isshin-Ryu Northwest Okinawa Karate Association

In the vein of Dave Lowry, a thought-provoking collection of short vignettes that entertains while it educates. Packed with straightforward, easy, and quick to read sections that range from profound to insightful to just plain amusing, anyone with an affinity for martial arts can benefit from this material. This book educates, entertains, and ultimately challenges every martial artist from beginner to black belt.

Martial Arts Instruction (Kane)

"Boeing trains hundreds of security officers, Kane's ideas will help us be more effective." – **Gregory A. Gwash**, Chief Security Officer, The Boeing Company

While the old adage, "those who can't do, teach," is not entirely true, all too often "those who can do" cannot teach effectively. This book is unique in that it offers a holistic approach to teaching martial arts; incorporating elements of educational theory and communication techniques typically overlooked in *budo* (warrior arts). Teachers will improve their abilities to motivate, educate, and retain students, while students interested in the martial arts will develop a better understanding of what instructional method best suits their needs.

The Way of Kata (Kane/Wilder)

"This superb book is essential reading for all those who wish to understand the highly effective techniques, concepts, and strategies that the *kata* were created to record." – **Iain Abernethy**, British Combat Association Hall of Fame member

The ancient masters developed *kata*, or "formal exercises," as fault—tolerant methods to preserve their unique, combat-proven fighting systems. Unfortunately, they also deployed a two-track system of instruction where only the select inner circle that had gained a master's trust and respect would be taught the powerful hidden applications of *kata*. The theory of deciphering *kata* was once a great mystery revealed only to trusted disciples of the ancient masters in order to protect the secrets of their systems. Even today, while the basic movements of *kata* are widely known, the principles and rules for understanding *kata* applications are largely unknown. This groundbreaking book unveils these methods, not only teaching you how to analyze your *kata* to understand what it is trying to tell you, but also helping you to utilize your fighting techniques more effectively.

The Way of Martial Arts for Kids (Wilder)

"Written in a personable, engaging style that will appeal to kids and adults alike."
– **Laura Weller**, Guitarist, *The Green Pajamas*

Based on centuries of traditions, martial arts training can be a positive experience for kids. The book helps you and yours get the most out of every class. It shows how just about any child can become one of those few exemplary learners who excel in the training hall as well as in life. Written to children, it is also for parents as well. After all, while the martial arts instructor knows his art, no one knows his/her child better than the parent. Together you can help your child achieve just about anything… The advice provided is straightforward, easy to understand, and written with a child-reader in mind so that it can either be studied by the child and/or read together with the parent to assure solid results.

The Way of Sanchin Kata (Wilder)

"This book has been sorely needed for generations!" – **Philip Starr**, National Chairman, Yiliquan Martial Arts Association

When karate was first developed in Okinawa it was about using technique and extraordinary power to end a fight instantly. These old ways of generating remarkable power are still accessible, but they are purposefully hidden in *sanchin kata* for the truly dedicated to find. This book takes the practitioner to new depths of practice by breaking down the form piece-by-piece, body part by body part, so that the very foundation of the *kata* is revealed. Every chapter, concept, and application is accompanied by a "Test It" section, designed for you to explore and verify the *kata* for yourself. *Sanchin kata* really comes alive when you feel the thrill of having those hidden teachings speak to you across the ages through your body. Simply put, once you read this book and test what you have learned, your karate will never be the same.

Journey: The Martial Artist's Notebook (Kane/Wilder)

"Students who take notes progress faster and enjoy a deeper understanding than those who don't. Period." – **Loren W. Christensen**, Martial Arts Masters Hall of Fame inductee

As martial arts students progress through the lower ranks it is extraordinarily useful for them to keep a record of what they have learned. The mere process of writing things down facilitates deeper understanding. This concept is so successful, in fact, that many schools require advanced students to complete a thesis or research project concurrent with testing for black belt rank, advancing the knowledge base of the organization while simultaneously clarifying and adding depth to each practitioner's understanding of his or her art. Just as Bruce Lee's notes and essays became *Tao of Jeet Kune Do*, perhaps someday your training journal will be published for the masses, but first and foremost this notebook is by you, for you. This is where the deeper journey on your martial path toward mastery begins.

The Way to Black Belt (Kane/Wilder)

"It is so good I wish I had written it myself." – **Hanshi Patrick McCarthy**, Director, International Ryukyu Karate Research Society

Cut to the very core of what it means to be successful in the martial arts. Earning a black belt can be the most rewarding experience of a lifetime, but getting there takes considerable planning. Whether your interests are in the classical styles of Asia or in today's Mixed Martial Arts (MMA), this book prepares you to meet every challenge. Whatever your age, whatever your gender, you will benefit from the wisdom of master martial artists around the globe, including Iain Abernethy, Dan Anderson, Loren Christensen, Jeff Cooper, Wim Demeere, Aaron Fields, Rory Miller, Martina Sprague, Phillip Starr, and many more, who share more than 300 years of combined training experience. Benefit from their guidance during your development into a first-class black belt.

Wolves in Street Clothing (Wilder/ Hollingsworth)

"Teaches folks to rekindle tools that are already in us—already in our DNA—and have been there for thousands of years." – **Ron Jarvis**, Tracker, Outdoorsman, Self-Defense Instructor

This book gives you a new light in which to see human predatory behavior. As we move farther and farther from our roots insulating ourselves in technology and air-conditioned homes we get disconnected from the inherent and innate aspects of understanding the precursors to violent behavior. Violence is not always emotionally bound, often and in the animal kingdom is simply a tool to access a needed resource—or to protect an essential resource. Distance, encroachment, and signals are keys to avoiding a predator. Why would a cougar attack a man after a bike ride? Why would a bear attack a man in a hot tub? Why would a thug rob one person and not another? The predatory animal mind holds many of the keys to the answer to these questions. Learn drills that will help you tune your focus and move through life safer and more aware of your surroundings.

70-Second Sensei (Kane/Wilder)

"I'll let you in on a secret. The *70-Second Sensei* is a gateway drug. It's short, easy to read, and useful. It has stuff in it that will make you a better instructor. Even a better person." — **Rory Miller**, Chiron Training

Once you have mastered the physical aspects of your martial art, it is time to take it to the next level—to lead, to teach, to leave a legacy. This innovative book shows you how. Sensei is a Japanese word, commonly translated as "teacher," which literally means "one who has come before." This term is usually applied to martial arts instructors, yet it can signify anyone who has blazed a trail for others to follow. It applies to all those who have acquired valuable knowledge, skills, and experience and are willing to share their expertise with others while continuing to grow themselves. After all, setting an example that others wish to emulate is the very essence of leadership. Clearly you cannot magically become an exemplary martial arts instructor in a mere 70-seconds any more than a businessperson can transform his or her leadership style from spending 60-seconds perusing The One Minute Manager. You can, however, devote a few minutes a day to honing your craft. It is about giving back, offering your best to others so that they can find the best in themselves. And, with appreciation, they can pay it forward…

The Contract Professional's Playbook (Nyden/Kane)

"While early career practitioners may understand the value of drafting, negotiating, and managing exceptional contracts, they often struggle to master the requisite skills. This comprehensive manual helps structure the negotiation process, thereby minimizing the perilous process of trial-and-error, expediting competency with leading practices and tools that can help reduce risk and speed outcomes for both buy-side and sell-side alike." — **Gregg Kirchhoefer**, P.C., IAOP Leadership Hall of Fame Member

Ever increasing demand for performance- and outcome-based agreements stems from pressure for enterprises to drive greater value from their strategic customer/supplier relationships. To achieve expected performance, contractual relationships are increasingly complex and interdependent, requiring more stakeholders be involved in the decision making. Unfortunately for contract professionals held accountable to these requirements there has been little in the way of resources that answer their "how to" questions about drafting, negotiating, and managing performance- and outcome-based agreements. Until now! *The Contract Professional's Playbook* (and corresponding eLearning program) walks subject matter experts who may be new to complex contracting step-by-step through all aspects of the contract life cycle. Invaluable competencies include identifying and managing risk, increasing influence with stakeholders, developing pricing models, negotiating complex deals, and governing customer-supplier relationships to avoid value leakage in the midst of constant change. It's an invaluable resource that raises the bar for buy-side and sell-side practitioners alike.

There are Angels in My Head! (Wilder)

"This is not a book on doctrine, dogma or collection of creeds to memorize in order to impress others with knowledge. This is a practical application of your participation in a new experience. Here you will find your questions answered even before they are asked." – **Br. Rich Atkinson**, Order of St. Francis

The unexplainable has happened. A prayer has been answered, a gift has been given, a communication has occurred... Is it the voice of God, or the voices in your head? Here's how to find out: In this groundbreaking book, you will discover the organization of the mystical experience. Based on the classic works of G. B Scaramelli, an 18th Century Jesuit Priest, Wilder brings modern relevance to any person to apply to their journey as they seek the Divine. Using examples and principles from Christianity and other religions, Wilder demonstrates that mankind's profound mystical experience crosses all cultures and religions.

Fiction Books:

Blinded by the Night (Kane)

"Kane's expertise in matters of mayhem shines throughout." – **Steve Perry**, bestselling author

Richard Hayes is a Seattle cop. After 25 years on the force he thinks he knows everything there is to know about predators. Rapists, murderers, gang bangers, and child molesters are just another day at the office, yet commonplace criminals become the least of his problems when he goes hunting for a serial killer and runs into a real monster. The creature not only attacks him, but merely gets pissed off when he shoots it. In the head. Twice! Surviving that fight is only the beginning. Richard discovers that the vampire he destroyed was the ruler of an eldritch realm he never dreamed existed. By some archaic rule, having defeated the monster's sovereign in battle, Richard becomes their new king. When it comes to human predators, Richard is a seasoned veteran, yet with paranormal ones he is but a rookie. He must navigate a web of intrigue and survive long enough to discover how a regular guy can tangle with supernatural creatures and prevail.

Legends of the Masters (Kane/Wilder)

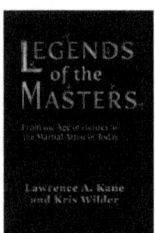

"It is a series of (very) short stories teaching life lessons. I'm going to bring it out when my nephews are over at family dinners for good discussion starters. A fun read!" – **Angela Palmore**

Storytelling is an ancient form of communication that still resonates today. An engaging story told and retold shares a meaningful message that can be passed down through the generations. Take fables such as *The Boy Who Cried Wolf* or *The Tortoise and the Hare*, who hasn't learned a thing or two from these ancient tales? This book retools Aesop's lesser-known fables, reimagining them to meet the needs and interests of modern martial artists. Reflecting upon the wisdom of yesteryear in this new light will surely bring value for practitioners of the arts today.

DVDs:

121 Killer Appz (Wilder/Kane)

"Quick and brutal, the way karate is meant to be." – **Eric Parsons**, Founder, Karate for Life Foundation

You know the *kata*, now it is time for the applications. *Gekisai (dai ni)*, *Saifa*, *Seiyunchin*, *Seipai*, *Kururunfa*, *Suparinpei*, *Sanseiru*, *Shisochin*, and *Seisan kata* are covered. If you ever wondered what purpose a move from a *Goju Ryu* karate form was for, wonder no longer. This DVD contains no discussion, just a no-nonsense approach to one application after another. It illuminates your *kata* and stimulates deeper thought on determining your own applications from the *Goju Ryu* karate forms.

Sanchin Kata: Three Battles Karate Kata (Wilder)

"A cornucopia of martial arts knowledge." – **Shawn Kovacich**, endurance high—kicking world record holder (as certified by the Guinness Book of World Records)

A traditional training method for building karate power, *sanchin kata* is an ancient form. Some consider it the missing link between Chinese kung fu and Okinawan karate. This program breaks down the form piece by piece, body part by body part, so that the hidden details of the *kata* are revealed. This DVD complements the book *The Way of Sanchin Kata*, providing in-depth exploration of the form, with detailed instruction of the essential posture, linking the spine, generating power, and demonstration of the complete *kata*.

Scaling Force (Miller/Kane)

"Kane and Miller have been there, done that and have the t—shirt. And they're giving you their lessons learned without requiring you to pay the fee in blood they had to in order to learn them. That is priceless." – **M. Guthrie**, Federal Air Marshal

Conflict and violence cover a broad range of behaviors, from intimidation to murder, and they require an equally broad range of responses. A kind word will not resolve all situations, nor will wristlocks, punches, or even a gun. Miller and Kane explain and demonstrate the full range of options, from skillfully doing nothing to applying deadly force. You will learn to understand the limits of each type of force, when specific levels may be appropriate, the circumstances under which you may have to apply them, and the potential cost of your decision, legally and personally. If you do not know how to succeed at all six levels, there are situations in which you will have no appropriate options. That tends to end badly. This DVD complements the book *Scaling Force*.

www.ingramcontent.com/pod-product-compliance
Lightning Source LLC
Chambersburg PA
CBHW081201170426
43197CB00018B/2890